IMAGES
of America

OXFORD

I0805868

On the Cover: This is a pre–World War II photograph of the well-dressed Oxford Fire Department. The volunteer fire departments in Oxford have an incredible record of service that dates back to 1824. The bow-tied man to the far left is Howard Bartlett. He had been the city's fire chief many years and was once Chenango County's Fireman of the Year. Bartlett was also elected chairman of the county firemen's association for 14 terms. A special award was given to Bartlett on his retirement after 25 years of service to Oxford. (Courtesy of the Oxford Historical Society.)

IMAGES
of America

OXFORD

Fred Lanfear

ARCADIA
PUBLISHING

ISBN 978-0-7385-7418-9

Published by Arcadia Publishing
Charleston, South Carolina

Printed in the United States of America

Library of Congress Control Number: 2010934333

For all general information, please contact Arcadia Publishing:
Telephone 843-853-2070
Fax 843-853-0044
E-mail sales@arcadiapublishing.com
For customer service and orders:
Toll-Free 1-888-313-2665

Visit us on the Internet at www.arcadiapublishing.com

Dedicated to Charlotte Stafford, an incomparable lady and scholar of great intelligence, skill, and wit, whose name will always be first mentioned when Oxford's history is the subject

Contents

Acknowledgments

During the late 1970s and 1980s, the first generation of hard workers in the Oxford Historical Society spent many hours organizing and storing the archives, which included hundreds of photographs that formed the core of the Oxford Historical Depot-Museum. The museum is housed in an authentic railroad depot, which served as the Delaware, Lackawanna & Western Railroad (DL&W) depot. Many people at the heart of the society helped produce this book: Charlotte Stafford, Charlotte Blenis, Marion Ross, Phyllis Wackford, Carolyn Honkomp, Esther Roach, Lyle Walsh, and Grant Gustin. The members and officers who work to organize programs, maintain the building, and arrange the materials of the society's collection deserve much gratitude.

Most of the photographs in the book are from the Oxford Historical Society's archives and are not specially noted. The following people have graciously loaned their photographs: Barbara Bogie, Vicky House, Kathi Mosher, Sarah Seaman, Anna Stark, and the Chenango County Historical Society (CCHC).

Keith Lanfear scanned the photographs and other materials, stored them on his computer, and arranged them for each chapter. This was crucial and is much appreciated.

INTRODUCTION

The Fort Stanwix Treaty of 1767 protected the lands owned by the Iroquois Nations from colonial settlement until after the Revolutionary War. That land west of the Unadilla River was inviting but unavailable for new settlement until Gov. George Clinton signed new treaties in the late 1780s. Then the settlers came—mainly from Massachusetts and Connecticut—to establish farms and towns in the lush valleys. One of the earliest towns was Oxford. This book is a brief account of its settlement, development, and present condition.

After all these years, Oxford is still a small town. Historians, playwrights, and poets tend to paint small towns with a broad brush, and their strokes often carry much truth. Edgar Lee Masters, for instance, wrote lasting impressions of small-town folks with his *Spoon River Anthology*. Many of the small-town clichés from our literary heritage describe Oxford. And yet, Oxford is memorably different and is a special little town. A visitor will quickly notice the attractive setting, the parks, and the architecture. A native resident develops a reservoir of experiences, relationships, and local lore to draw from. He or she senses that there is nowhere else just like Oxford. The photographs in this book, the scraps of history, and the people described here are what make this small town like no other.

The town's character is captured in its businesses, farms, and quarries. The theme is always the people and their times; they are the unique individuals who coped, survived, and left a mark. The early settlers were builders, farmers, preachers, inventors, businessmen, and educators. Oxford's women were in prominence as well, like Polly Knapp, Katherine Whitney, Charlotte Stafford, and Brandi Estelow. They have shaped and inspired Oxford's story.

Oxford is set in the Chenango Valley, and it lies approximately mid-way between Binghamton and Utica. The town prospered from the combination of good farmland, other natural resources, and early improvements in transportation. Oxford's history, which spans over 220 years, can be organized in four periods based on the dominant modes of transportation. Oxford's first period was filled with paths and crude roads that were fit only for walking or jostling oxcarts and horse-drawn wagons. The next period was of the Chenango Canal, which was a quiet mode of travel that brought to Oxford new goods from around the world and carried out the products of local labor. Next came the railroad, and it was a time filled with hissing engines that practically whisked passengers and products in and out of the community. Finally, the automobile arrived. The automobile pervaded Oxford's daily life, and it epitomized the mixed blessings and ramifications of modern life.

Each period shaped the community and left its marks. The village streets and parks remind residents of earlier years. Reminders of the past periods are found in the town's infrastructure and buildings, like Canal Street, other canal remnants, railroad tracks, the old depot, and abandoned businesses. There are many marks of the automobile age as well, from the concrete highways, traffic signals, gas stations, and many other manifestations that affect our jobs, health, and safety.

The institutions that developed here in Oxford have provided much strength and continuity for the town. Although this is a brief book, and certainly it is not a complete history, it is an introduction to Oxford's story and a collection of pictures for a commendable American town.

One

The Early Years

In 1789, Elijah Blackman came to be Oxford's first settler. The next spring, Blackman brought his two sons and adopted daughter, 11-year-old Polly Knapp, over to Oxford from Unadilla. He cleared the site and built a cabin but was ousted by landowner Benjamin Hovey, who arrived in November. Blackman was given 128 acres that were upriver for his labors.

In 1791, Hovey built a cabin and moved his family to Oxford from Massachusetts. Twelve more families arrived that year, and they had needed skills and different interests. John Bartle, for instance, settled near Bowman Creek and opened the first tavern in town. In 1792, forty-six families came to Oxford, and the town rapidly began to take the shape. By 1795, there were 150 households, and the Yankee pattern of the settlement was indelible from the parks, streets, and their names. By January 1793, an application for Oxford Academy had already been submitted to the New York State Legislature, and it was approved in January 1794. The man most responsible for the establishment of the academy was Uri Tracy. Tracy was an extraordinary man who had a profound influence on religion and education in Oxford.

The early years of development were difficult in Oxford because of the tools at hand and the arduousness of travel. Most of the residents had to work by hand cutting trees, hewing and pit-sawing beams and timbers for buildings, shaving shingles for roofs, and siding houses. During the first generation of Oxford, the residents had built more than 170 structures, including two large churches and three schools. By 1824, Henry R. Mygatt drew the first map of the village. During that time, Oxford had a well-established academy, organized churches, many retailer shops, and artisans, and the town's government was state chartered. Mills were built for grinding grain and sawing wood. It was a great start for a small town.

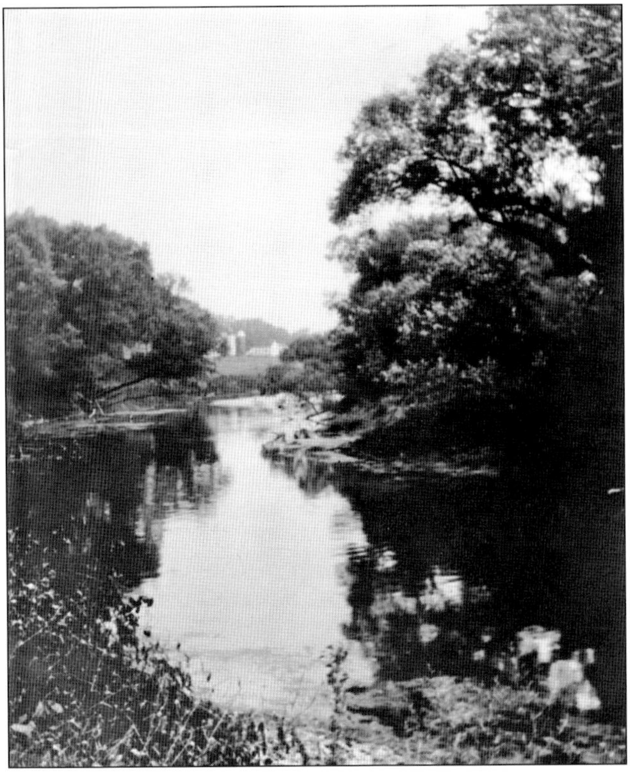

This tranquil scene on the Chenango River was photographed in 1938 near the bend near Cork Island, which was where the locally famous Cork Island Duel had taken place a century earlier.

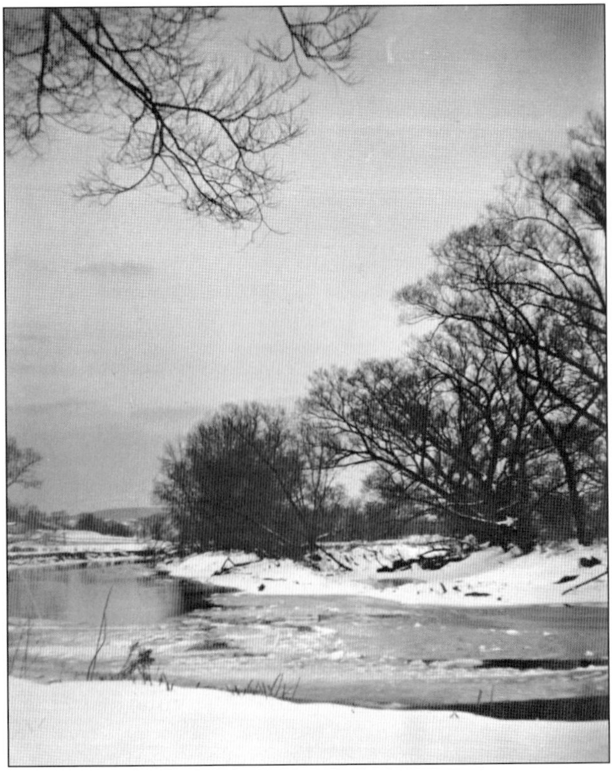

This winter scene was photographed in 1928, before the Crawford family's farm had new silos. The area looks exactly the same today except for the farm.

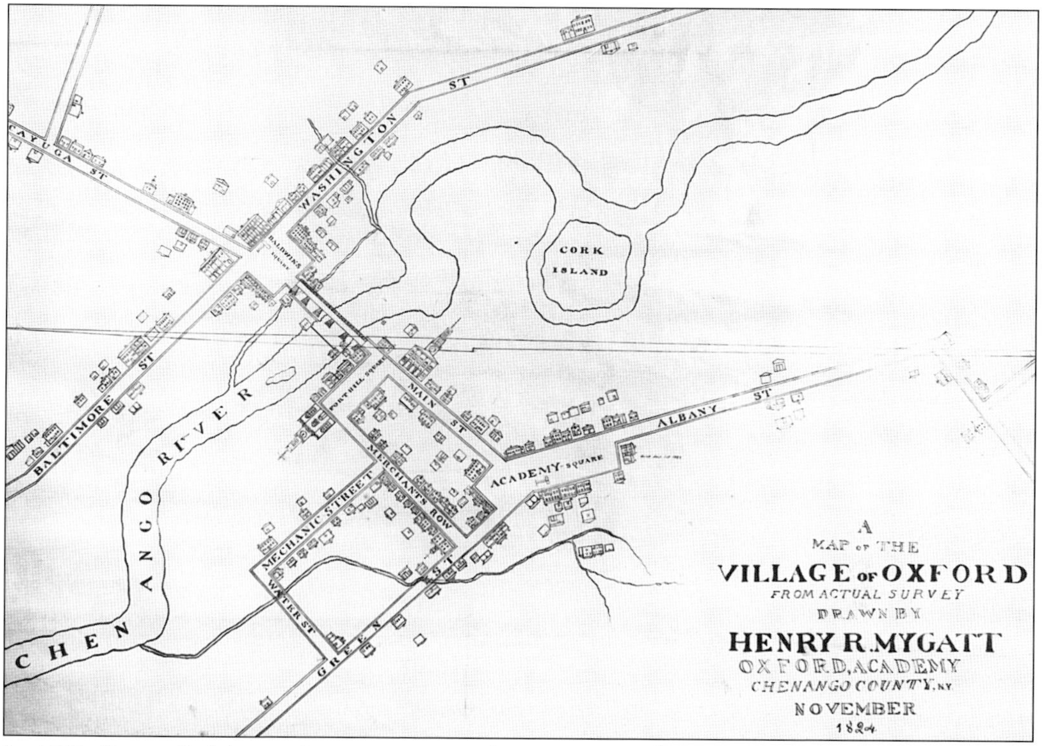

In 1824, Henry R. Mygatt drew a city map that represented the streets and buildings after 30 years of settlement. Nearly 180 buildings surrounded the three parks. Many of the buildings are still here today, although some street names have changed.

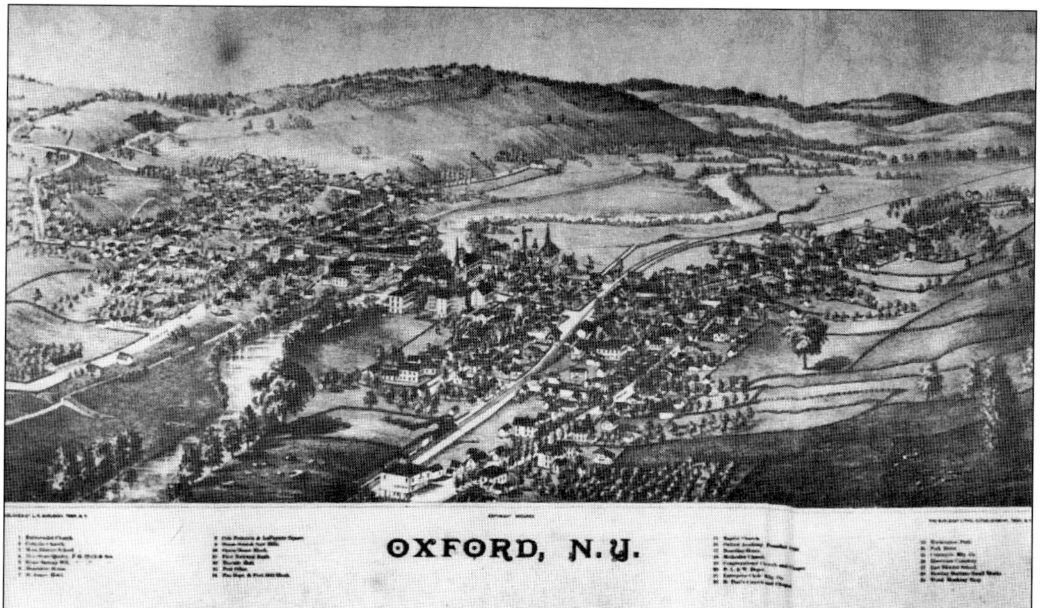

In 1883, Burleigh grew a map of the village after 90 years of settlement. By that time, the surrounding farms had cleared nearly all the trees. It took another century before Oxford enacted better management for the reforestation of the surrounding area.

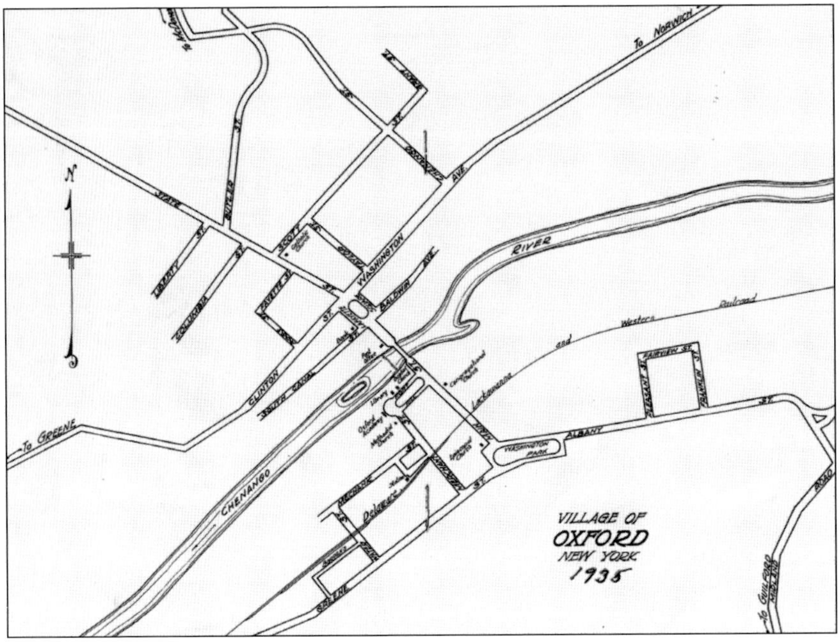

By 1935, the modern village still resembled the Mygatt map. Three new streets on the east side and six on the west side have completed the pattern. The three nice parks have been preserved; Cork Island at this point was covered with silt.

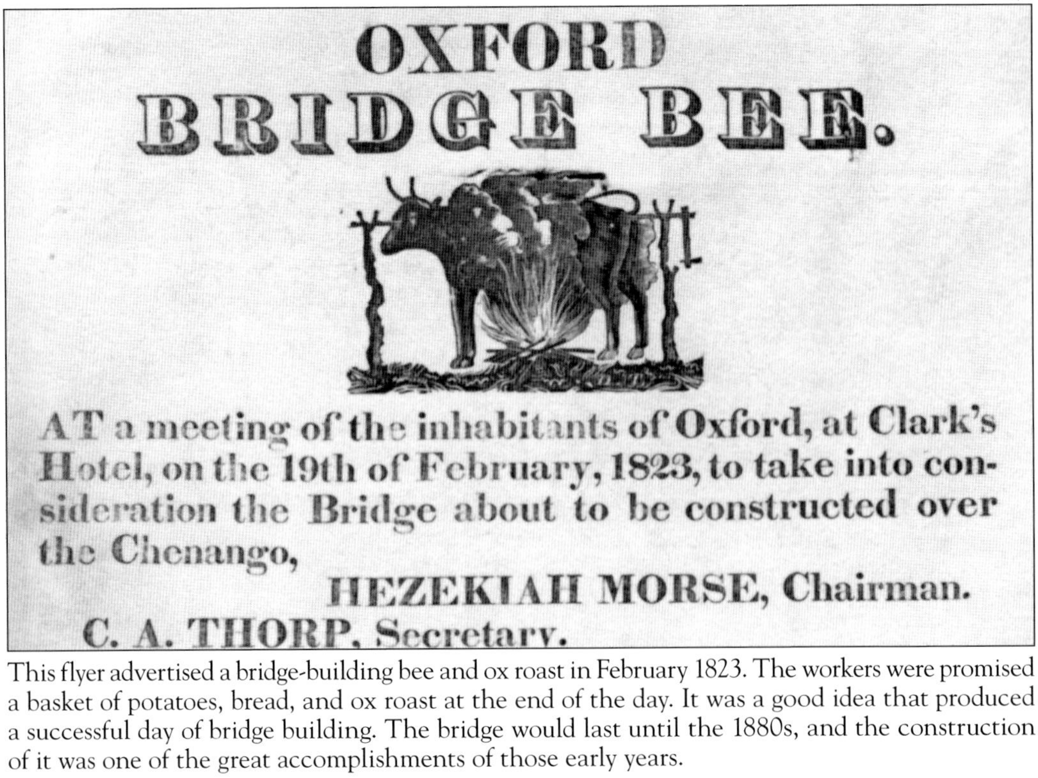

This flyer advertised a bridge-building bee and ox roast in February 1823. The workers were promised a basket of potatoes, bread, and ox roast at the end of the day. It was a good idea that produced a successful day of bridge building. The bridge would last until the 1880s, and the construction of it was one of the great accomplishments of those early years.

Two

THE CHURCHES

The first church formed in Oxford was the Congregational Church in 1799. A Presbyterian clergyman, Rev. John Camp, organized and conducted services in private homes until a church was built in 1823. The congregation thrived, and the church building was reconstructed in 1874 and repaired in 1904. In 1866, a parsonage had been purchased, and a separate chapel was built as a gift of the Miller family. The church has recently joined with the First Baptist Church, and they have become the United Church of Oxford; the churches shared the minister and facilities.

In 1815 and 1816, three churches were organized and began services. St. Paul's Episcopal Church met at home of Abijiah Lobdell. The Oxford Baptist Church was organized, and the Methodist Episcopal Church met in a barn on Albany Street. Nearly two centuries later, each church thrives and serves the community. The Universalist Church first met in a schoolhouse in 1833, and it was founded in 1834. In 1849, St. Joseph's Roman Catholic Church was built after the congregation met for a time in the home of James Flanagan. The first Mass was celebrated in Flanagan's home in 1848. The church rectory was for a time in the Burr mansion, but it is now the Oxford Memorial Library.

One of Oxford's Presbyterian clergymen, Uri Tracy, was a Yale graduate and a former missionary to the Indians, and he was successful in several secular posts. He was Oxford's first postmaster, the first principal of Oxford Academy, the first sheriff of Chenango County, and a one-term member of the New York State Assembly. Tracy also served six years in the US Congress. Finally, he was appointed the first judge of Chenango County, where he served until he was 60 years of age.

In the 1980s, the Faith Bible Church began holding services in the old Oxford Inn. From 1991 until 1999, the congregation met in the old freight depot near the Delaware, Lackawanna & Western Railroad (DL&W) tracks. A beautiful new church was later built, and it overlooked the valley from west of the village on New York State Route 220.

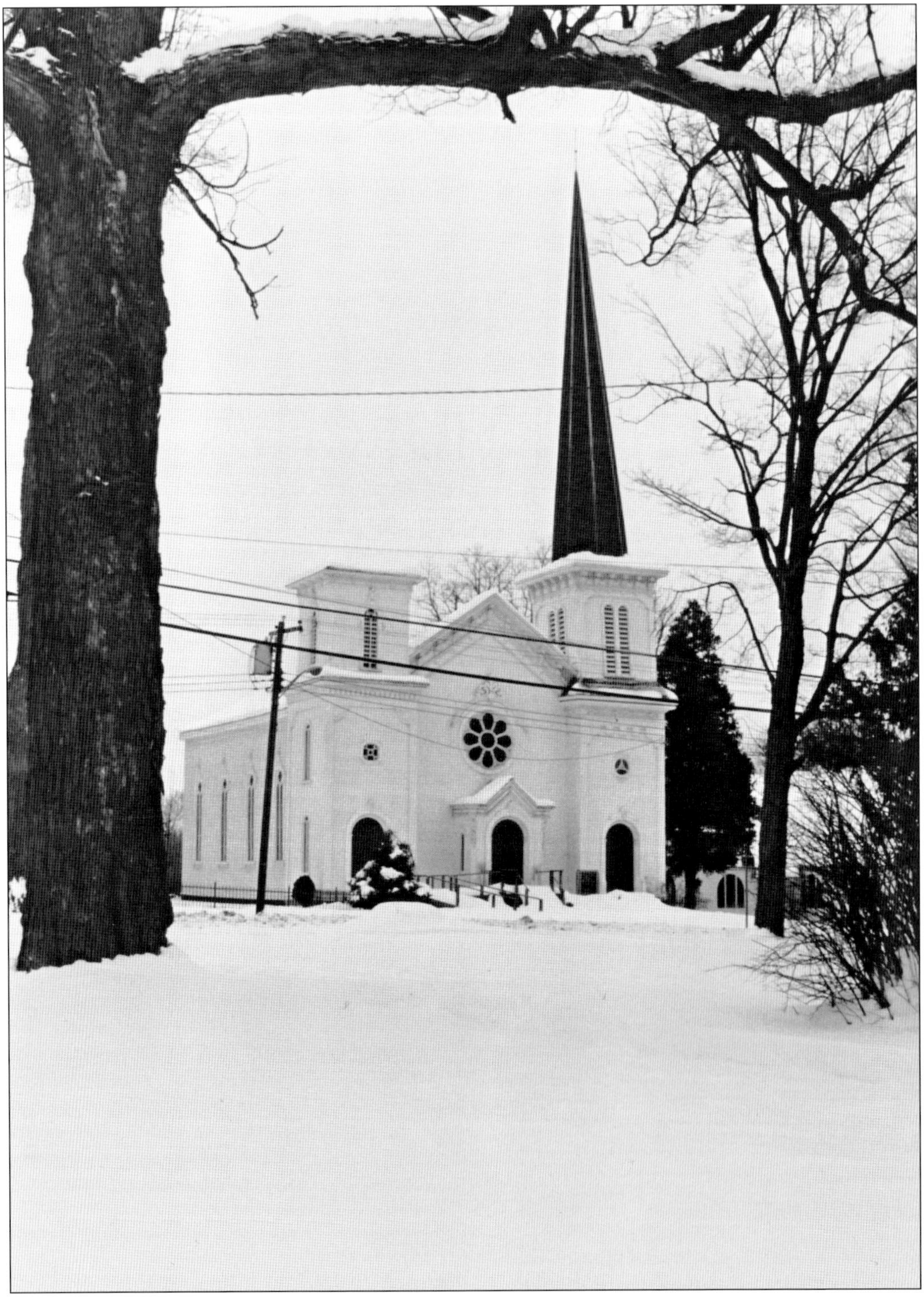

This photograph shows the First Congregational Church on East State Street, and on the right is the Miller Chapel. The left steeple was planned to match the other, but it was struck by lightning. The large parsonage is just to the left of the church building.

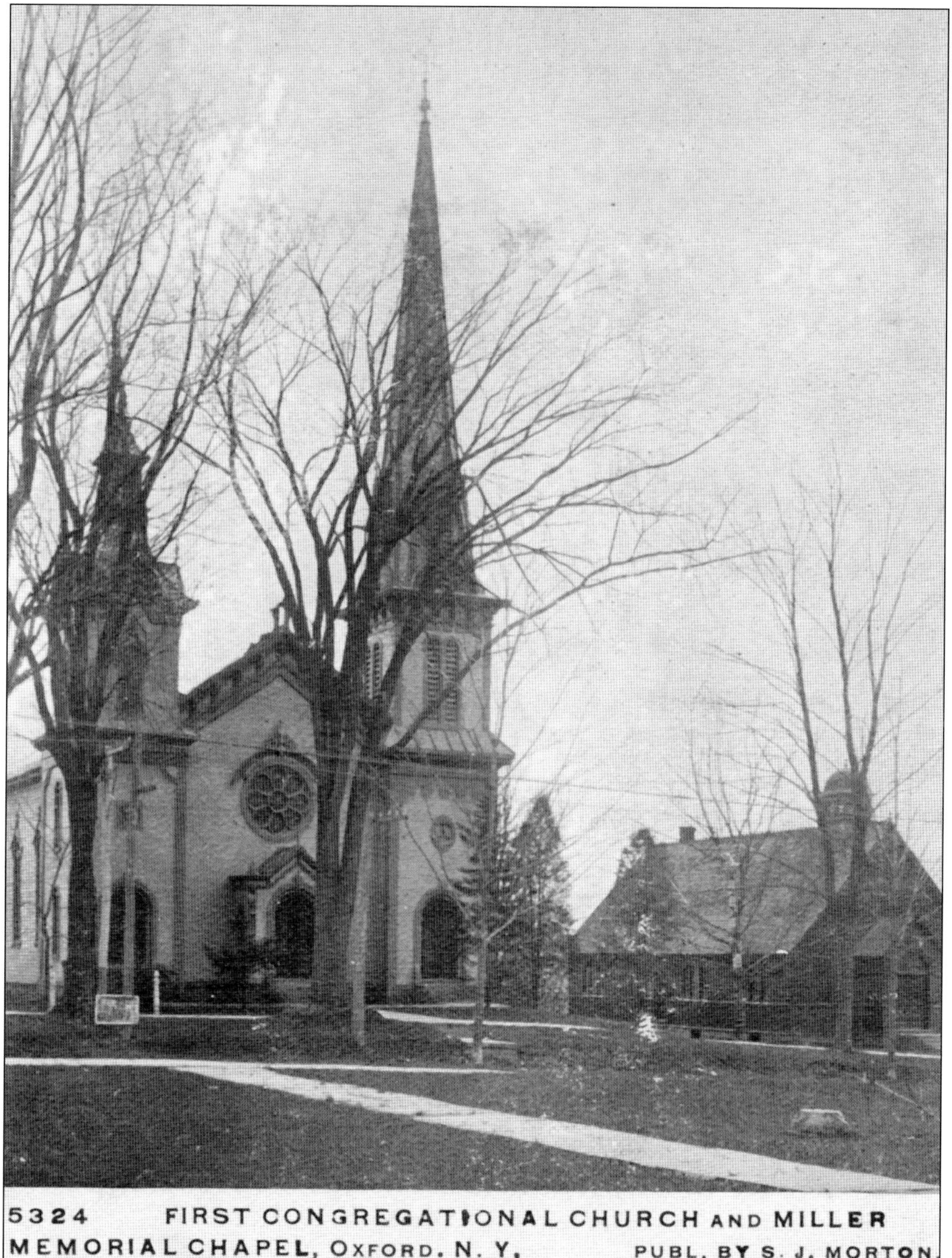

This photograph, which was taken by St. John Morton, shows the original steeple on the left before the lightning strike. The church was built and dedicated in 1824. In 1887, the Miller Memorial Chapel, which is to the right of the church, was a gift of Mrs. Henry L. Miller in memory of her husband. In 2010, it houses the Oxford Masonic Lodge.

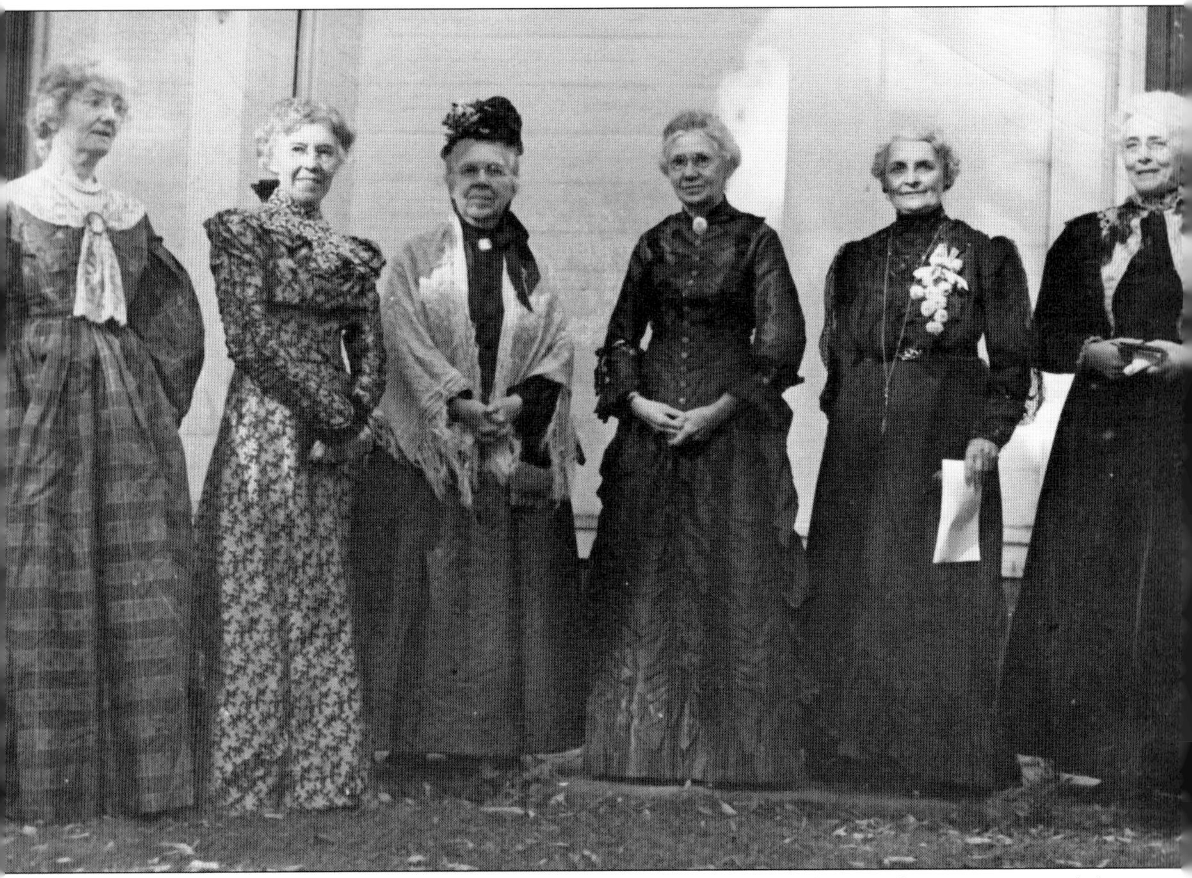

In 1949, six women are posing during a ceremony to celebrate the 150th anniversary of their church. From left to right they are Mae Young, Mabel Cowles, Laurina Baldwin, Mabel Leary, Bessie Payne, and Kittie Hogan. At the time (and presently), the Congregational Church was the second oldest in the Chenango County.

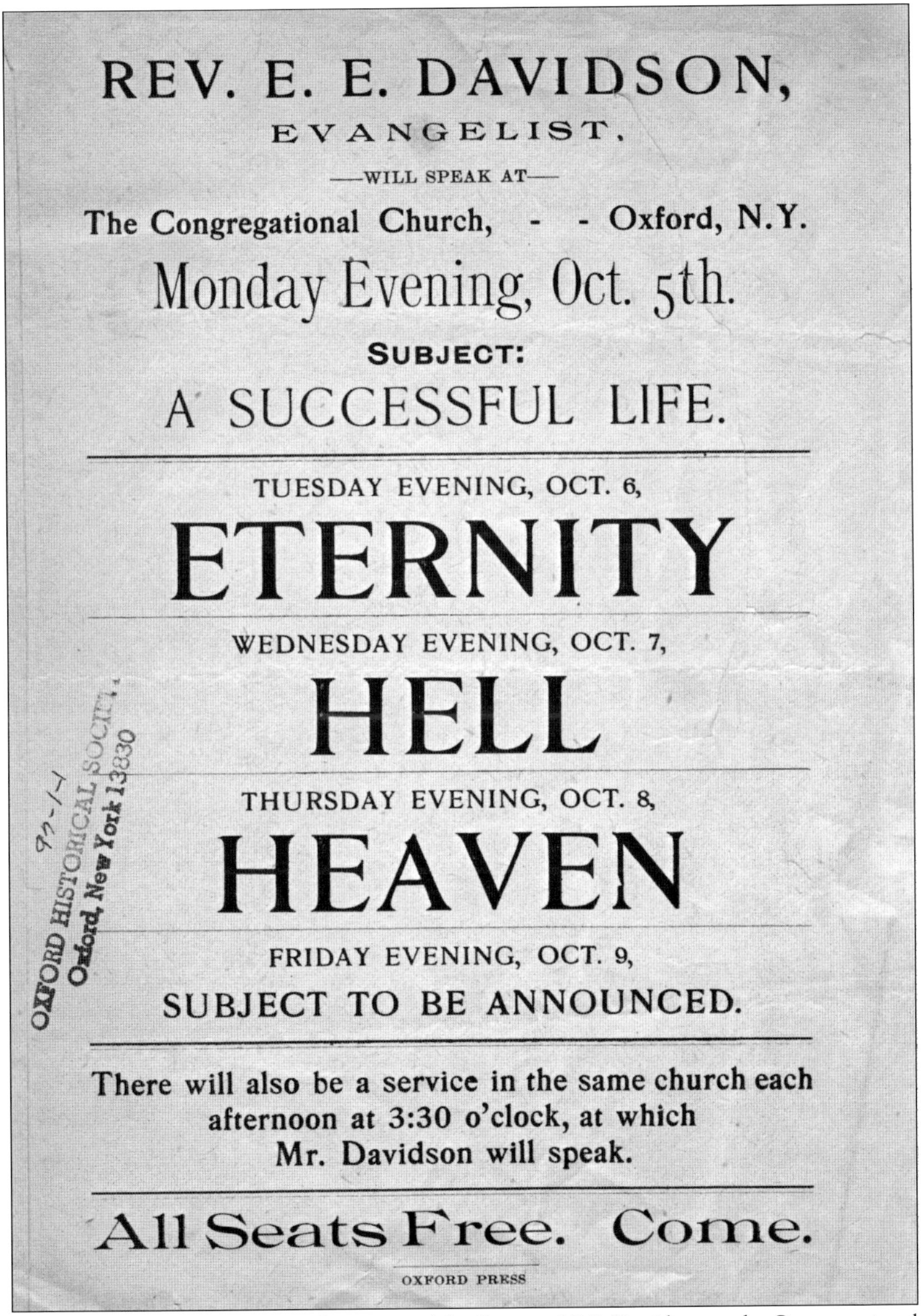

REV. E. E. DAVIDSON,

EVANGELIST.

—WILL SPEAK AT—

The Congregational Church, - - Oxford, N.Y.

Monday Evening, Oct. 5th.

SUBJECT:

A SUCCESSFUL LIFE.

TUESDAY EVENING, OCT. 6,

ETERNITY

WEDNESDAY EVENING, OCT. 7,

HELL

THURSDAY EVENING, OCT. 8,

HEAVEN

FRIDAY EVENING, OCT. 9,

SUBJECT TO BE ANNOUNCED.

There will also be a service in the same church each afternoon at 3:30 o'clock, at which Mr. Davidson will speak.

All Seats Free. Come.

OXFORD PRESS

This flyer advertises the visit and sermons of the Reverend E.E. Davidson to the Congregational Church in Oxford.

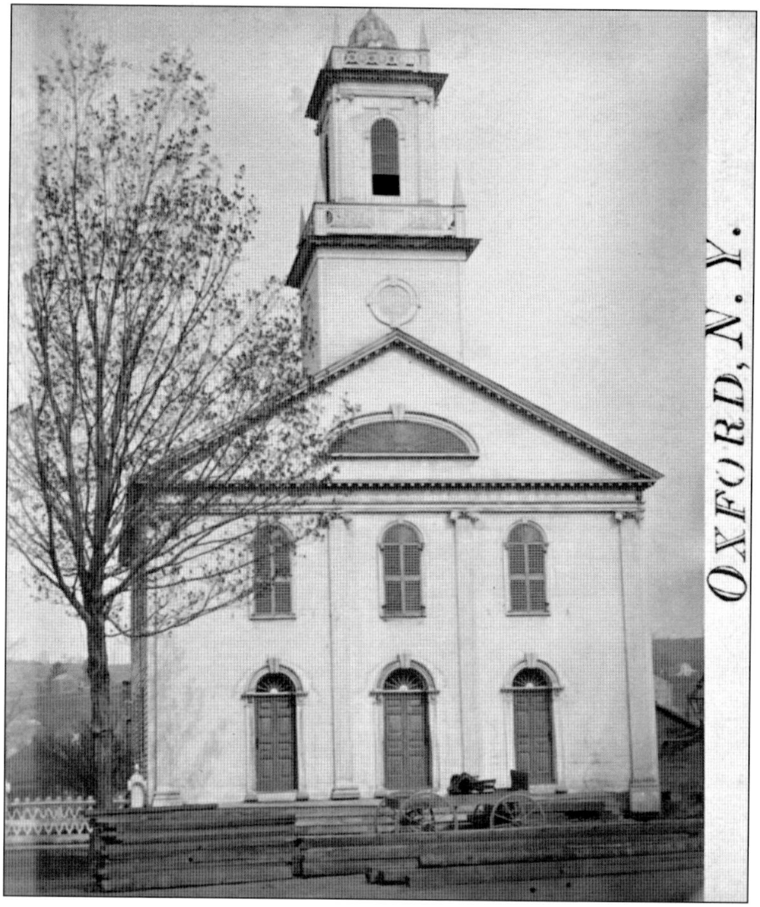

The First Baptist Church was built in 1832. It was remodeled in 1857, 1879, and 1953. In 1953, there was a dramatic moving of the church from its site. It was located behind the Ira Wilcox building on the west side of Fort Hill Park, but it has since moved to the east side and now stands there today. The Dexheimer Company of Guilford moved the church building with their huge trucks, rollers, and steel cables.

This photograph shows the First Baptist Church in 1993 and its new location on the east side of Fort Hill Park. It is still a beautiful building despite lacking the former high steeple.

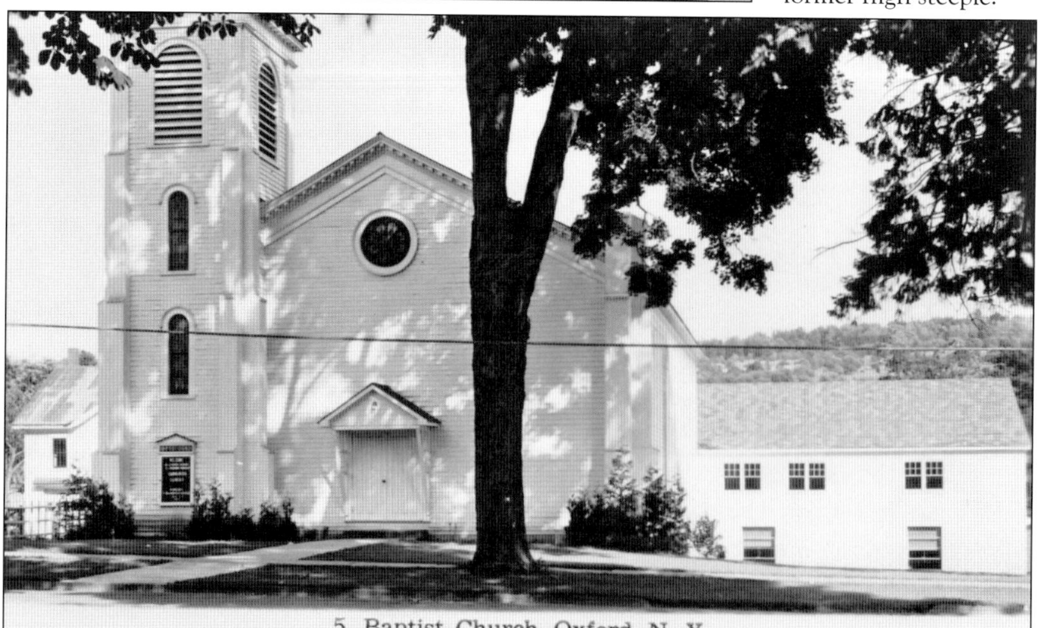

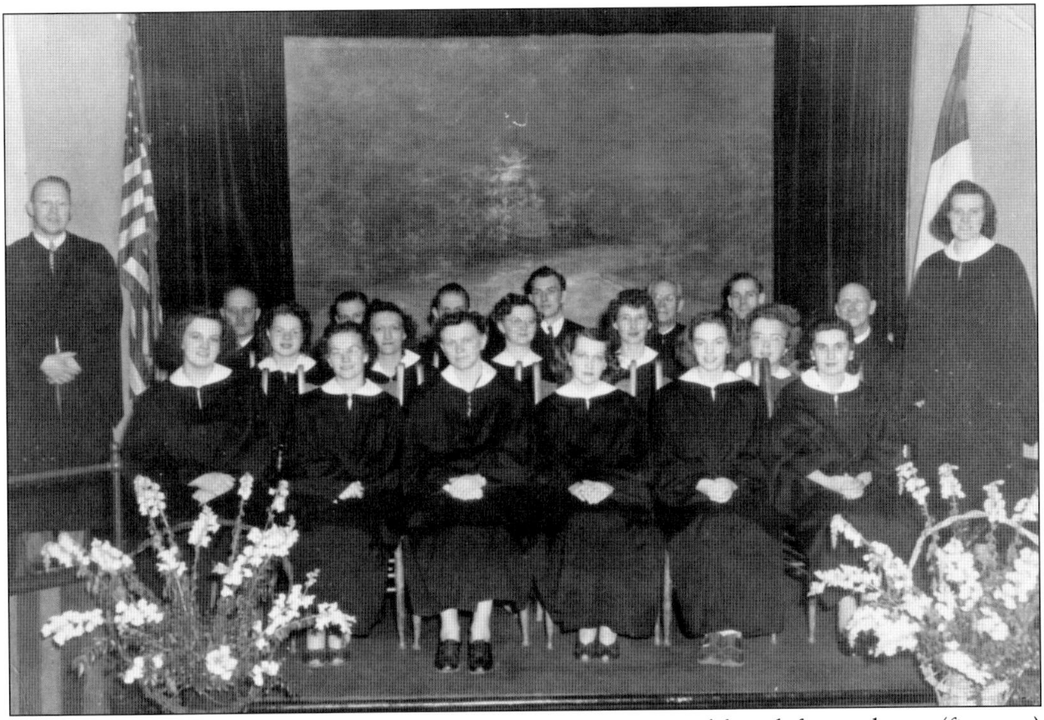

Here is the choir of the First Baptist Church around 1955. Pictured from left to right are (first row) Jean Westcott, Lois Wackford, Lena Maltzen, Eloise Nichols, Flora Adams, and Florence Race; (second row) Barbara Ardron, Jean Manzer, Sue Purdy, Helen Race, and Laura Adams; (third row) Floyd Elsbree, David Jones, Cyrus Sprague, John Walden, Lou Manzer, Oliver Manzer, and Carl Jones; (standing) Zerah Cone and Mrs. Cyrus Sprague.

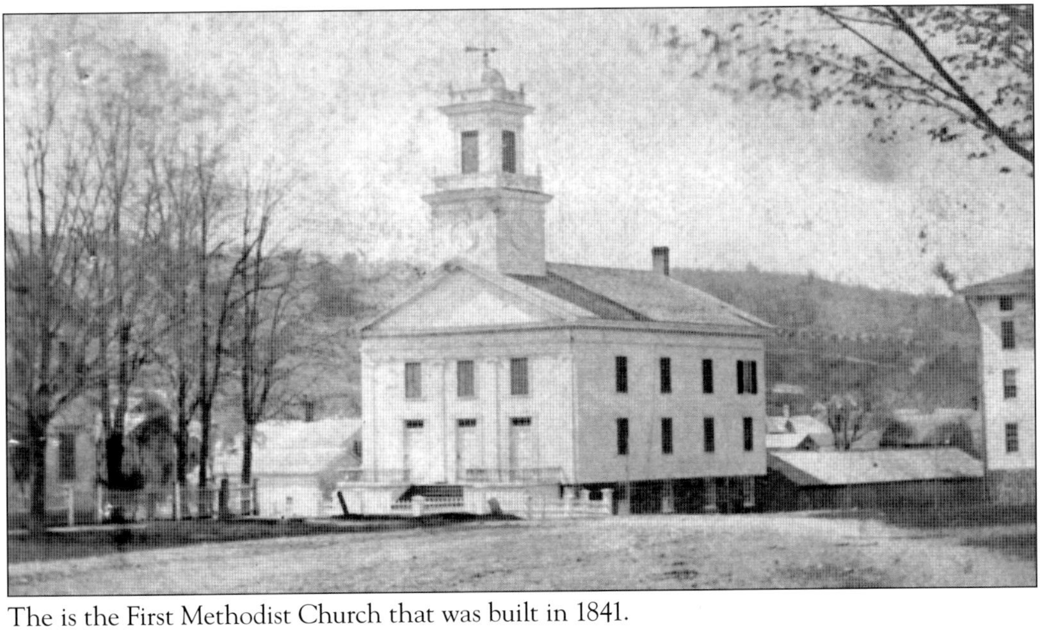

The is the First Methodist Church that was built in 1841.

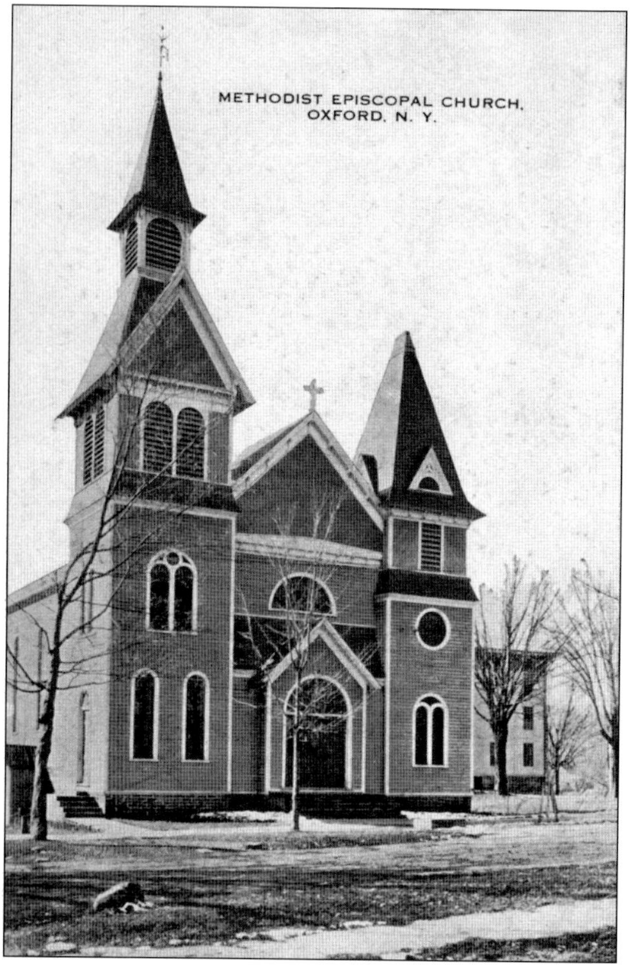

Pictured is the Methodist Episcopal Church after it was remodeled in the 1890s. After a church supper in 1964, the building accidentally burned down. A new church building was constructed on South Washington Avenue, and it was quickly completed and dedicated in 1966. Some of the necessary building funds were raised by a group of churchwomen. They salvaged the shards of stained-glass windows from the old church and made them into jewelry items. The jewelry became popular sale items during the fundraiser. This site seen in the photograph became a parking lot for the school.

The photograph shows the First Methodist Church on South Washington Avenue, which was built after the disastrous fire in 1965.

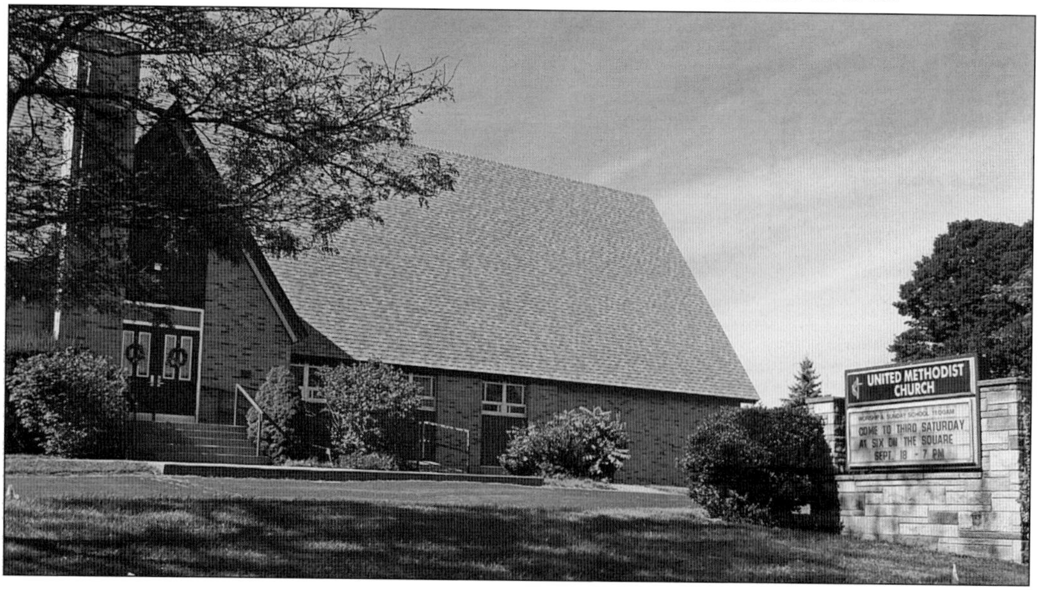

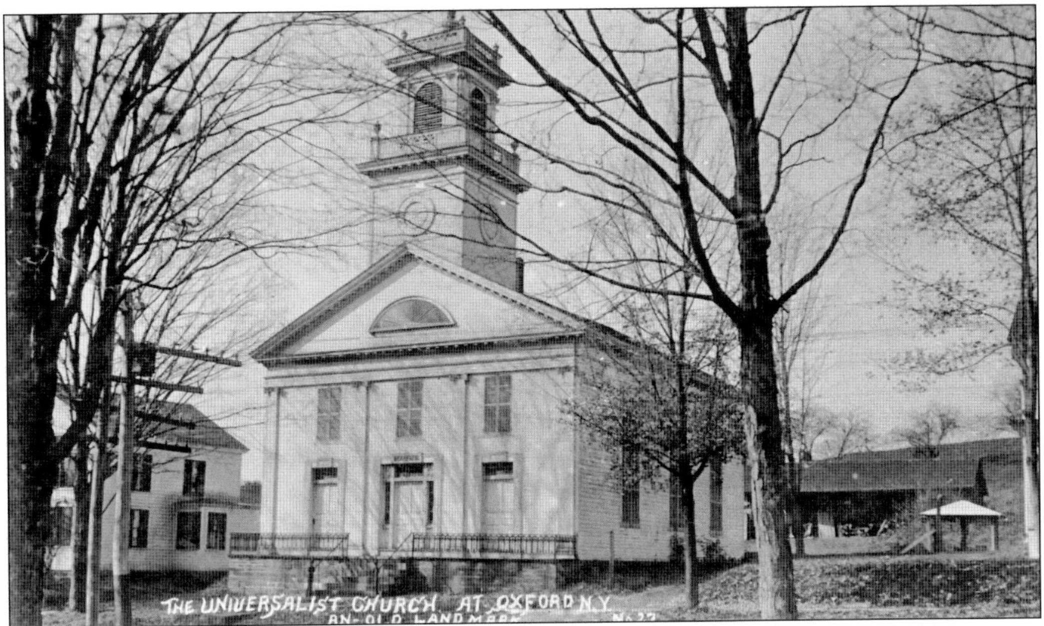

In 1833, the Universalist Church was organized, and for a time the congregation held meetings in the Parker House, which is now the Bida Nursing Home. In 1837, the new church building was constructed on North Washington Avenue.

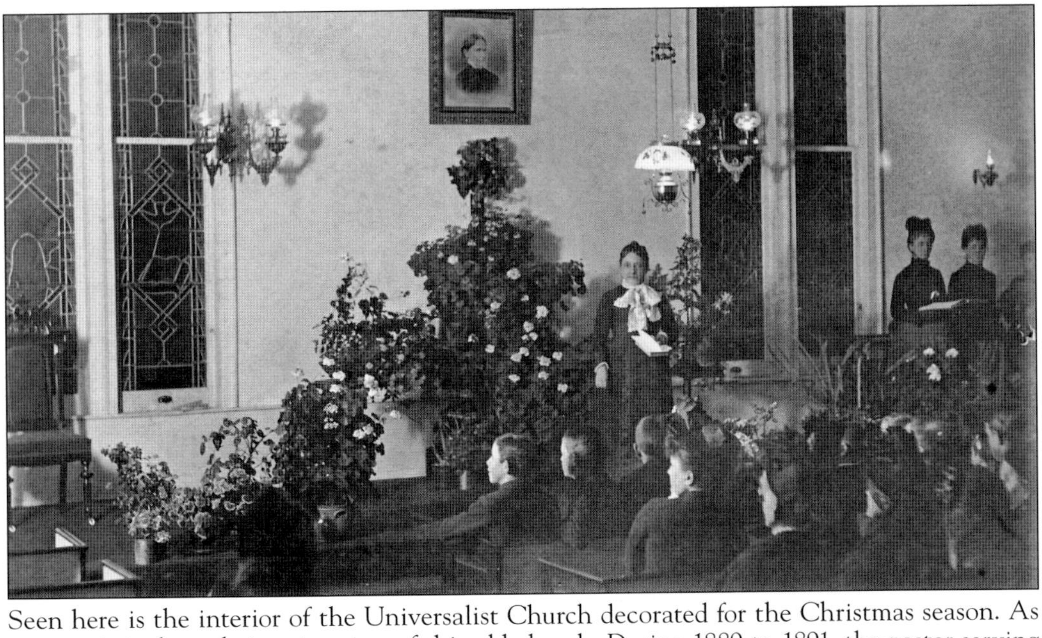

Seen here is the interior of the Universalist Church decorated for the Christmas season. As a rarity, it is the only interior view of this old church. During 1889 to 1891, the pastor serving the church was the Reverend Amanda Deyo, who was the first woman known to hold a clergy position in Oxford.

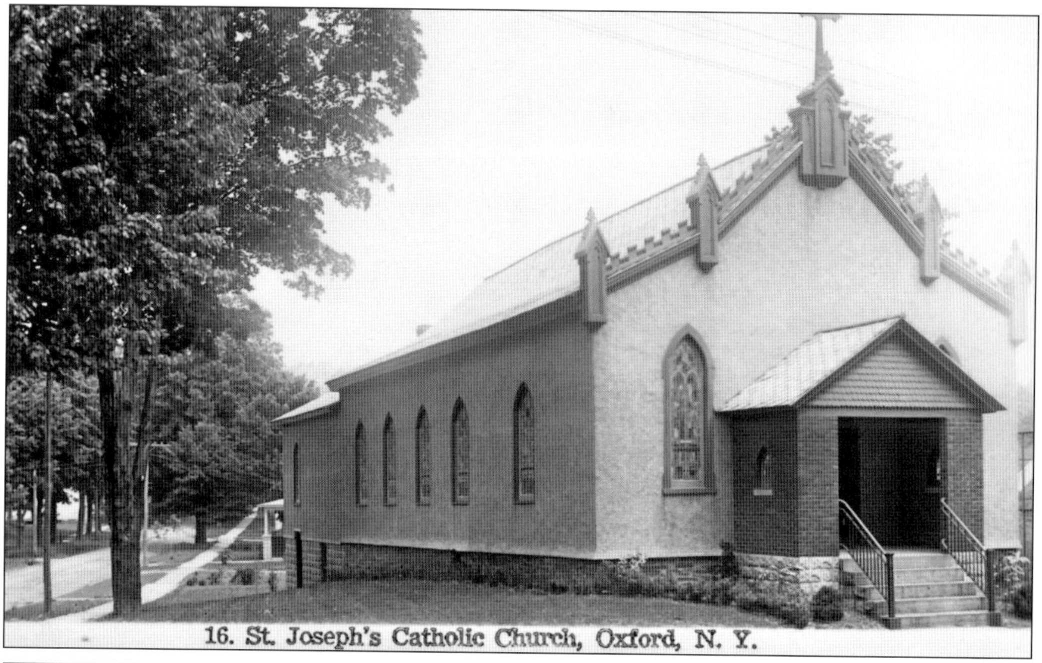

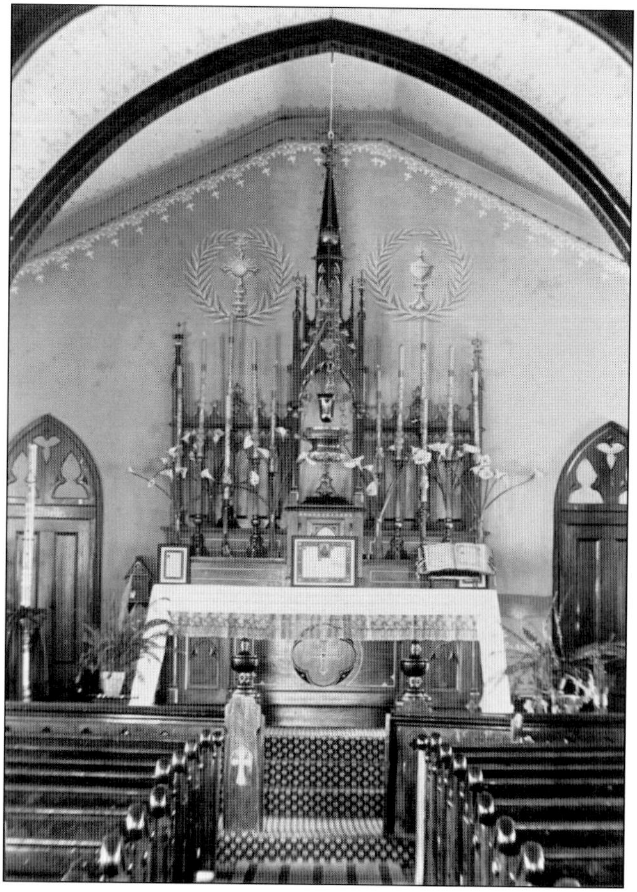

This photograph shows the St. Joseph's Catholic Church, which was built in 1849. The first priest was Fr. James Hourigan, who came from Binghamton. The church building had several renovations. The first one was in 1870 when the building was moved back on the lot, which added 16 feet in length. A new front was also built.

This is the interior of St. Joseph's Catholic Church before the altar was remodeled.

Pictured is St. Paul's Episcopal Church, which was built from 1856 to 1857. The church's old frame building, which was completed on the same site in 1816, was the first church built in Oxford. In 1818, the building was the first to have a church bell in Chenango County. The structure was built of Oxford bluestone under the direction of architect Henry C. Dudley.

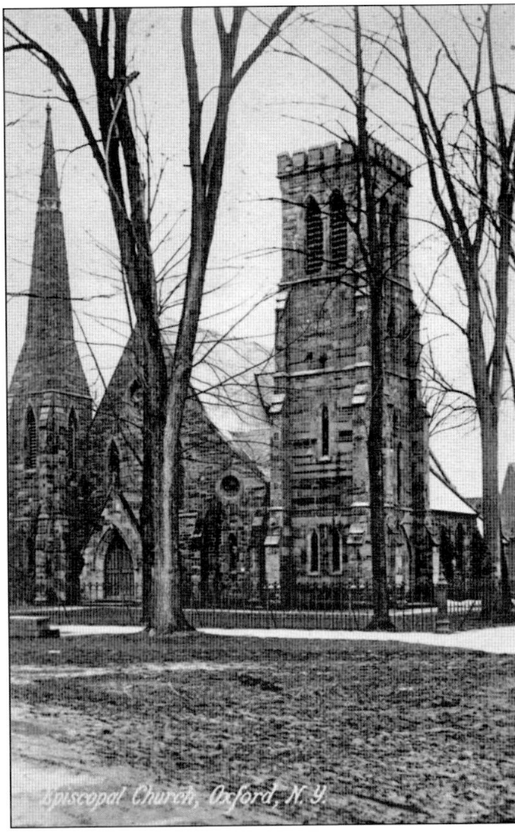

This is an image of St. Paul's Episcopal Church from Washington Park. The church rectory is on the left. The church is the most sketched, painted, and photographed building in Oxford.

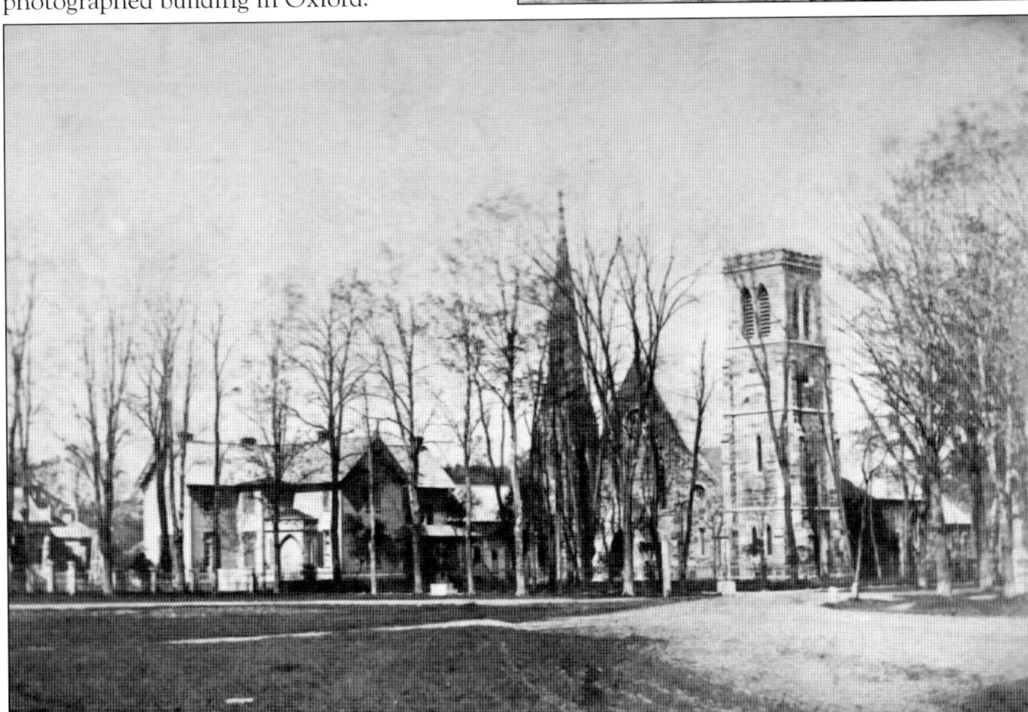

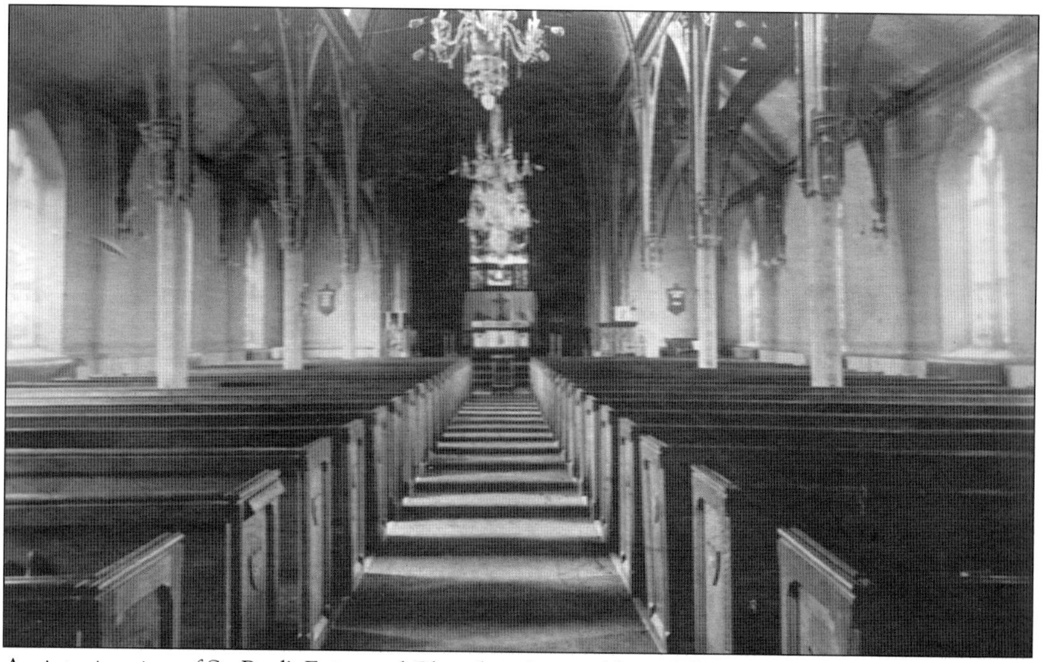

An interior view of St. Paul's Episcopal Church is depicted here. The Waterford crystal chandeliers are from Trinity Church in New York City; they had hung the crystal chandeliers in St. George's Chapel during the time before the Revolutionary War. The chandeliers' relocation to Oxford was made possible because of an appeal by the daughters of Gerrit Van Wagonen after St. George's Chapel was moved.

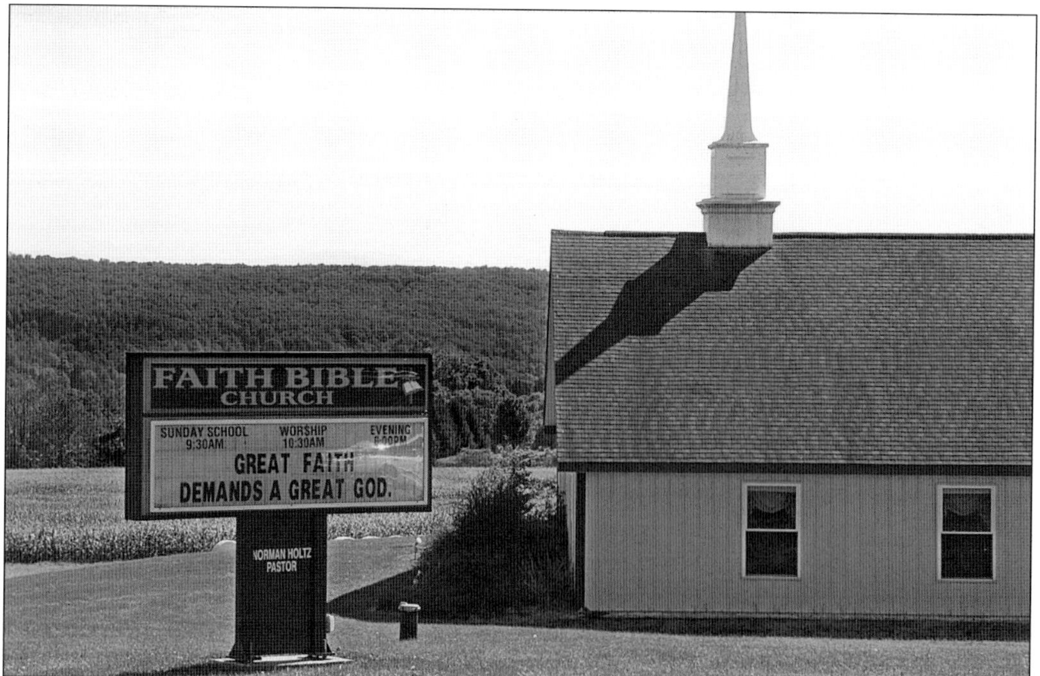

This photograph shows Oxford's newest church. The Faith Bible Church overlooks the valley, and it is located near New York State Route 220, northwest of the village.

Three

Business Big and Small

Oxford has always been known for its businesses. Dairy farming was the largest producer of wealth in town. In the beginning, each family produced its own food, flax, and wool for clothing. Only a fraction of produce was sold for cash or traded for goods and services. With better tools, livestock, and farming methods, the farmers' margin for cash steadily increased. In the 1870s, two new railroads were built, and farmers began to sell and trade their produce. Finally, in 1889, the Borden's milk processing plant opened.

Demand for fresh milk in the rapidly growing eastern cities was high, and prices stayed steady until the 1930s. During that time, the competition increased but demand was low, and the Great Depression caused milk prices to plummet. The low point came in August 1939. Farmers organized a strike against Borden's and its milk, which was priced at 1.5¢ per quart. The strike was dissipated, and milk prices remained low until World War II. The war brought up the demand for milk, which rejuvenated the dairy business. However, the industry has seen the majority of dairy farms go under. Only the big, efficient farms have survived.

For a period of time, roughly during 1870 to 1930, the quarrying and shipping of Oxford bluestone was considered big business. In Oxford, several quarries were opened, and the two owned by the F.G. Clarke Blue Stone Company were the largest in the world. Because of the popularity of city sidewalks, curbs, and public monuments, Oxford bluestone was in high demand. There were many orders from Boston, Philadelphia, and New York City, which allowed Clarke's quarries to employ over 300 workers.

After World War I, the competition from Portland cement lowered the demand for Oxford bluestone, and the Great Depression was the death knell for the big quarries; by 1930, they were all closed. A popular golf course was built on Clarke property called the Bluestone Golf Course.

The Oxford Basket & Manufacturing Company factory was a shot in the arm for the Oxford economy. From the 1890 to 1930, it employed around 70 workers and purchased thousands of logs from local farmers.

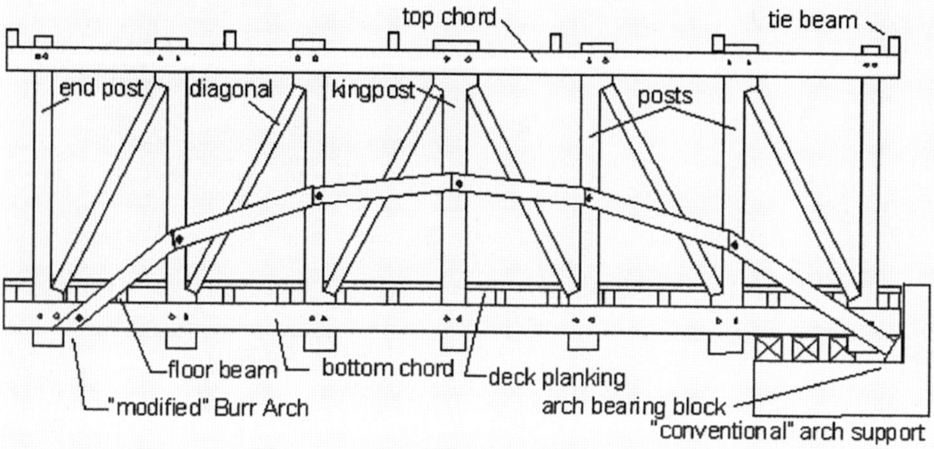

THE BURR ARCH TRUSS BRIDGE

In 1793, the self-taught engineer Theodore Burr moved to Oxford from Connecticut. He was a man with extraordinary skills, ingenuity, and energy. He designed and built the first gristmill on the Chenango River, and he also oversaw the building of the first bridge. Burr then designed the Burr Arch Truss Bridge, his crowning achievement, which was later patented. The arch nearly doubled the strength of a standard wooden bridge, and the new townships were eager to buy. By 1818, he had built 45 bridges and was a wealthy man. Burr had built his own mansion, which now houses the Oxford Memorial Library. In the 1820s, he moved to Pennsylvania to supervise the construction of even more spans that crossed the Susquehanna River in several places, most notably a bridge at Harrisburg.

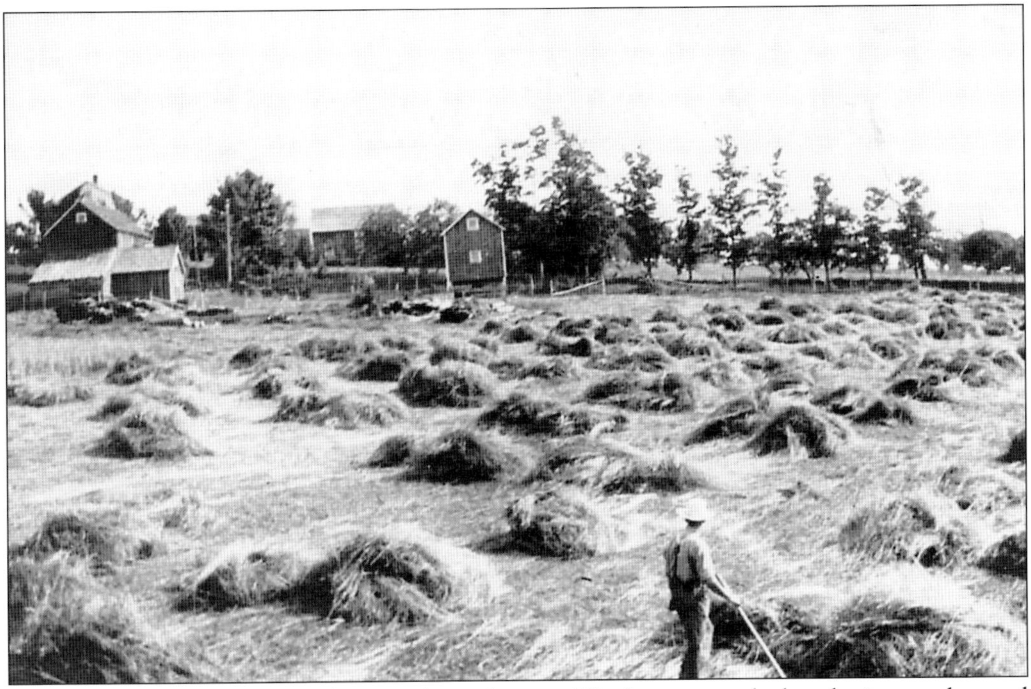

This photograph shows haymaking in the early years. The hay was cut by hand using scythes and was stacked up to cure in the field. It was hard, slow work.

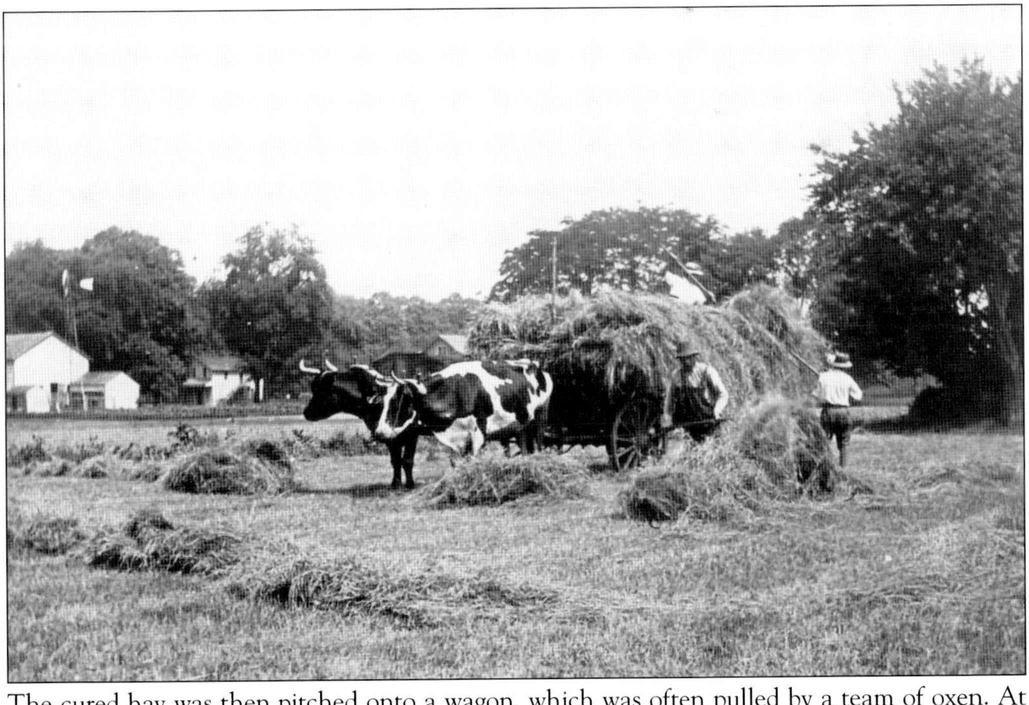

The cured hay was then pitched onto a wagon, which was often pulled by a team of oxen. At the barn, it would be pitched up into a mow. Finally, the hay was pitched down as animal fodder during the winter.

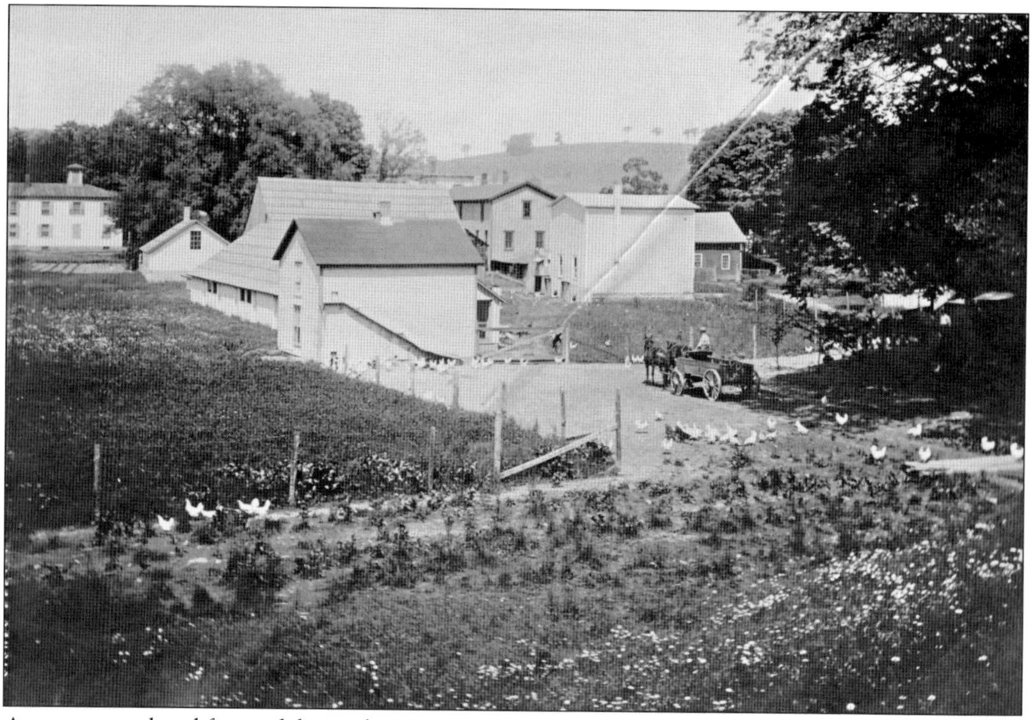

A prosperous local farm of the mid-1880s is featured here. It is a mixed farm with cows, chickens, and various activities. It is a view that might remind one of Currier and Ives prints.

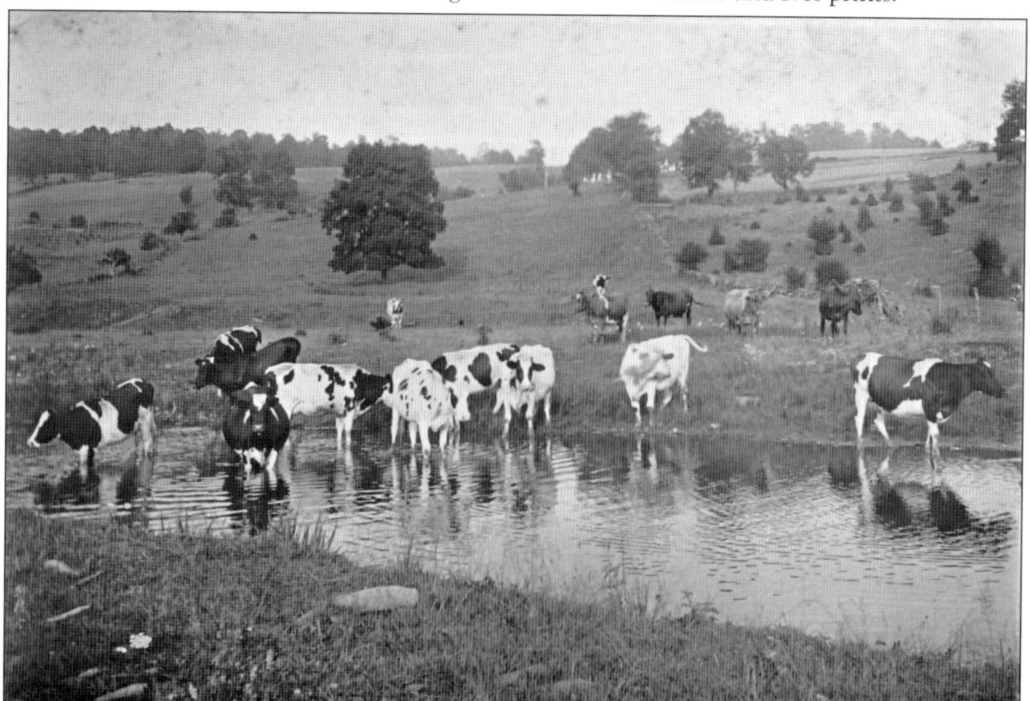

Here is another farm scene from the 1880s. During those days, larger herds of cows were common. The quality of livestock had not improved much, and most extra milk was sent to cheese factories.

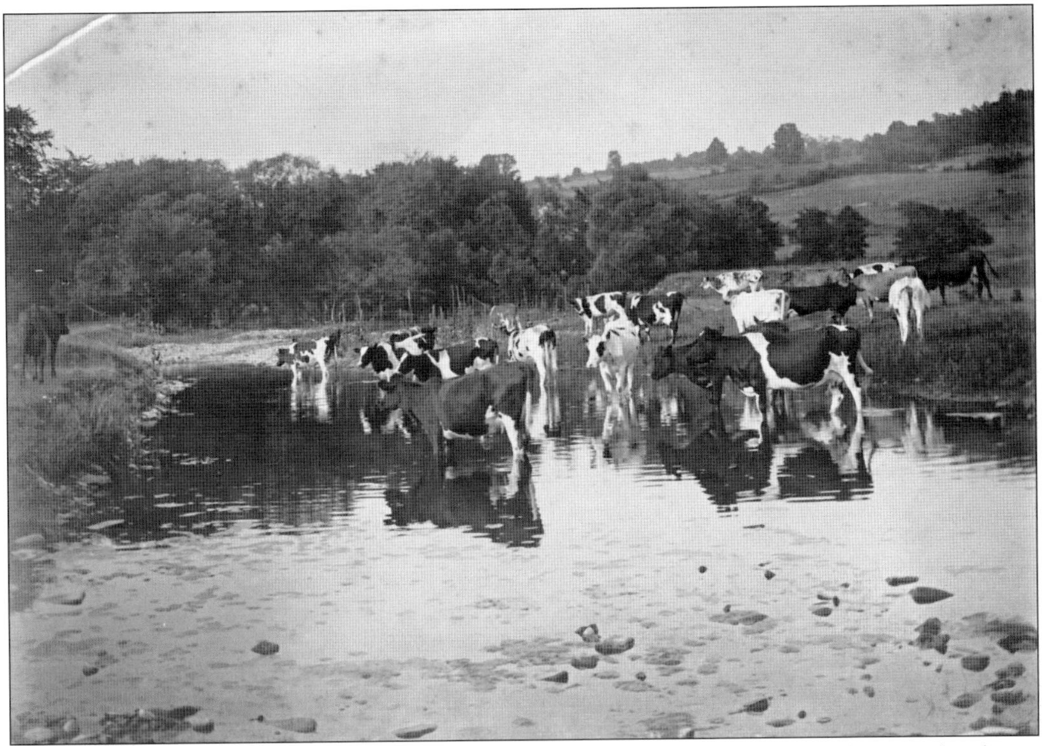

This photograph shows an open field and an attractive view of what may be the same herd.

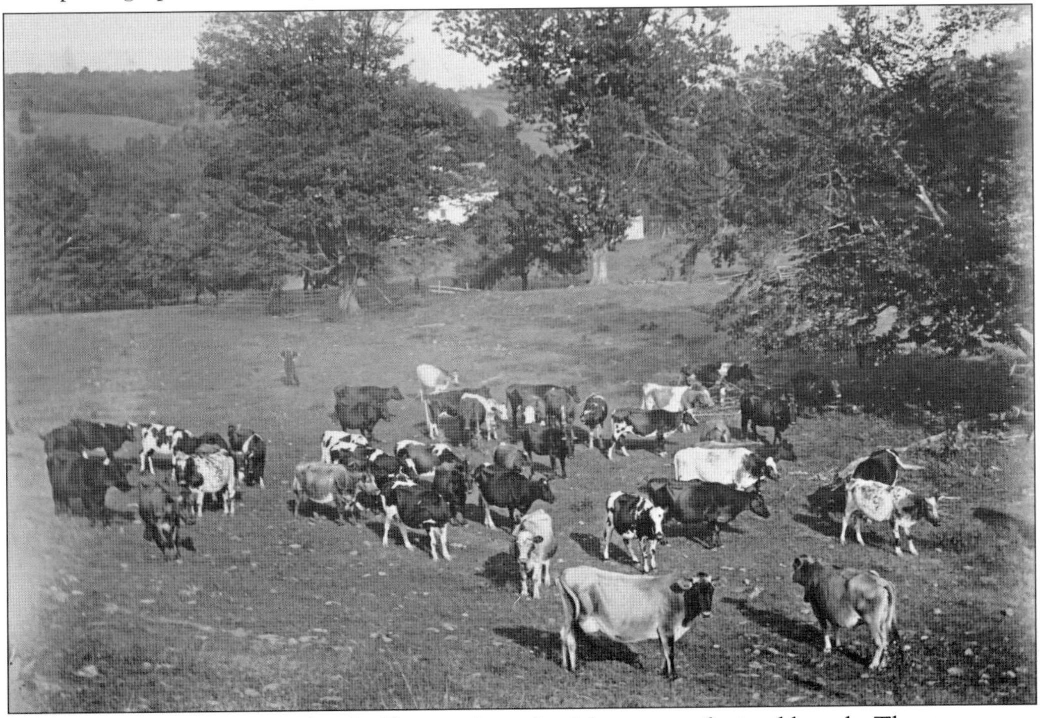

A farmer observes his large herd of livestock—a healthy group of mixed breeds. These cows are not part of the 20th-century herds that produced large amounts of milk.

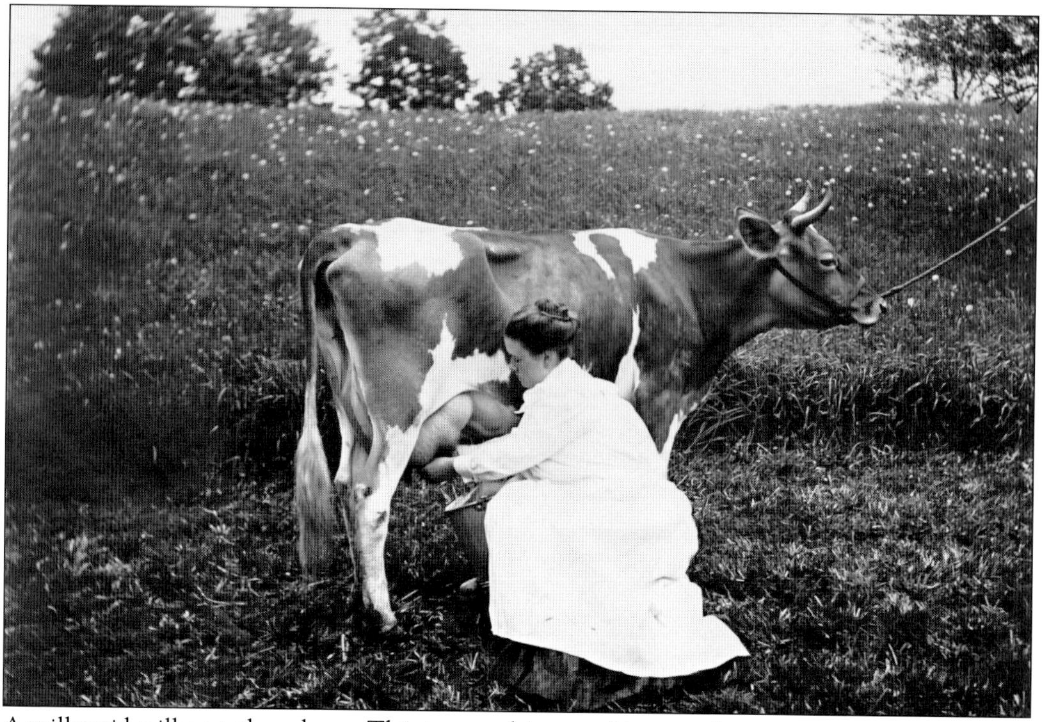

A milkmaid milks a tethered cow. This is a touching rural image of an uncommon occurrence—cows were usually milked in the barn.

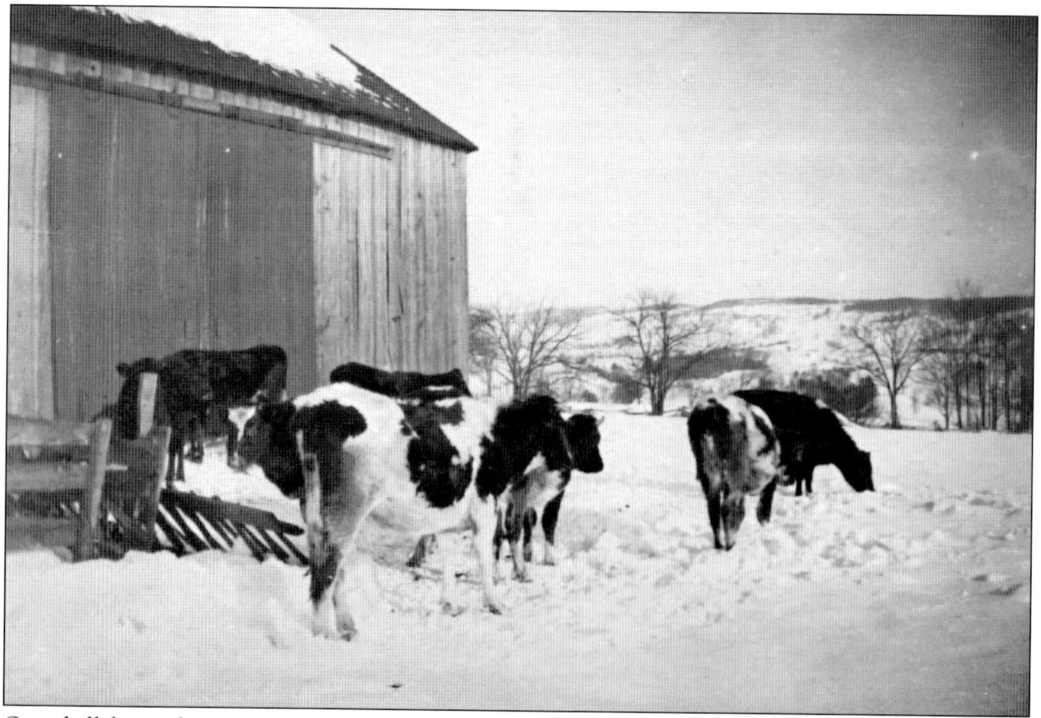

On a hill farm, these cows have been left out on a winter day in the 1920s; they all appear to be Holsteins. The cows are all large, and they portray a 20th-century herd.

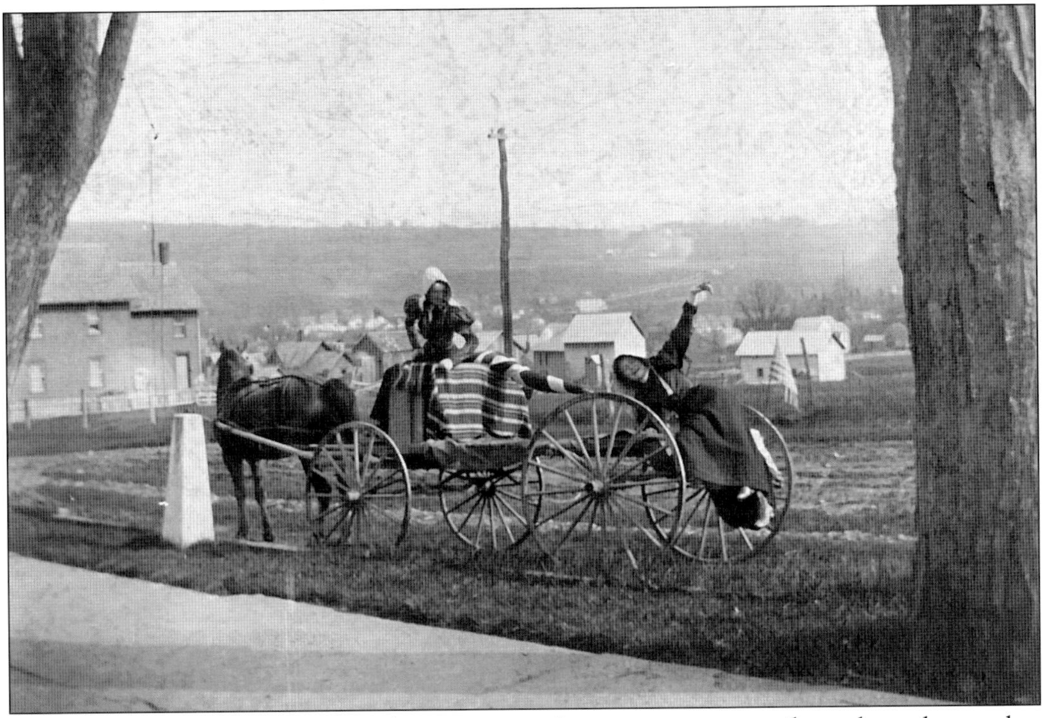

This photograph shows a daughter clowning around on a wagon near a mile marker as her mother looks on.

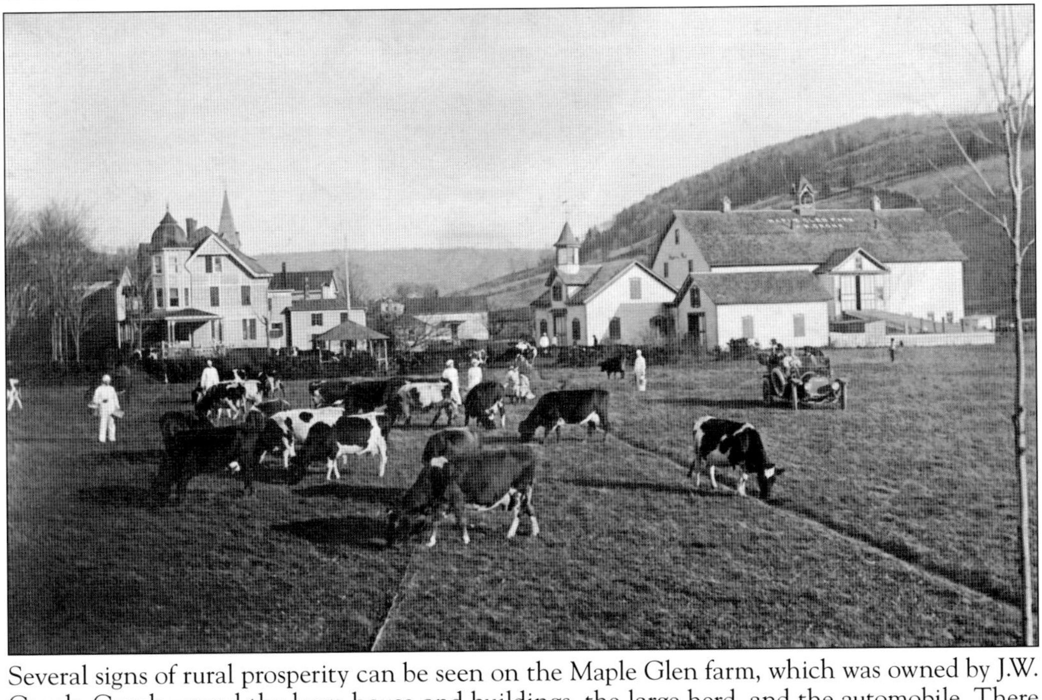

Several signs of rural prosperity can be seen on the Maple Glen farm, which was owned by J.W. Cronk. Cronk owned the large house and buildings, the large herd, and the automobile. There seems to be several visitors observing the livestock. The white outfits and caps hint that these may be Borden's inspectors.

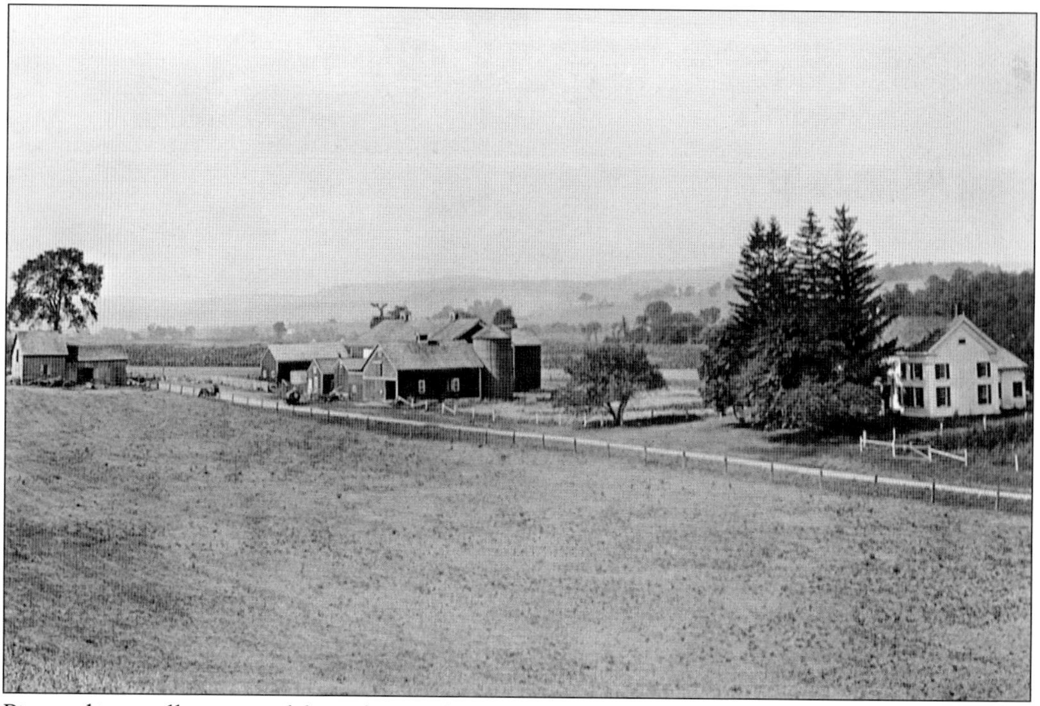

Pictured is a well-organized farm during the turn of the century. Scenes such as this typified the township at that time, and these images still come to mind when farming is mentioned.

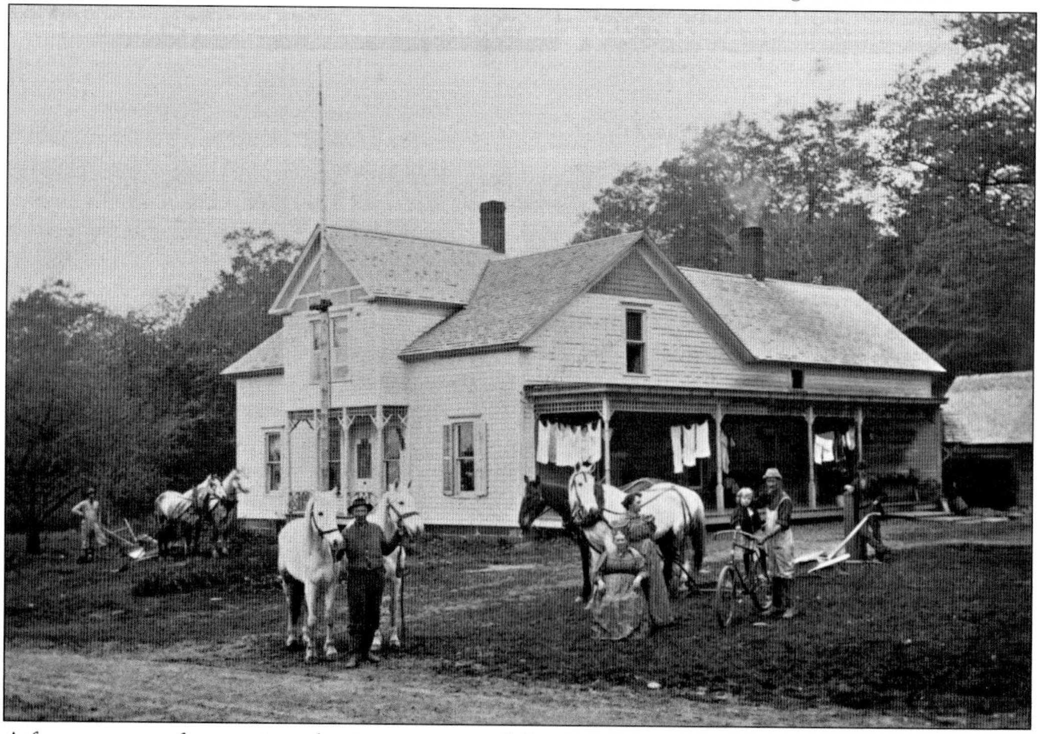

A farmer pauses from spring plowing to pose with his family in 1899. Two working teams of horses and a young in-training team of horses appear with the seven family members.

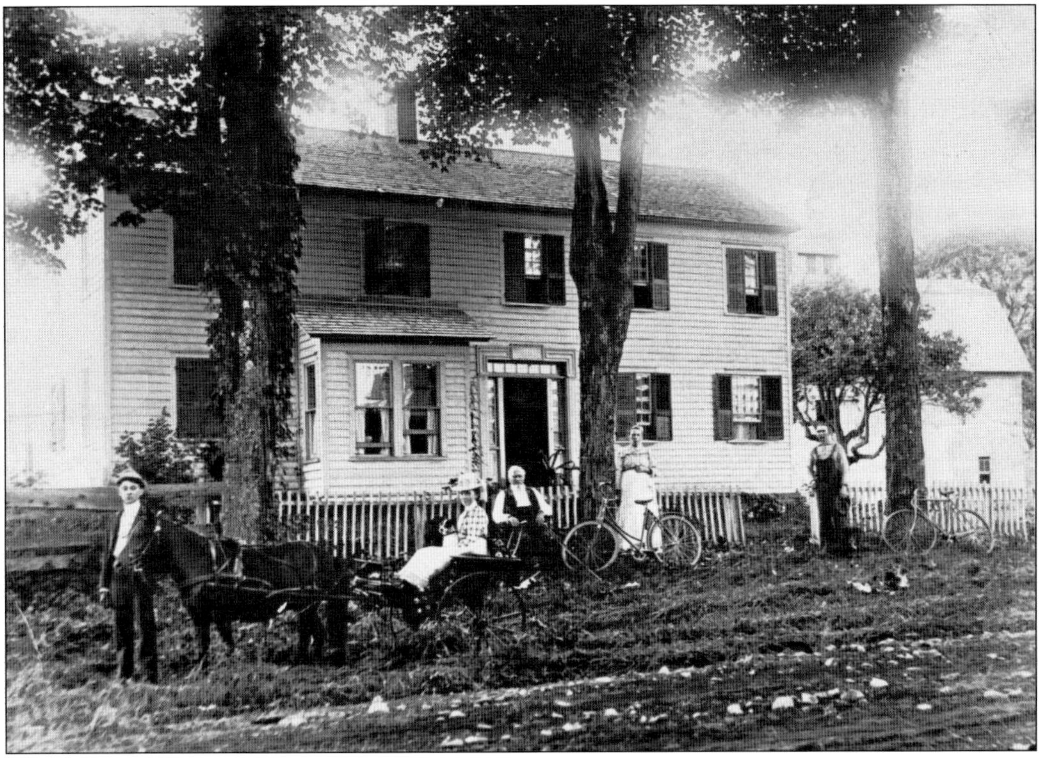

Taken in 1901, the Wells family poses on their farm, which was near the village, in this photograph. The young girl and her brother are quite proud of their bikes and pony cart, and they are dressed for the special occasion.

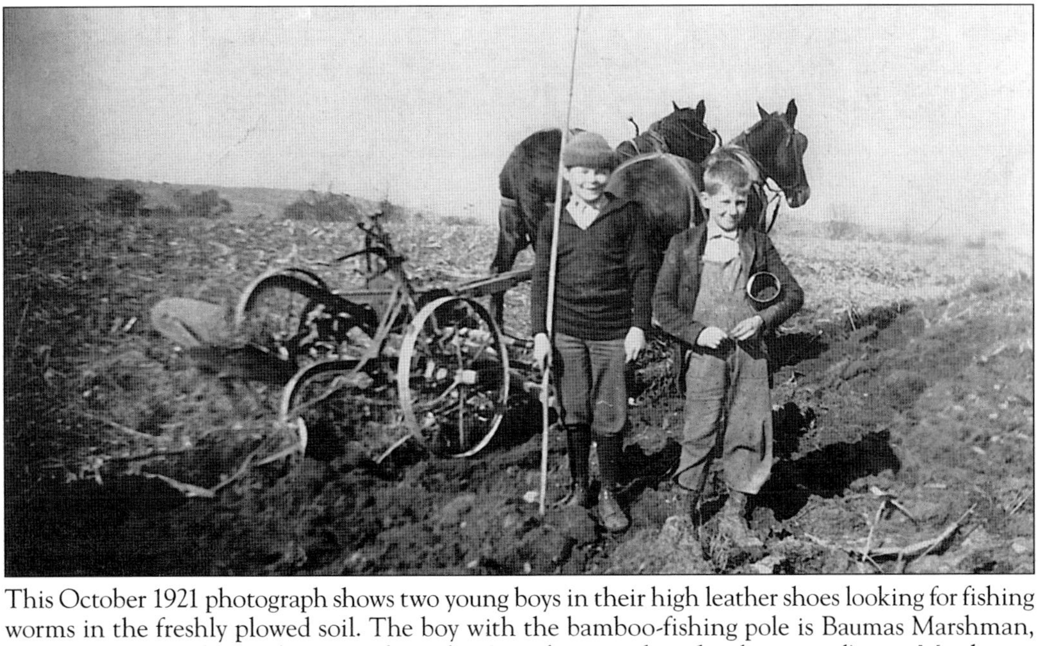

This October 1921 photograph shows two young boys in their high leather shoes looking for fishing worms in the freshly plowed soil. The boy with the bamboo-fishing pole is Baumas Marshman, and his friend Paul Benedict is on the right. Benedict was the school principal's son. Marshman was the grandson of Jacob Marshman, who founded the Marshman Farms.

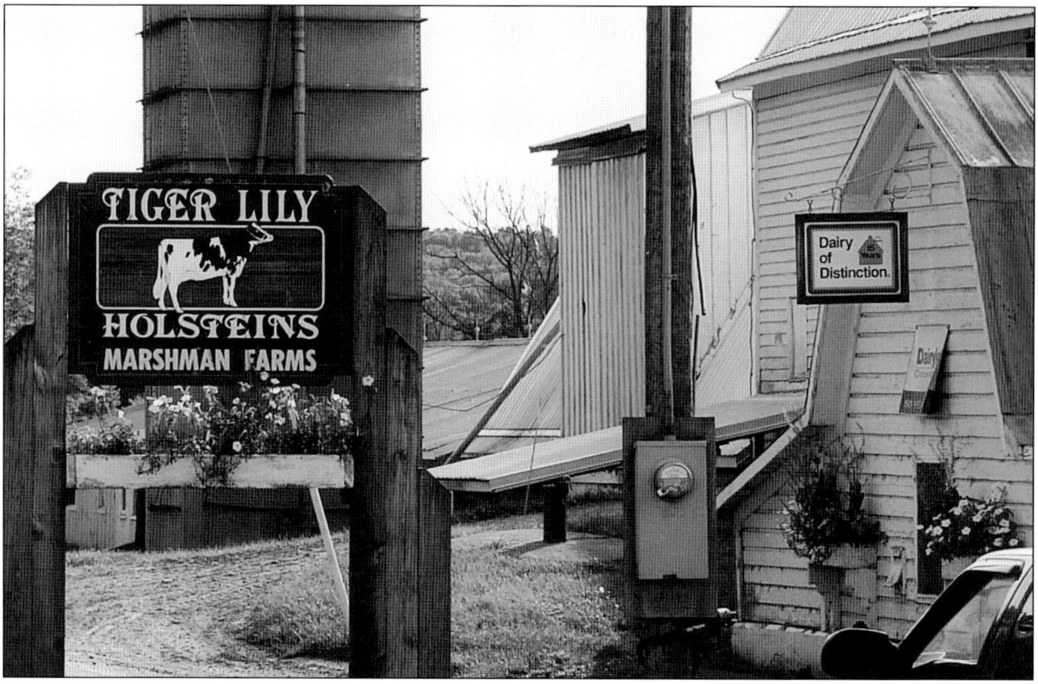

Seen here is a current scene at Marshman Farms; it has become an efficient modern operation. Today, the dairy farm houses 400 of the finest Holstein cows. The average milk production per cow is 300 percent higher than the cows that were owned by farmers during the 1930s.

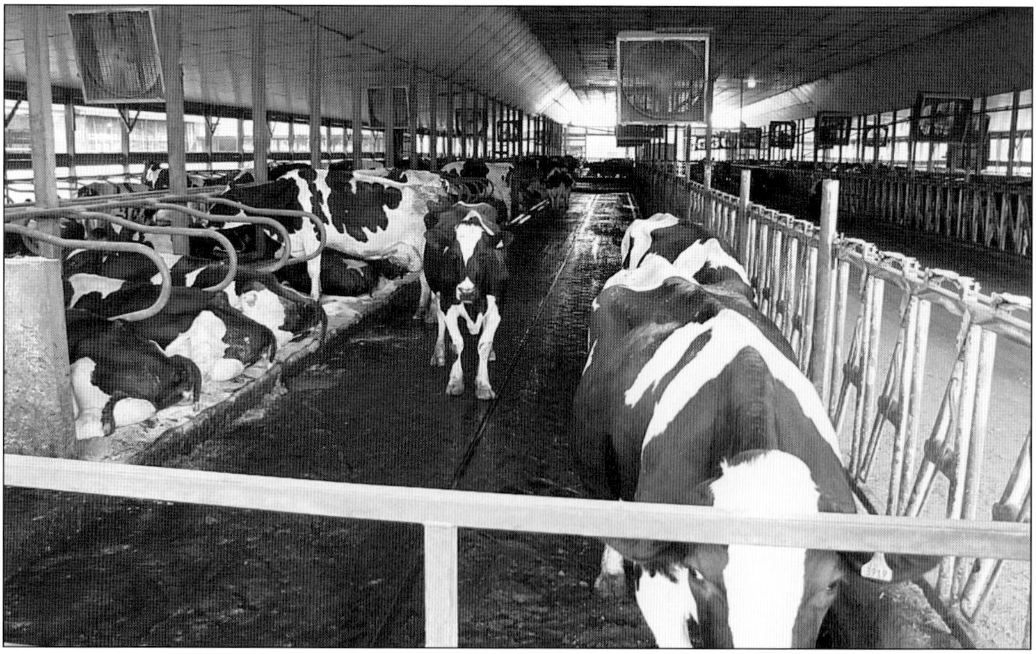

This photograph shows another view of Marshman Farms. The farm is capital intensive, which means that it requires high investment in equipment, machinery, and buildings. It also means that the farm operates under a modern, computer-assisted management team, which is made up of three generations of the family. Just like the old days, children are involved early with farming.

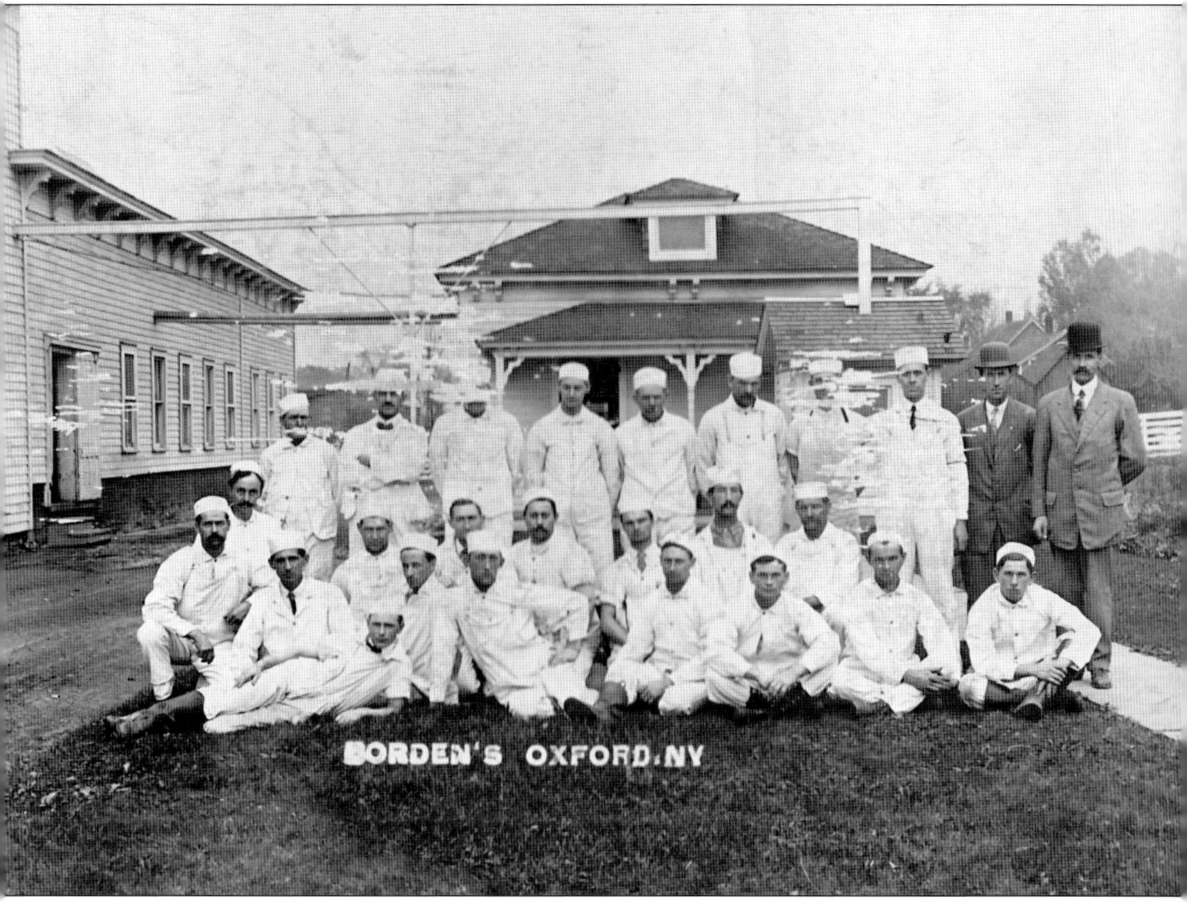

This is the oldest photograph of Borden's workers in the Oxford Historical Society archives and dates back to 1889 or 1890. All the workers are identified in an accompanying list, as are most of the workers in Borden's photographs. The clean uniforms and caps indicate the strict cleanliness of plant operations. Borden's enacted strict rules and ordered that fresh uniforms needed to be worn daily and all equipment be steam-cleaned at the end of each shift. This kept the bacteria count down, and it brought fresher and longer-lasting milk to the customer, which maintained Borden's excellent reputation with consumers. Pictured here are ? Graufe, M. Bartlett, S. Tiffany, J. Cotton, G. Wilcox, C. Brown, J. Dunn, A. Mead, ? Sharp, C. Cronk, ? Bassett, F. Miles, V. Root, C. Foster, J. Brown, A. Cotton, M. Nightengale, G. Lamb, J. Root, M. Dolan, N. Niles, F. Martin, E. Brown, W. Savage, ? Greenleaf, and W. Austin.

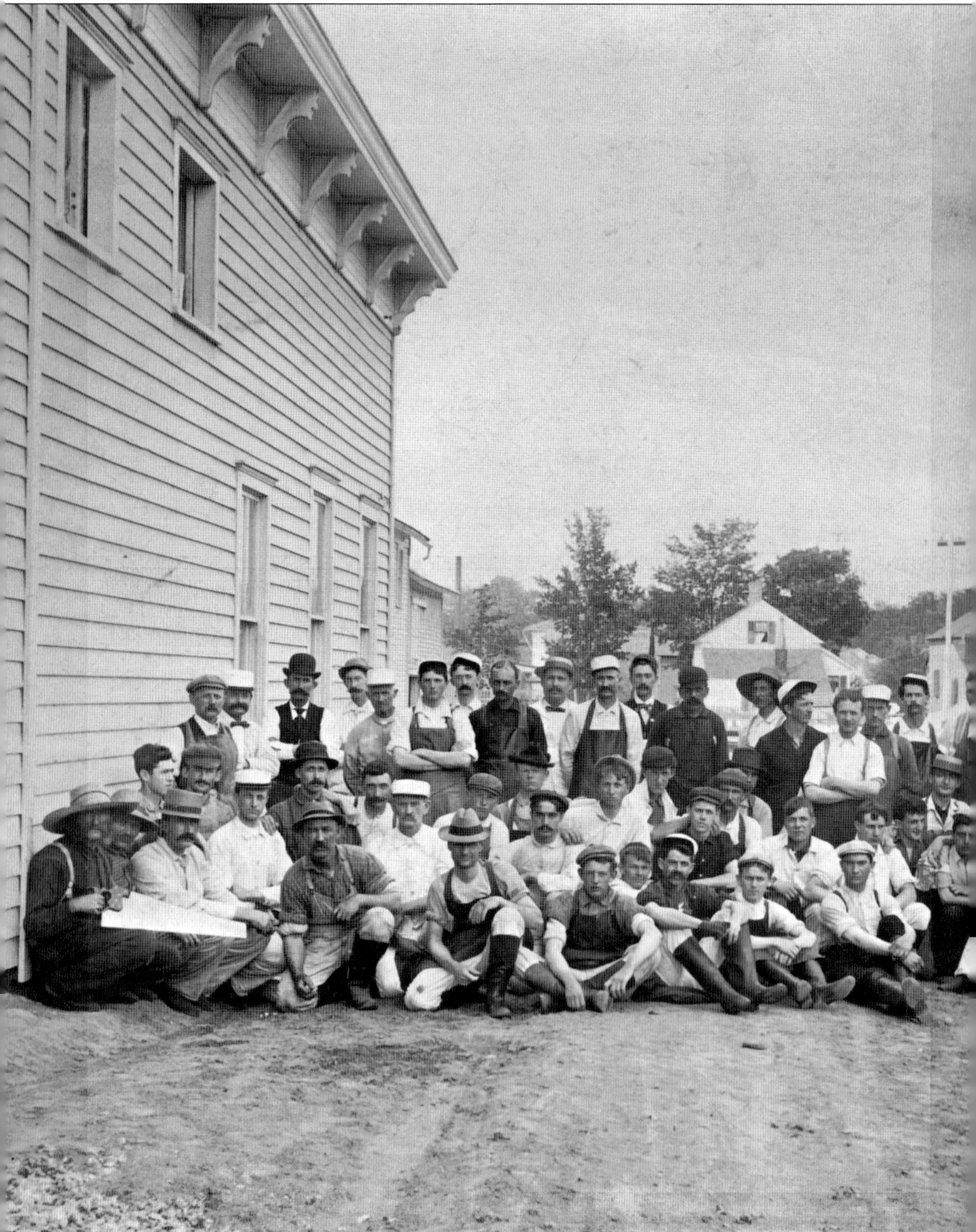

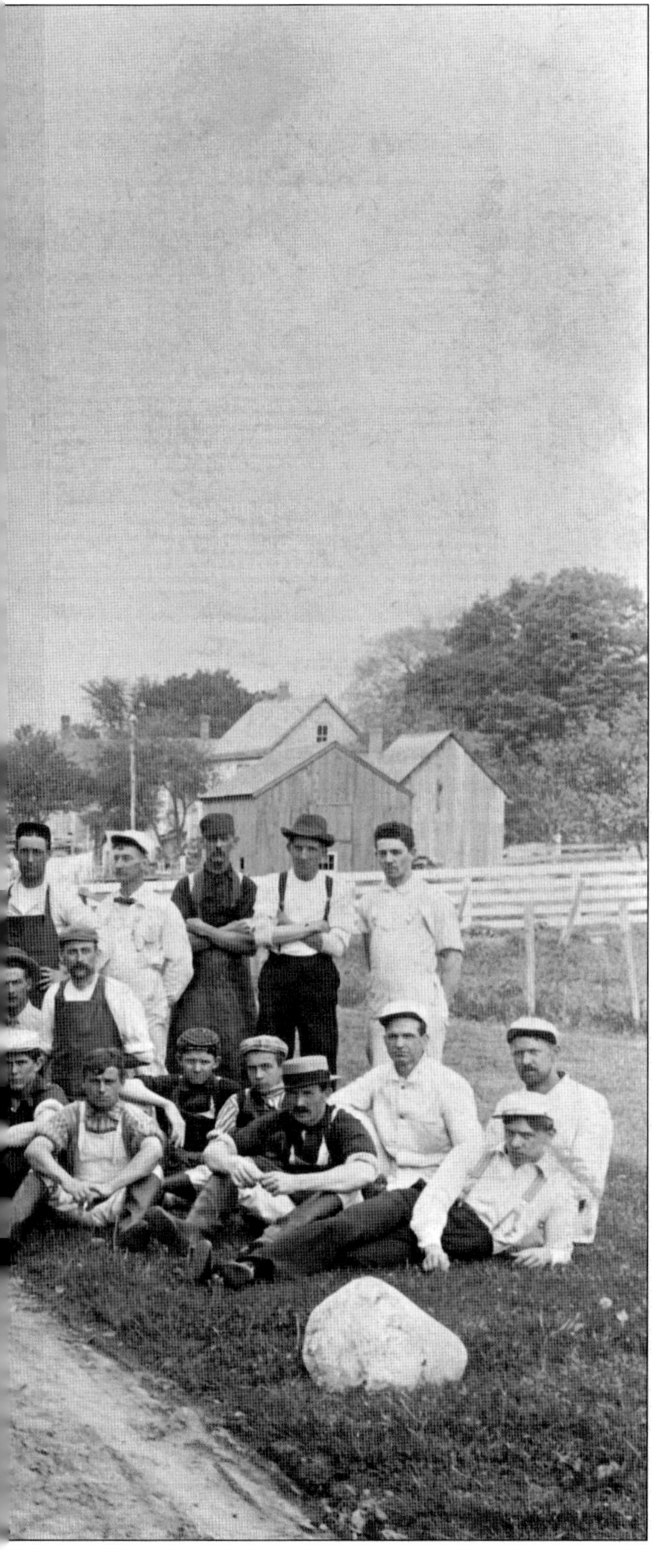

A 1898 photograph shows 64 Borden's workers. During those days, a regular shift was from 6:00 a.m. until 3:00 p.m. Most farmers brought their own milk to Borden's for inspection. The milk was dumped into a hopper where it was weighed, and a sample was taken to test for bacteria. The farmer received a receipt from Borden's, and the steam-cleaned milk cans were returned at the far end of the plant. Monthly milks checks were sent to farmers, and they were based on the weight of milk and butterfat content. Borden's regularly sent inspectors to their members' farms.

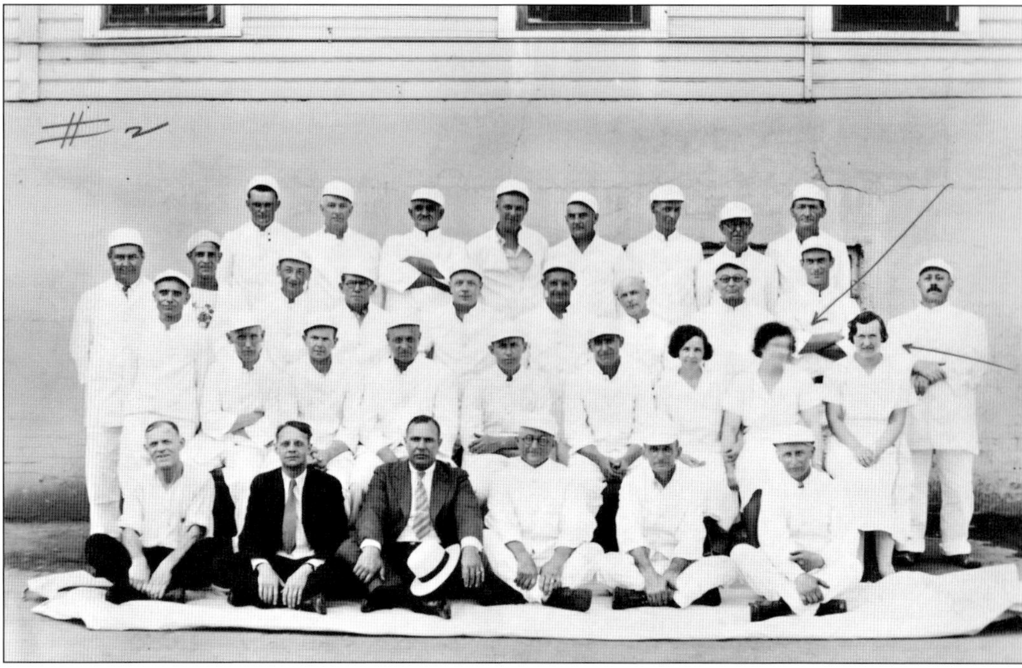

Borden's staff poses here in 1920. During this time, there were fewer workers. Only three women were on the staff, and here they appear to be correctly dressed.

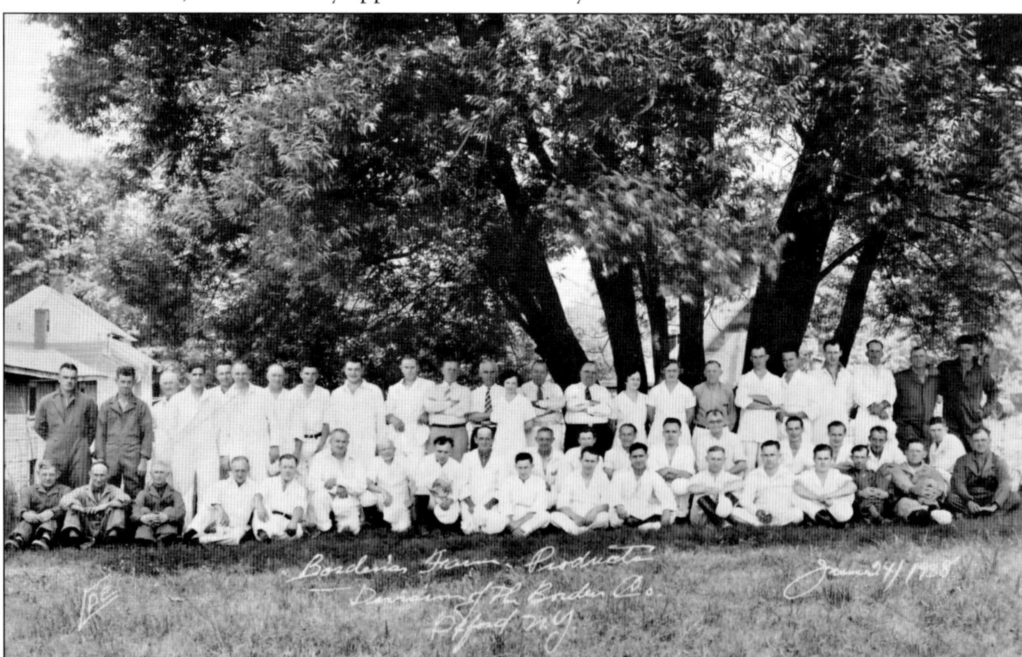

This 1938 photograph shows 53 workers, including three women. The staff is large, but during the time it was not beneficial. Milk prices were in a steady decline in the 1930s, only half of what they had been in 1910; it only got worse in the summer of 1939. When the prices went under $1 per centum weight, farmers went on strike and dumped tons of milk in the streets of Oxford. The next day, state troopers arrested 52 farmers, and the strike was dissipated.

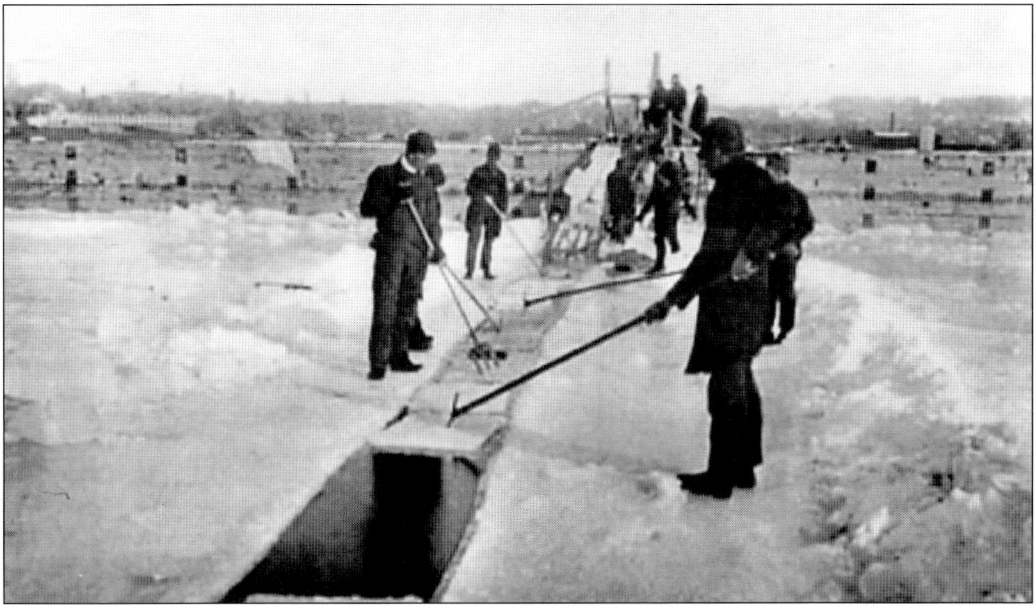

Taken in 1894, this photograph shows locals harvesting ice, which was mostly done on Rugg's Pond located on Midland Hill. The pond was where Borden's obtained most of its ice. Big sled loads were brought in for storage in the ice barns. In the photograph, it shows the channel that was cut on the pond. Later, the ice blocks were pushed to the edge for loading.

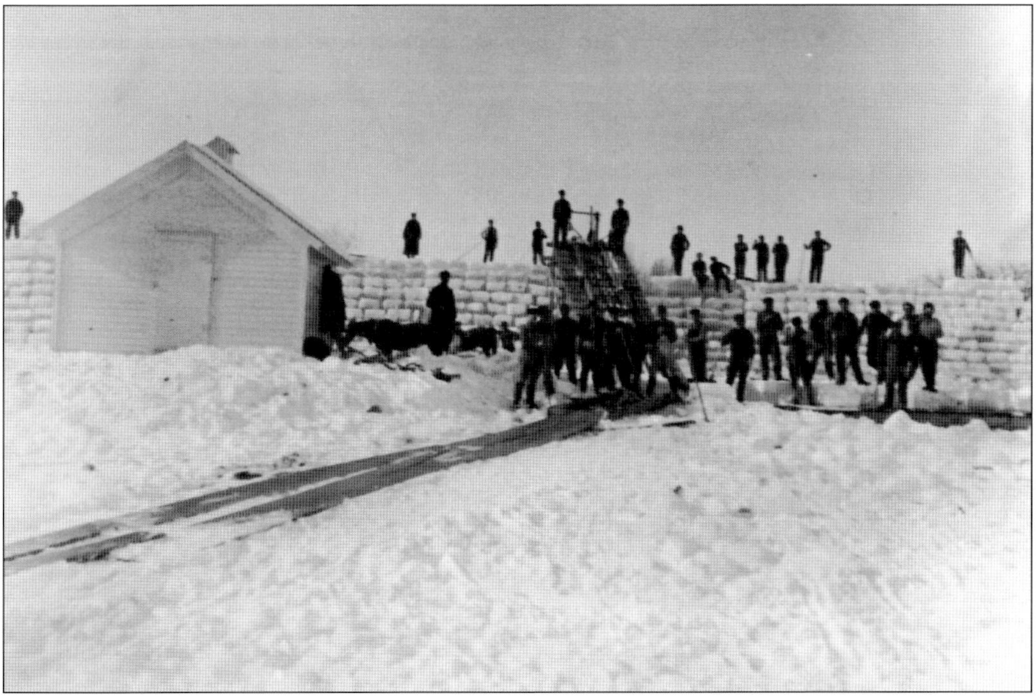

Using an elevator, men are seen stacking large ice chunks near the plant, which was probably for winter and spring use. Summer ice was stored in large barns and layered with straw or sawdust to preserve them. This was a big annual job that required many hours, because Borden's regularly harvested and stored over 8,000 tons of ice.

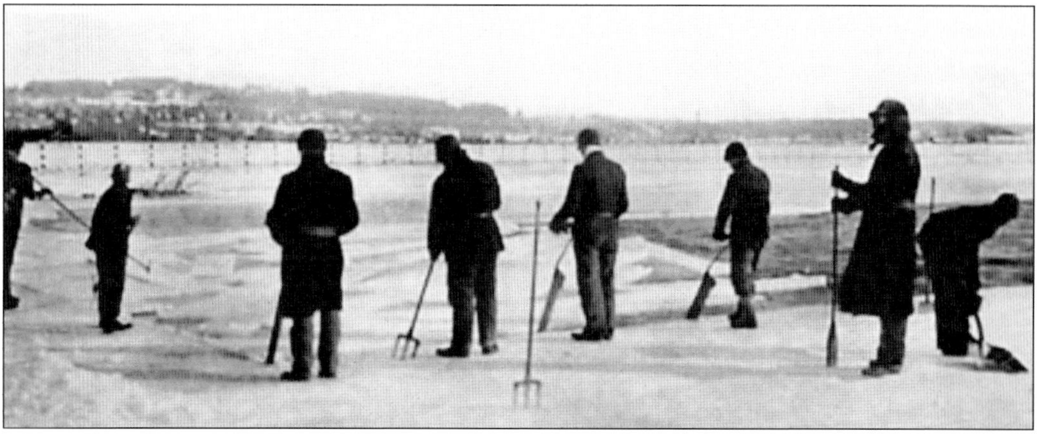

This image depicts ice saws that were used for cutting the channels and blocks of ice. The Oxford Historical Museum has a horse-drawn saw that was used to cut ice, which was a gift from Joe Knoll. In the museum, an early engine for powering an ice elevator, along with a full description of the Rugg's Pond operation, are on display. They were gifts from Russell Stafford and Bernard Stafford.

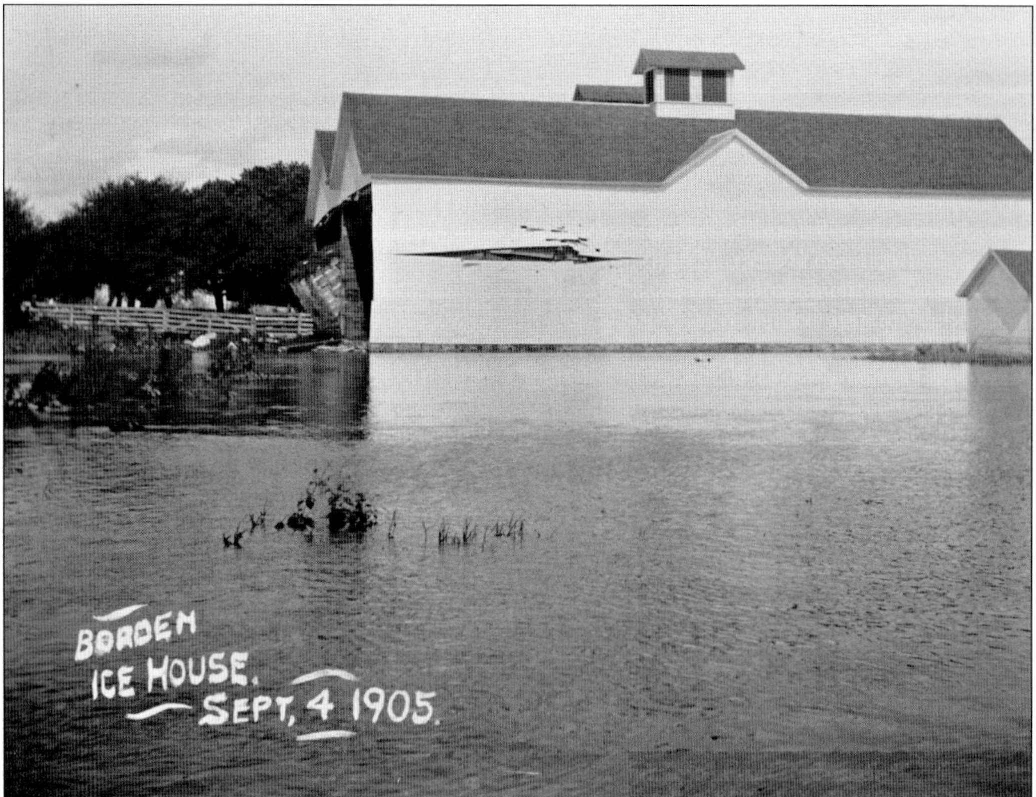

In September 1905, several hundred tons of ice shifted in the storage barns, which caused the flooding of the lowest tier of ice and considerable damage to two barns.

Taken in 1905, this photograph shows the straw cap that insulated the stored ice. Damage to the lower barn can be clearly observed. Several well-dressed onlookers have gathered to inspect the scene.

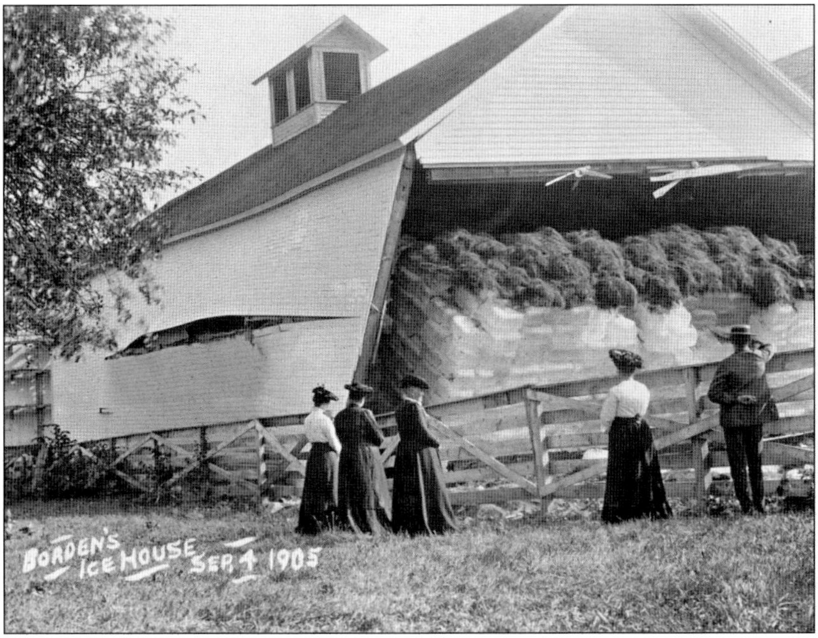

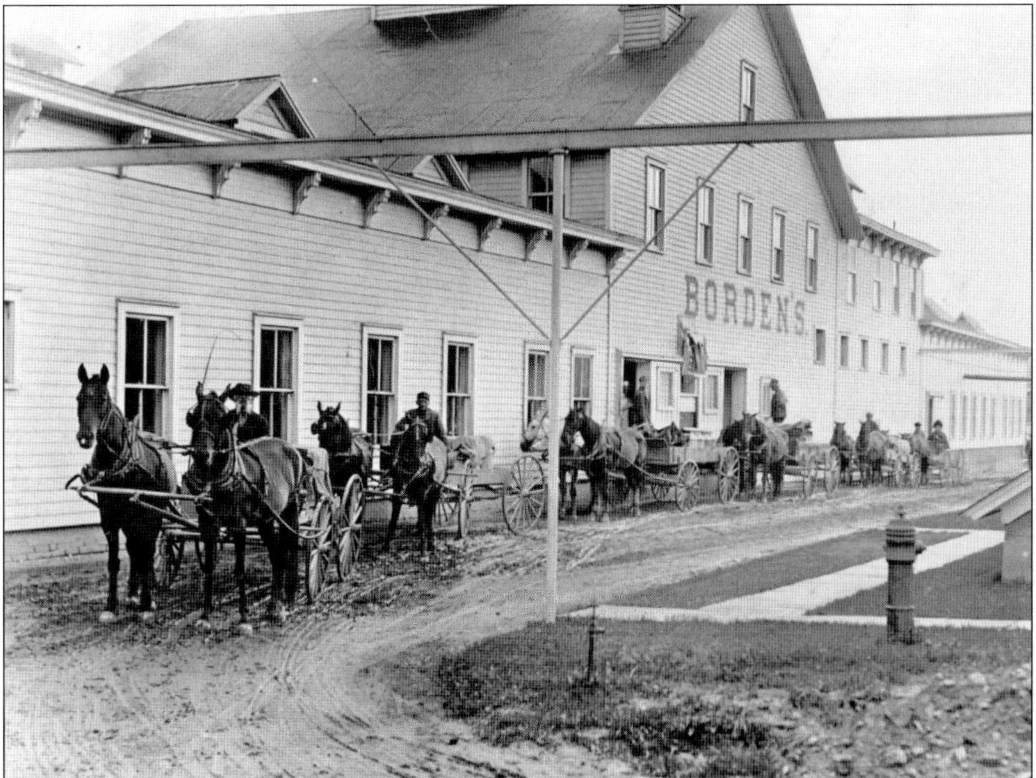

In this c. 1905 photograph, farmers with teams of horses are seen delivering milk to Borden's in the morning.

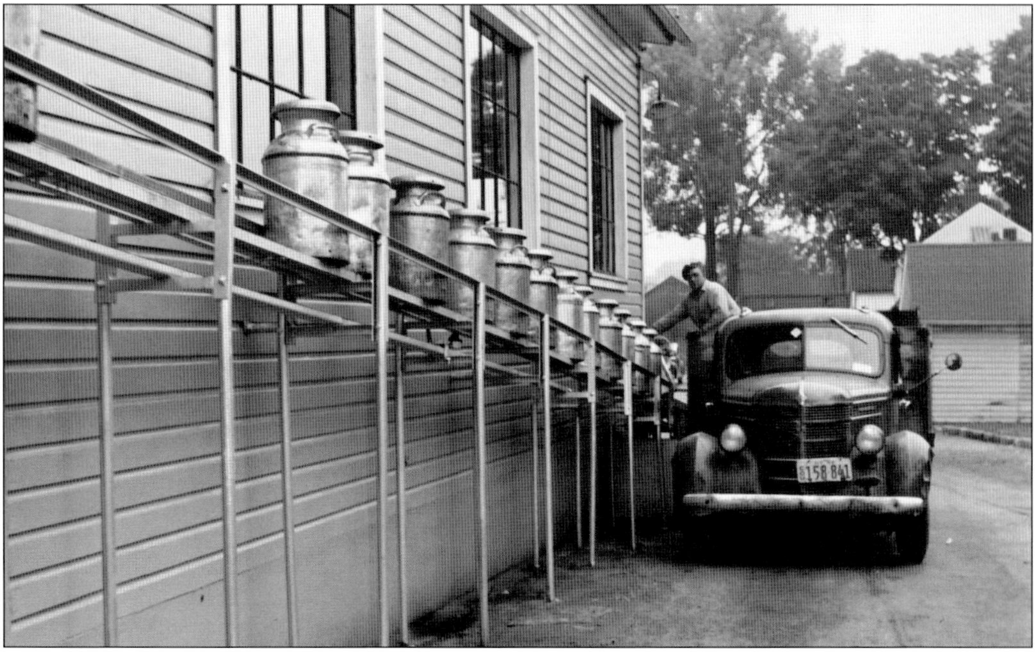

By the 1940s, most milk was brought to Borden's by hired truckers. In the photograph, the driver is collecting numbered cans that have been steam-cleaned. He is returning the cans to the farmers, which were then used for the next morning's pick-up. Farmers owned their milk cans, and sometimes a double set was needed.

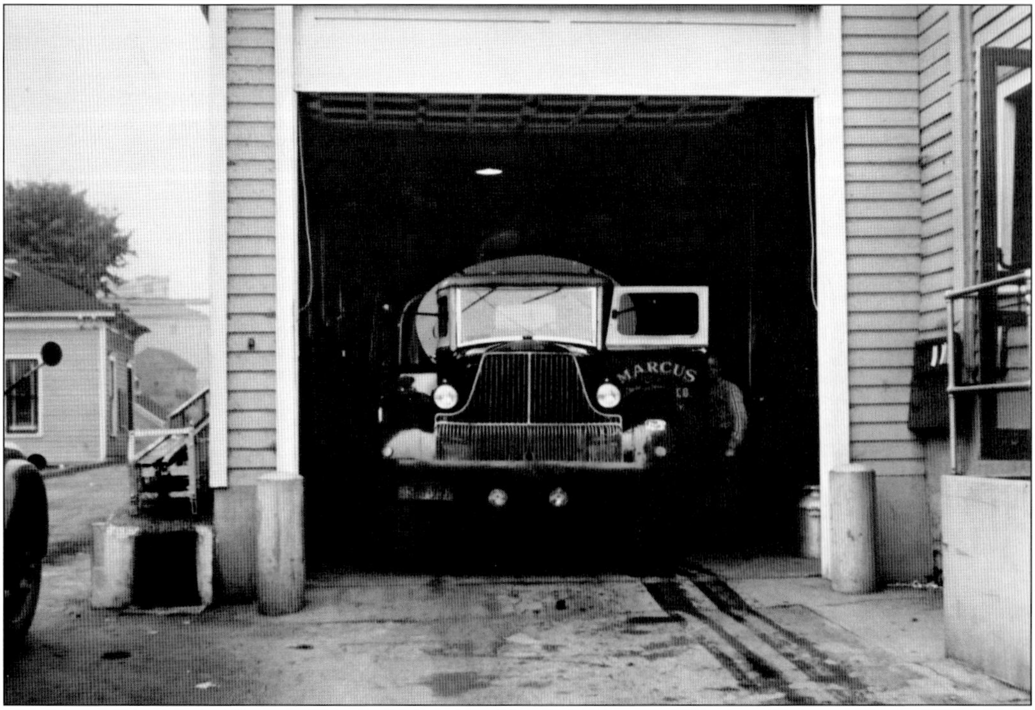

During the 1940s, large tank trucks delivered ice-cold pasteurized milk to cities for bottling. Borden's had ceased its bottling operations by August 1939.

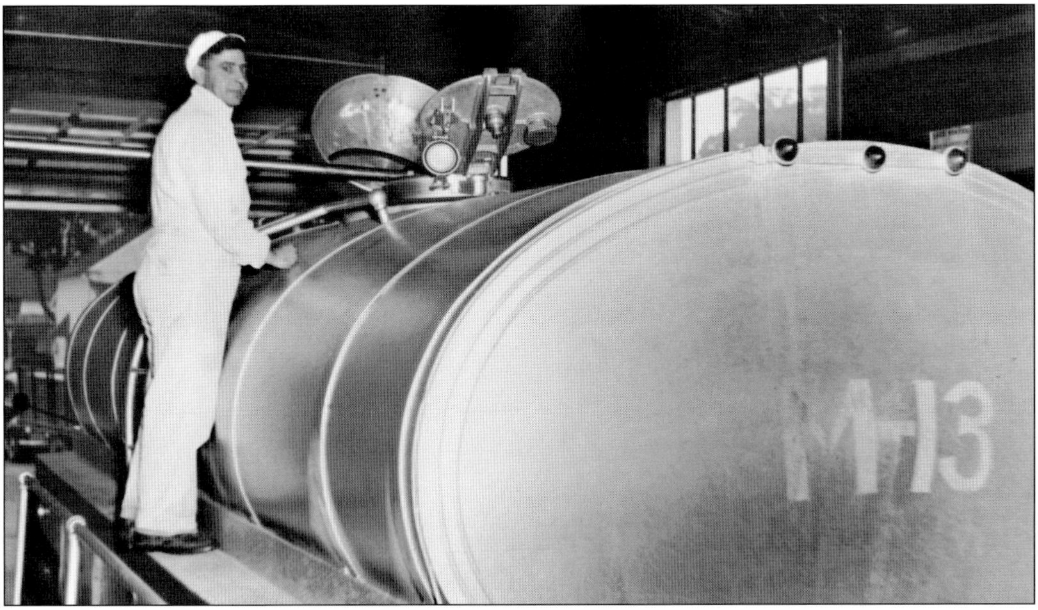

A tanker is filled with pasteurized milk before it is capped and sealed for shipment. Borden's milk was always certified and top grade. This quality brought it a national reputation. On June 18, 1939, the Oxford facility received two important orders. One order was for heavy cream (grade A) to be sent to Hyde Park. The second order was from the home of President Roosevelt; the king and queen of England were staying over that particular weekend, and they wanted to try Borden's milk.

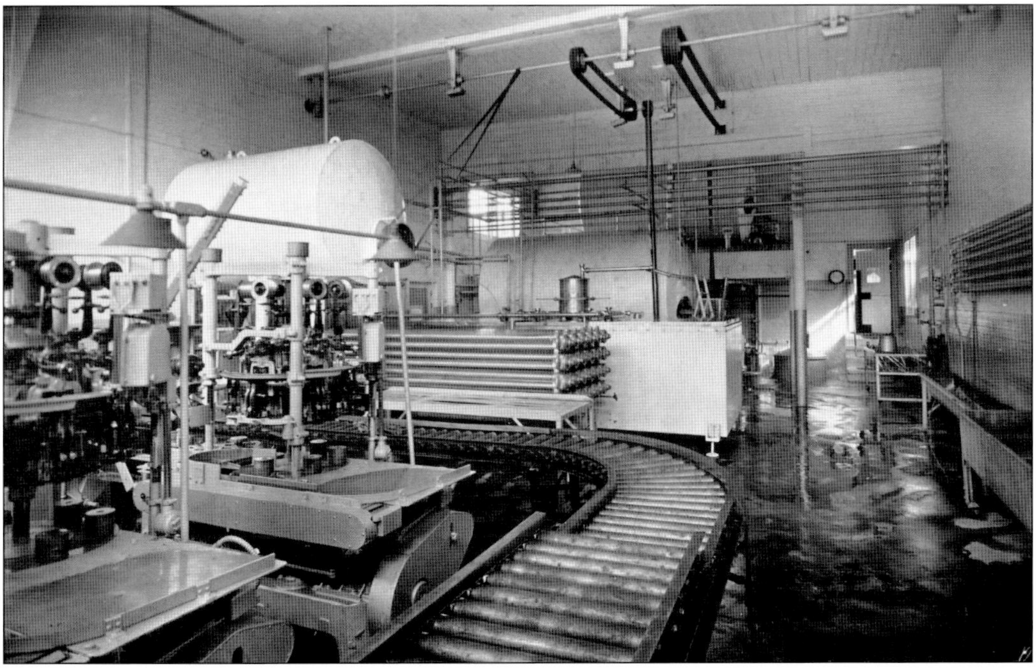

This photograph shows a conveyor belt winding past two of the old capping machines. Quart bottles of pasteurized milk were capped, crated, and shipped to New York City on ice. Fresh milk could be on urban breakfast tables less than 24 hours after the farm milking.

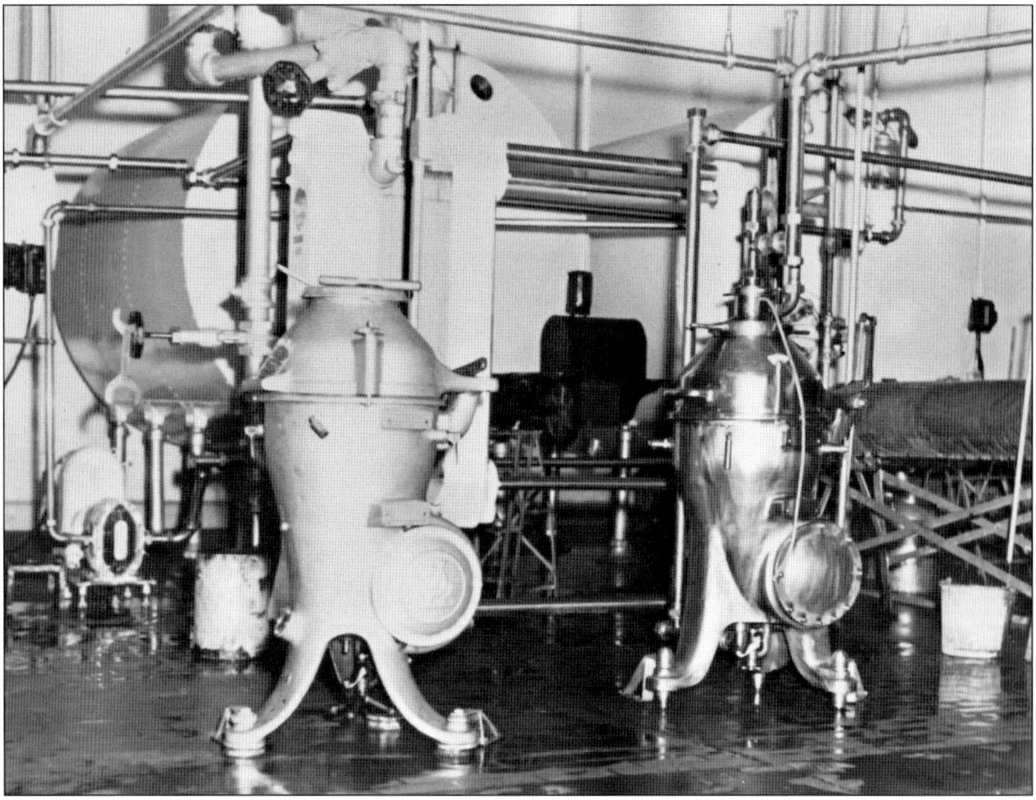

Two high-speed centrifuges separated cream from the milk. Three grades of milk were shipped: whole milk, light cream, and heavy cream.

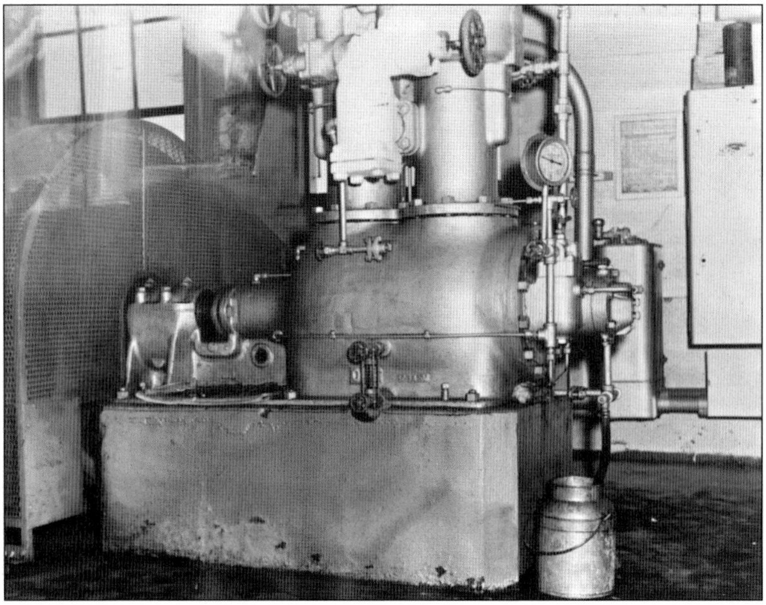

Steam was produced from water and pressurized in the boiler. These interior photographs of the Borden's Milk Plant show much of the processing of milk that provided employment for nearly 100 people in Oxford. Everything that touched milk (cans, bottles, truck tanks, and machinery) was steam-cleaned after every shift.

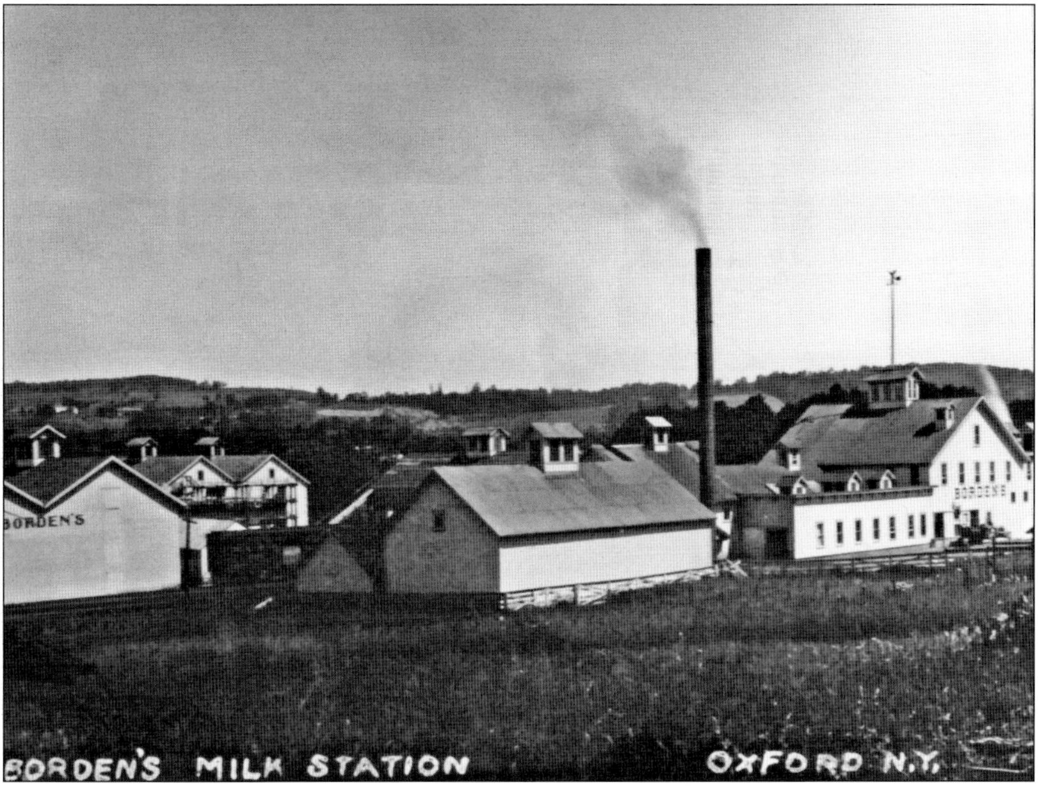

A 1920s photograph shows the complex of Borden's buildings that made up the Oxford site. The view is from the east of the buildings, and it shows the northeastern landscape.

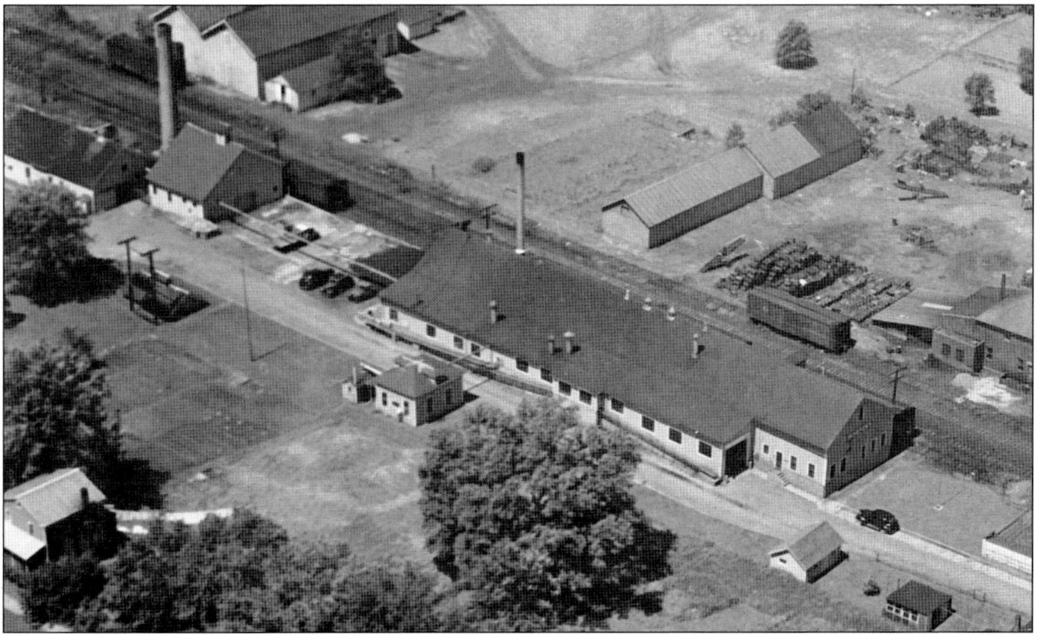

This 1939 aerial view of Borden's looks southwest from the east side of the DL&W tracks. The boxcar in the scene shows the size of Borden's.

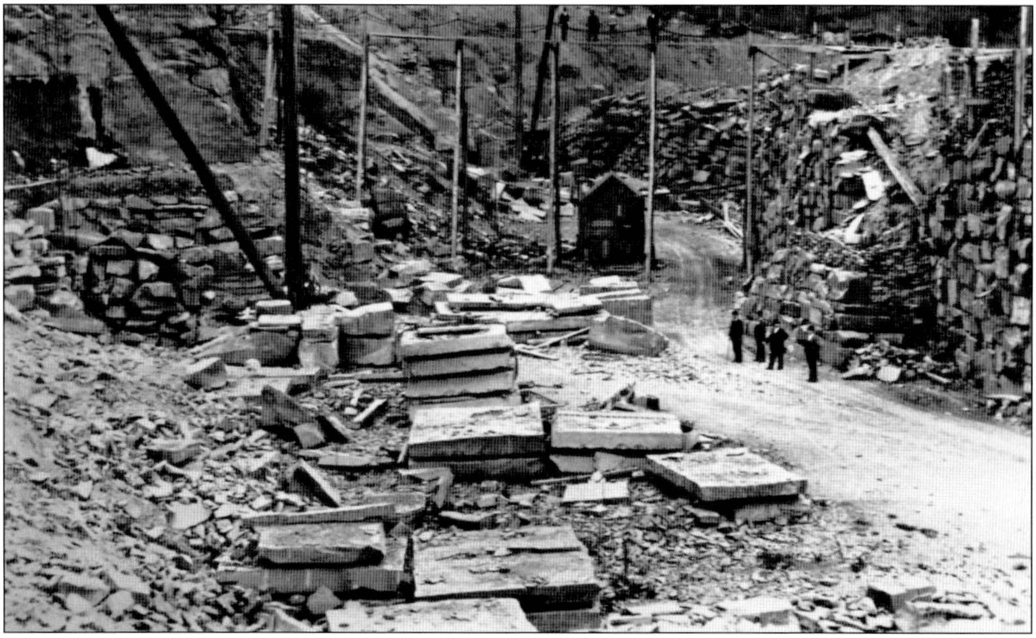

Seen here is a view of the south quarry that was owned by F.G. Clarke Blue Stone. Several undressed slabs are stacked and ready for dressing and shipping. The four men in the center of the photograph portray the grand size of the bluestone. A dressed stone is one that has been cut, trimmed to size, and polished on one side.

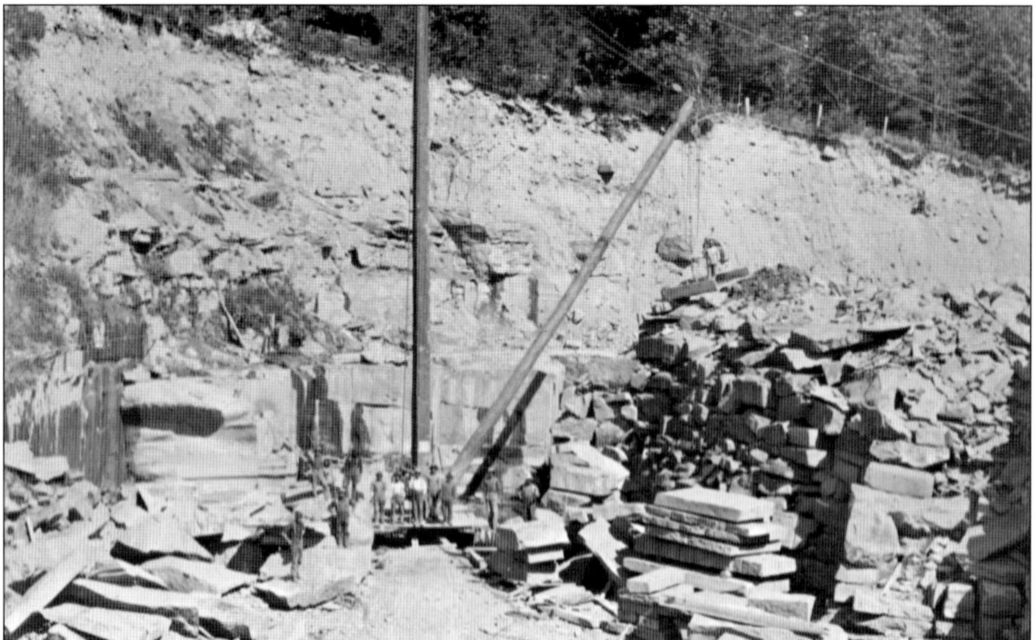

A shot of Clarke's north quarry shows cut and uncut slabs. The photograph also shows the huge crane with steel cables that hoisted the slabs onto sturdy, horse-drawn wagons that transported the slabs to the Clarke dock on the DL&W tracks. The 11 men in the center of the photograph provide a scale that shows the size of the slabs and the crane.

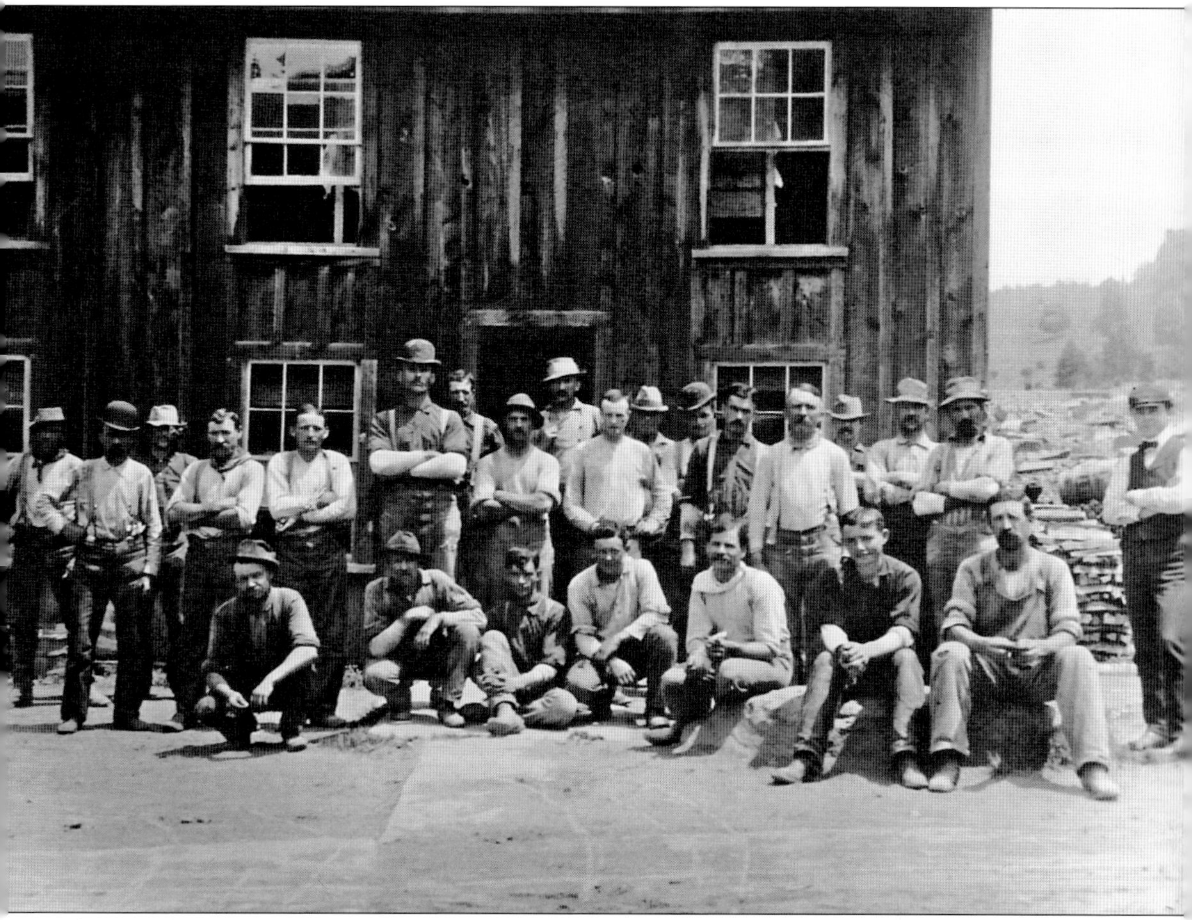

These workmen near the south quarry are as impressive as the quarry itself. They worked 10 hours a day, six days a week. The wages were certainly not high, but the total payroll for nearly 300 men was important to the community. The stones that these men quarried were used for Grant's Tomb in New York City, the sidewalks of Wall Street, and the cement in front of Trinity Church in Oxford, the Trinity Church in Binghamton, and the First National Bank in Oxford—all built with Oxford bluestone. St. Paul's Episcopal Church was built with bluestone from several nearby quarries. (Courtesy of CCHS.)

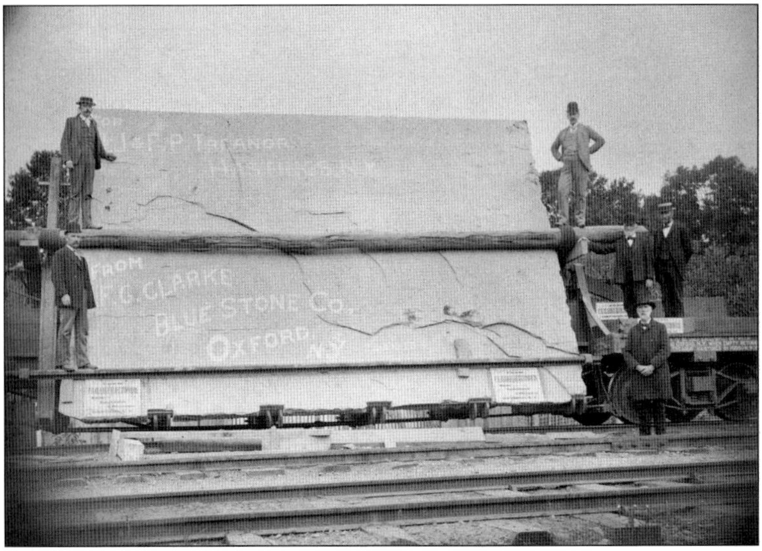

This photograph shows a huge slab of undressed bluestone, which was loaded on a special car that was invented to transport Oxford bluestone. The bluestone was being sent to Hastings, New York, and its destination can be clearly seen on the face of the slab. (Courtesy of CCHS.)

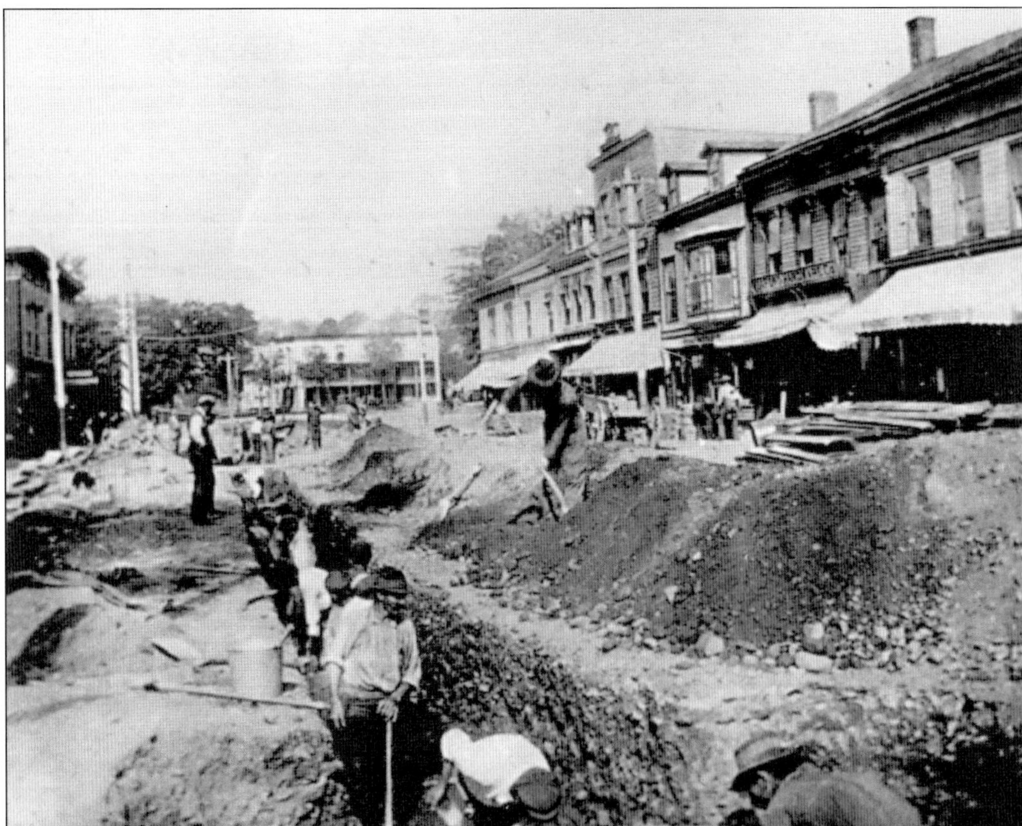

In 1902, the bluestone sidewalks were put in place on the Navy Island Block. This photograph shows the street pavement operation in progress and the ditch for the water main that was on the east side of the village. All the major equipment at the quarry was powered by steam, from the huge cranes and pneumatic drills to the saws and polishers. Gaslights were used to illuminate the work area whenever it was necessary. (Courtesy of Vicky House.)

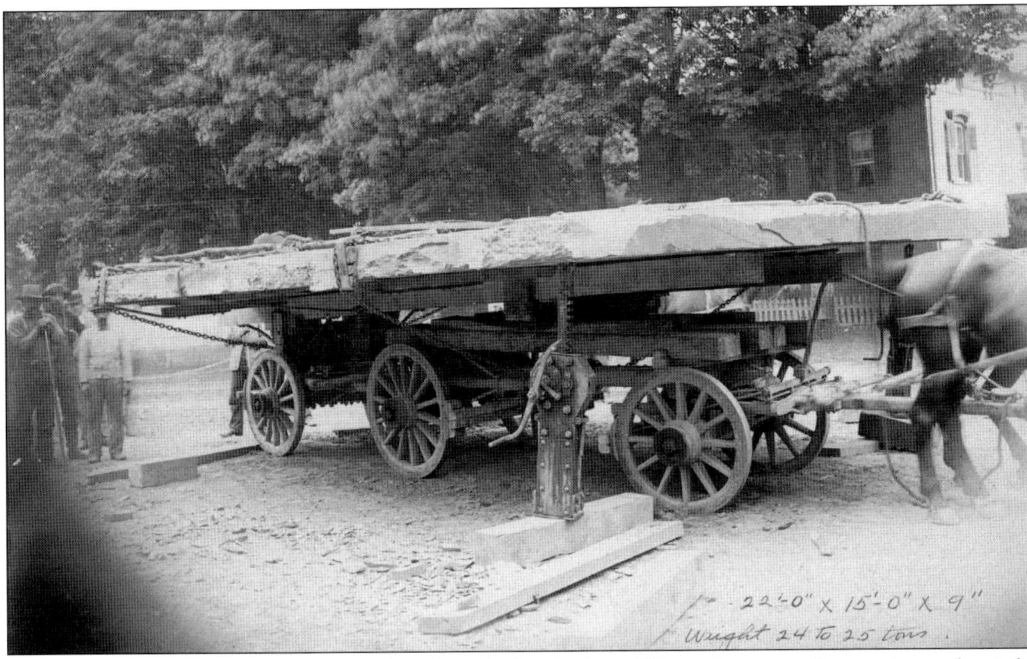

A platform rock is being transported to the Clarke dock on Water Street, and its estimated weight at 24 or 25 tons. Often, workers used the number of horses, which were needed to pull the stone on a wagon, to gauge the weight of large stones. According to their method, a 10-horse stone or 12-horse stone was considered very big. (Courtesy of CCHS.)

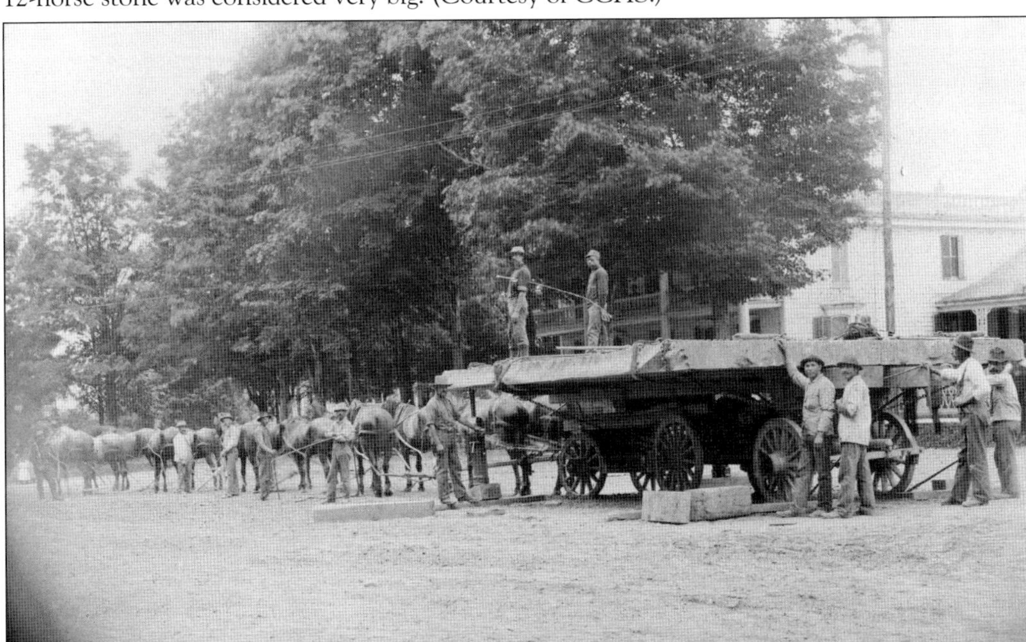

This photograph shows another large platform stone parked in front of the Corbin family's home, which is now the Oxford Memorial Library at Fort Hill Park. The wagon may have parked in order to give the horses a brief break. The large platform seemed to have been a 12-horse stone. (Courtesy of CCHS.)

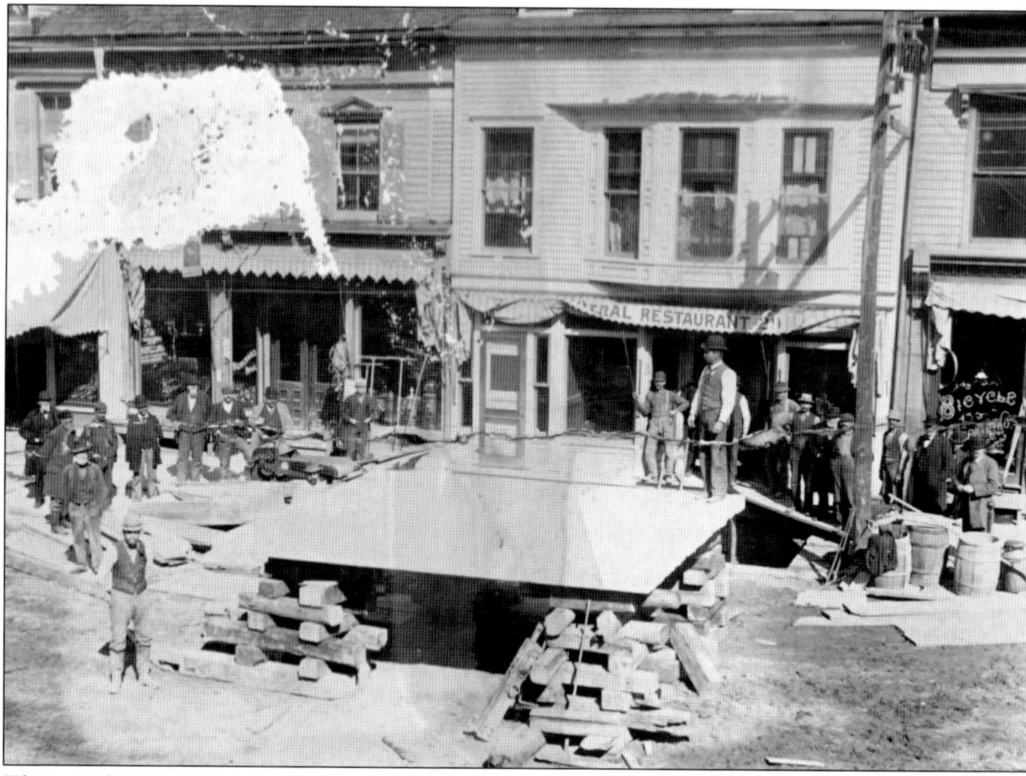

This is a large, well-dressed stone being lowered into place at the Central Restaurant on East Main Street. The stone extended from the front steps to the street. In the photograph, several of the men appear to be Clarke workers, onlookers, or kibitzers.

THE PENNANT.

F. G. Clarke Blue Stone Co.

Oxford, Chenango County, N. Y.

MINERS, MANUFACTURERS AND WHOLESALERS.

Rock, Platforms,
Sills, Lintels,
Steps, Flagging,
Gutter and Crossings.

Sawed, Planed,
Rubbed and Finished
STONE.

Estimates Furnished on Finished Work.

Stone Shipped to all Points.

Tests of Stone made at the New York State Museum by Hon. J. C. Smock:

Specific gravity	2.7113	Percentage of gain in weight in CO_2 gas	0.0024
Weight, per cubic foot	168.97	Weight increased in lbs. (per cubic ft.)	0.0041
Percentage of water absorbed	1.11	Percentage of gain in sulphurous acid	0.064
Weight of water per cubic foot	1.876	Weight increased per cubic foot	0.108

Freezing and thawing test—No effect.

F.G. Clarke advertised extensively, and this advertisement from the *Academy Pennant* is typical. Most of the time, Clarke advertisements included a complete list of quarry products along with some scientific support.

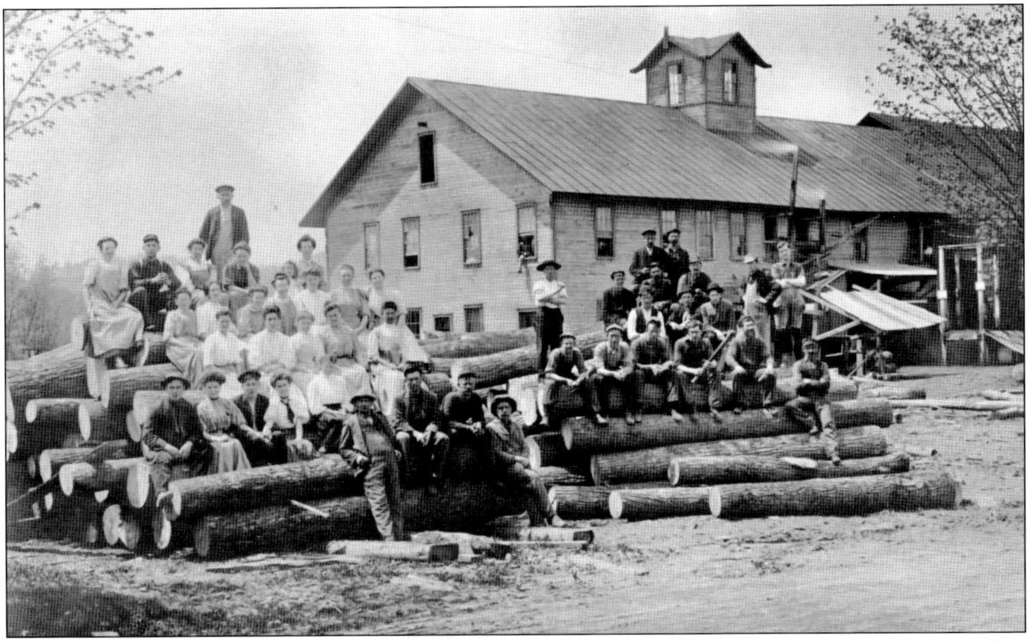

In 1889, during the same year that Borden's began shipping milk, the Ohio Basket Factory moved its operations to Oxford from Ashtabula, Ohio. The company changed its name to Oxford Basket & Manufacturing Company and was located on a railroad siding at the end of Pleasant Street. Taken around 1898, the photograph shows 45 workers from the Oxford Basket & Manufacturing Company factory. The company even hired a few women as workers. (Courtesy of Anna Stark.)

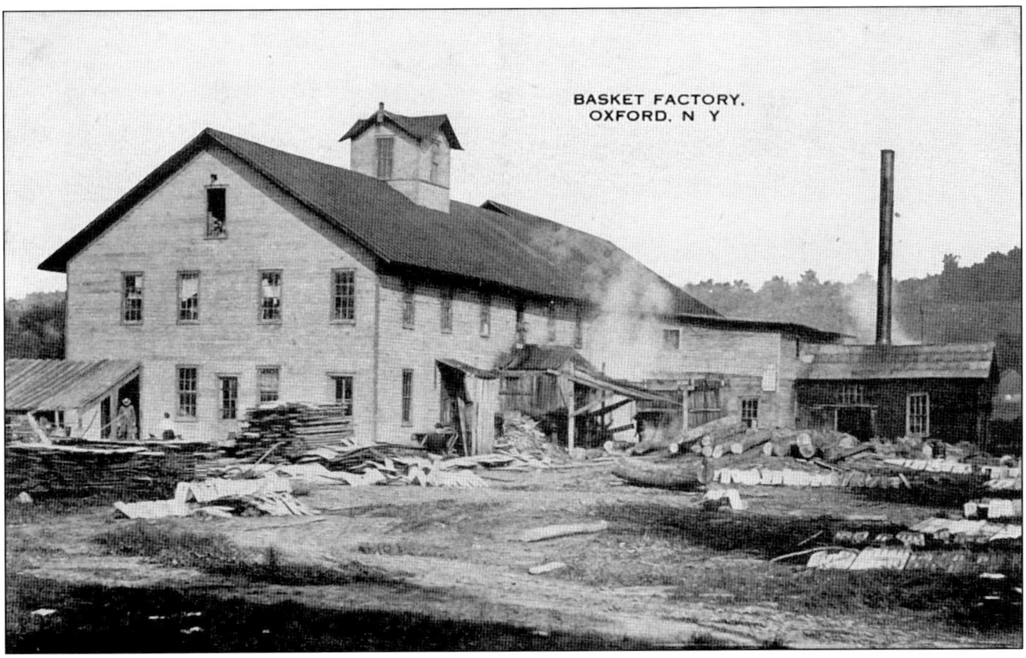

Taken in 1919, the photograph shows the Oxford Basket & Manufacturing Company factory in bad shape. On October 13, 1922, a fire burned the entire building to the ground. In just 13 months, though, the company built a new factory and installed new machinery.

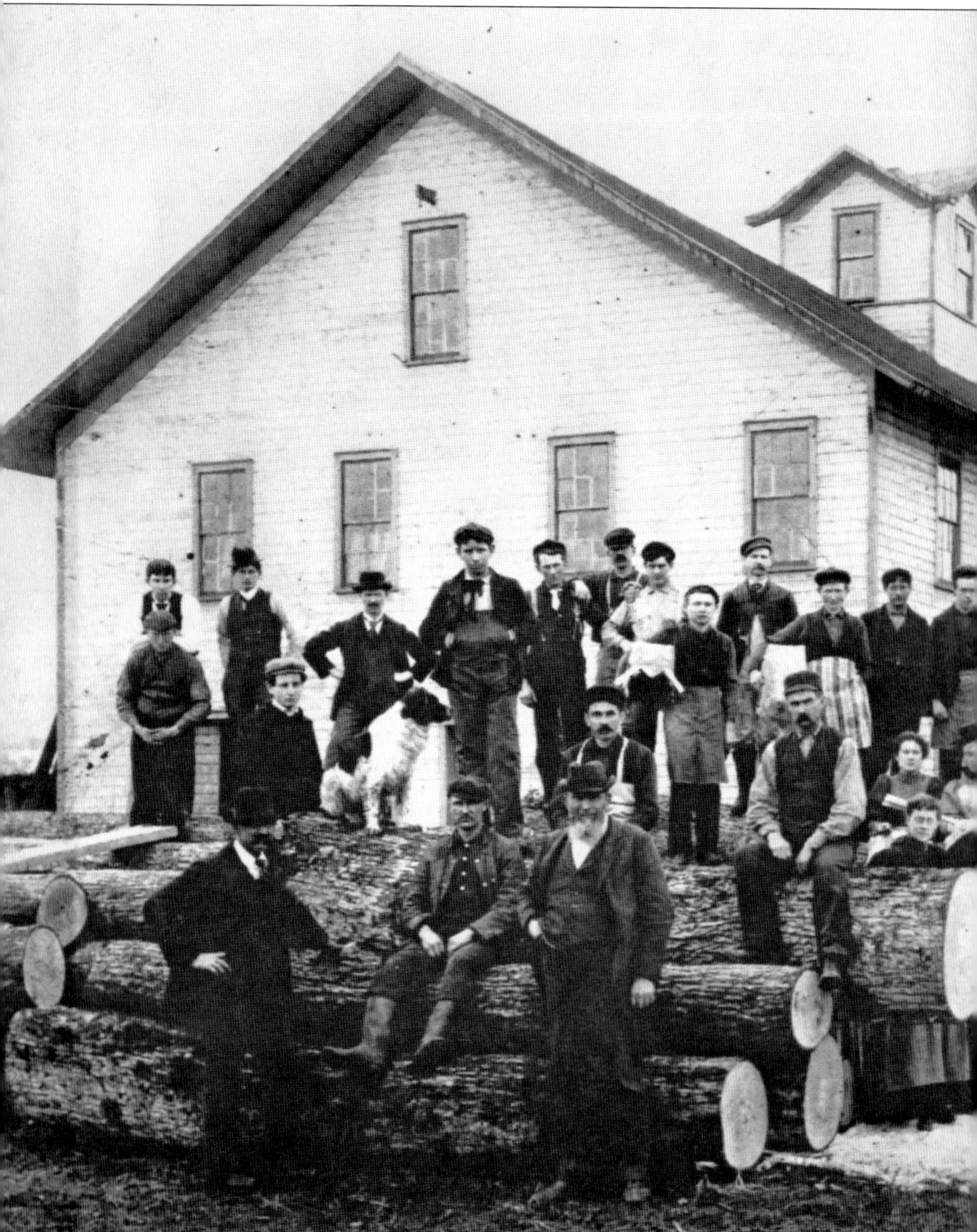

Basket workers pose for a photograph taken on a winter day in 1895. The company had 43 employees present, including 20 women. For most of its 40 years, the factory provided steady employment

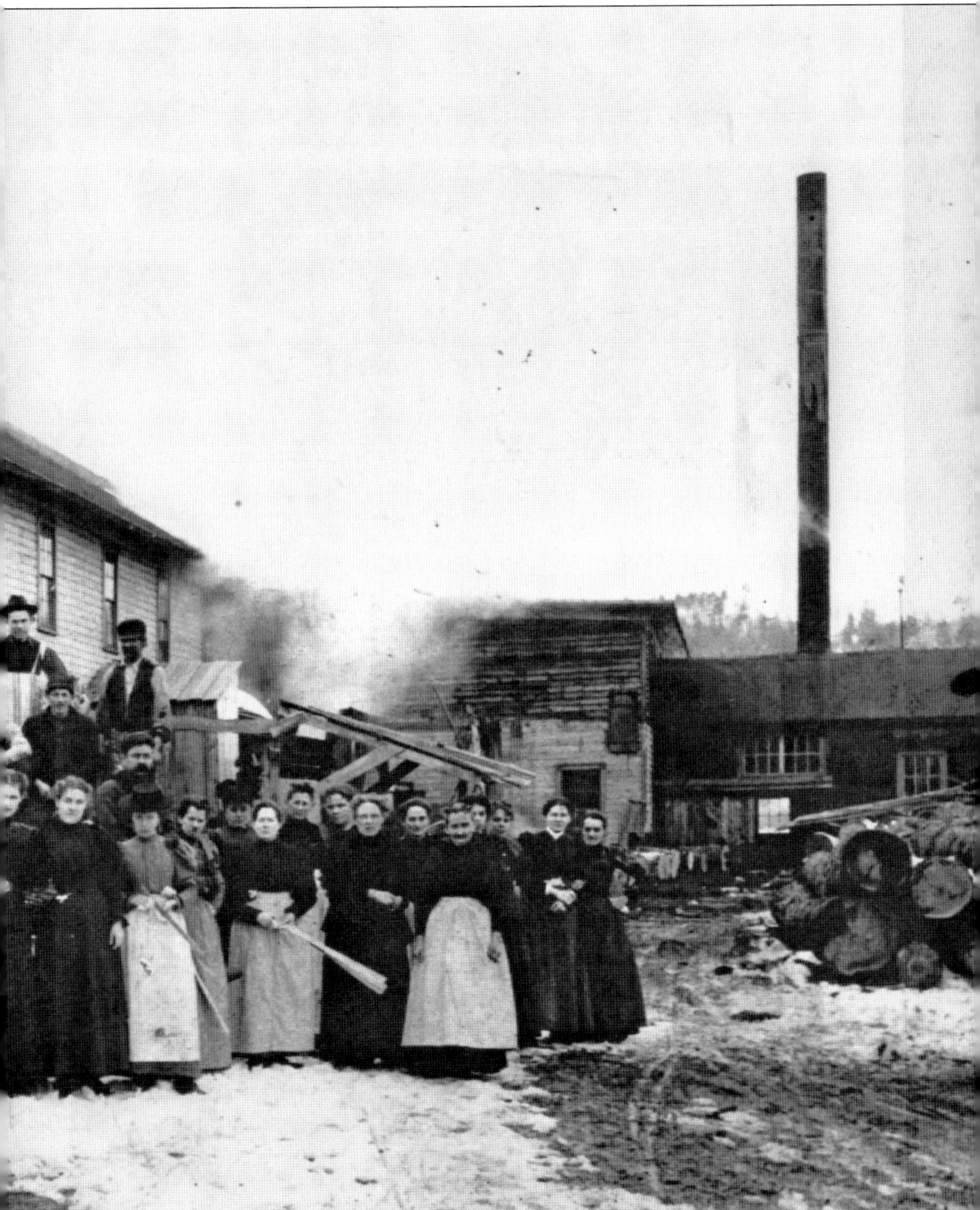

with current wages. Also, the image shows the large logs the factory needed to make baskets. Four teams worked full-time to pull them in and provide the company with a steady supply of logs.

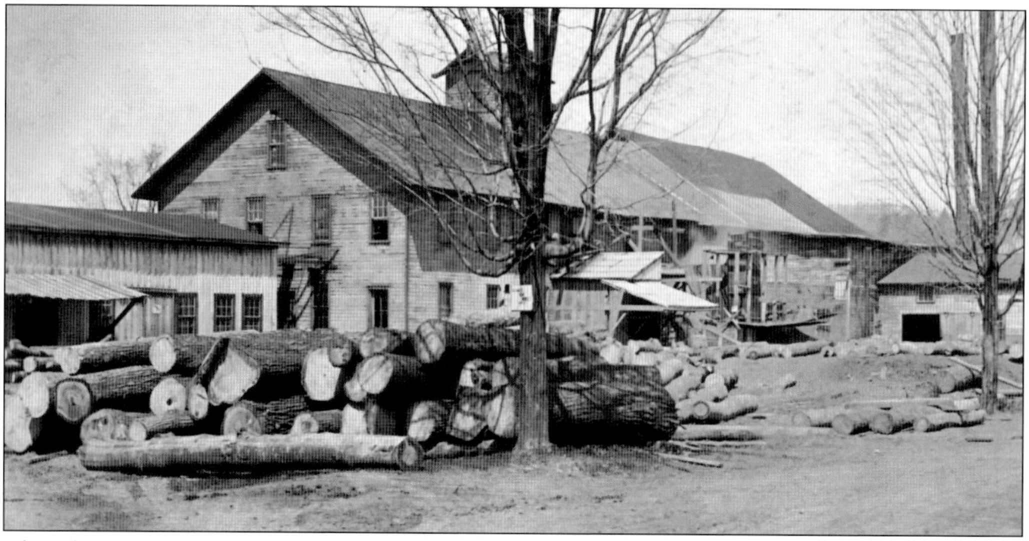

This photograph shows a typical stack of ash logs. The wood from the logs was preferred for most baskets. The factory used pressurized steam to boil the logs in big concrete vats for 12 to 18 hours. The loose bark was scraped off, and the logs were then skewered before being sliced by a sharp blade. The cutting process produced long sheets of veneer that had the desired thickness. These sheets were cut into strips and were weaved into a variety of baskets.

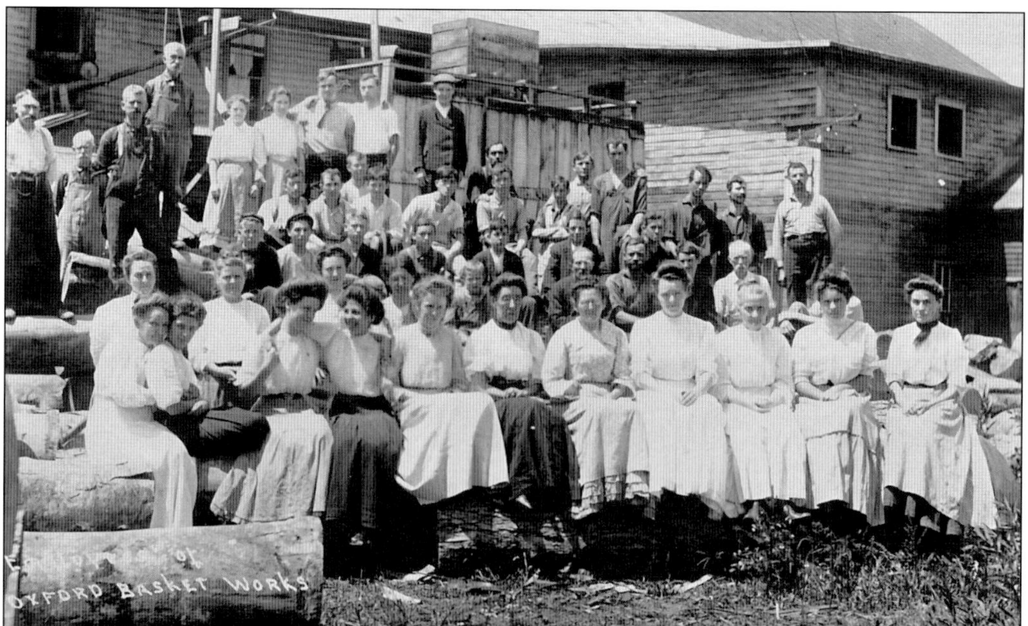

Fifty-one employees from the basket factory pose here, including 17 women; the employment rate ranged from 40 percent to a peak of 75 percent, which was during the time strawberry baskets were in high demand. Five to eight boxcars were sent out each week, three times a day. The company had indications of good morale despite the hard work it required. There were two breaks a day, a company song, camaraderie among the workers, and, of course, regular paychecks. (Courtesy of Anna Stark.)

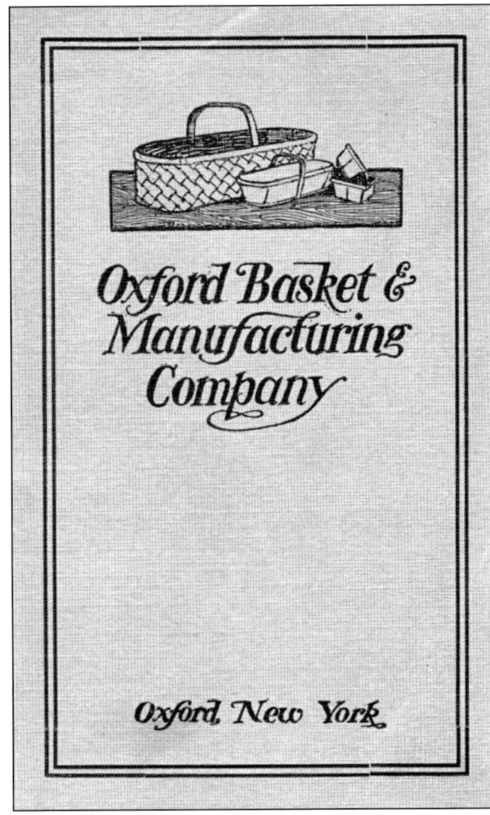

Oxford Basket & Manufacturing Company

Oxford, New York

This is the pristine catalog of Oxford Basket & Manufacturing Company's wares. The company had a large variety of products, and thousands of copies of the catalog were made and sent out over the years. At its annual meeting in January 1926, the company's directors reported that $25,000 had been paid to farmers for logs and $47,587 to employees in wages for the year. Today, the amounts would convert to over $300,000 and almost $600,000 respectively.

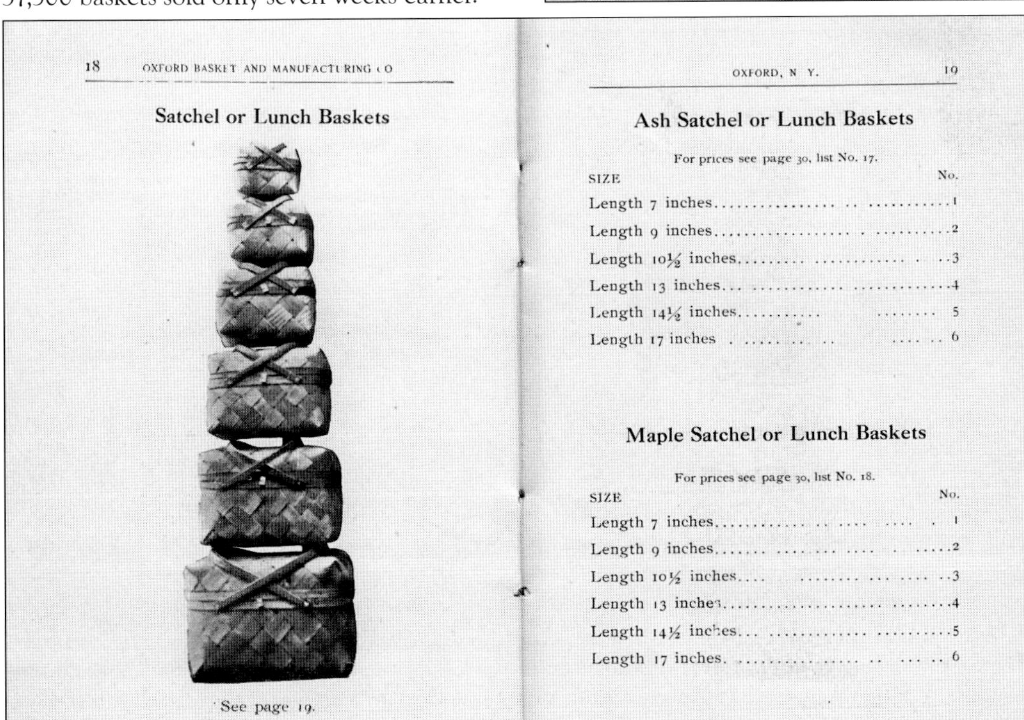

18 OXFORD BASKET AND MANUFACTURING CO

Satchel or Lunch Baskets

See page 19.

OXFORD, N. Y. 19

Ash Satchel or Lunch Baskets

For prices see page 30, list No. 17.

SIZE	No.
Length 7 inches	1
Length 9 inches	2
Length 10½ inches	3
Length 13 inches	4
Length 14½ inches	5
Length 17 inches	6

Maple Satchel or Lunch Baskets

For prices see page 30, list No. 18.

SIZE	No.
Length 7 inches	1
Length 9 inches	2
Length 10½ inches	3
Length 13 inches	4
Length 14½ inches	5
Length 17 inches	6

The famous diamond pattern was popular in several basket lines, as were the berry baskets. The biggest one-day record of production was 65,000 berry baskets on March 25, 1908, which broke the record of 37,500 baskets sold only seven weeks earlier.

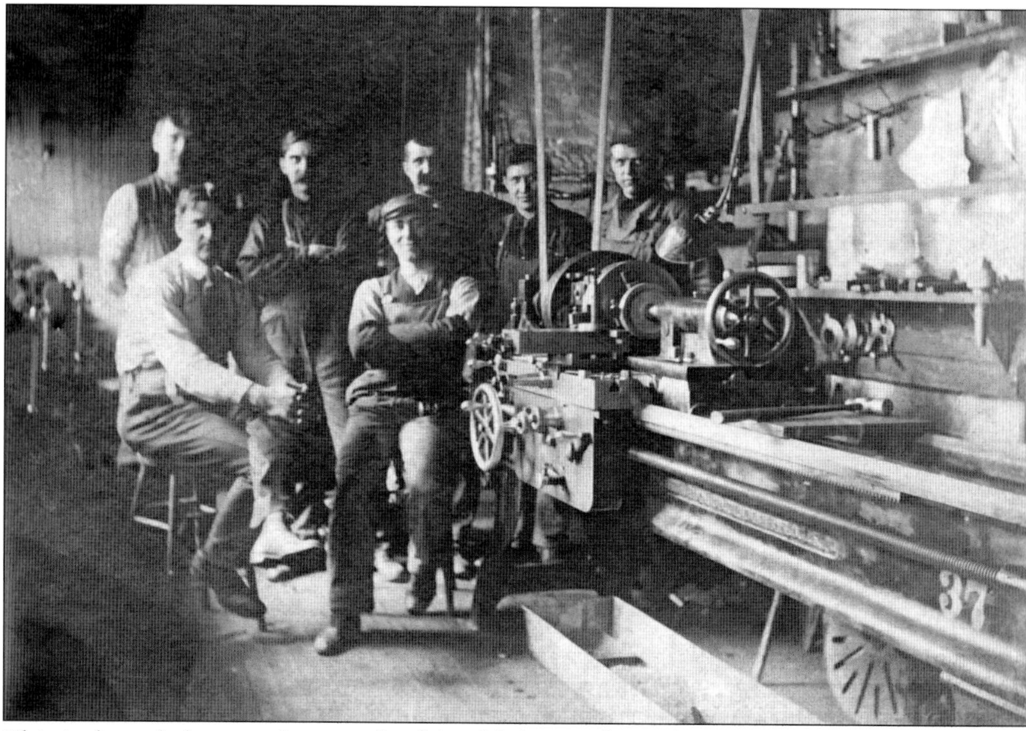

This is the only known photograph of Asa Hyde's machine shop, which was near the DL&W depot. The men there could make about anything: small tools, bicycle parts, chairs, and toys were just a few of the custom items.

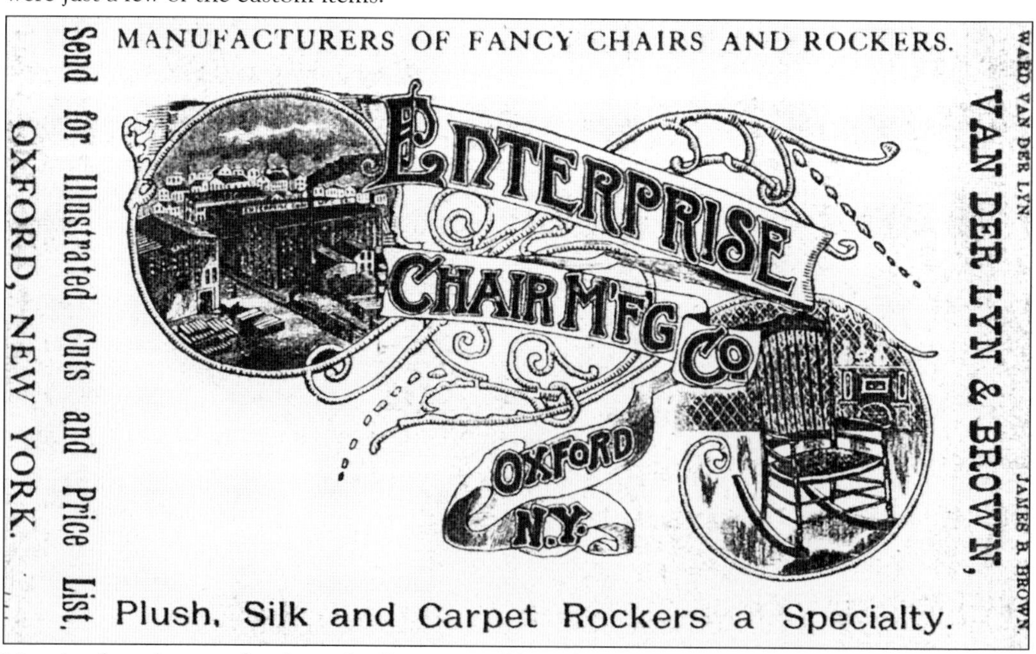

Here is a long-lost catalog from the Enterprise Chair Company, which sold a line of Shaker-style chairs in a spot next to Asa Hyde's machine shop. The Oxford Historical Museum has a vintage sample of its straight-back rocker.

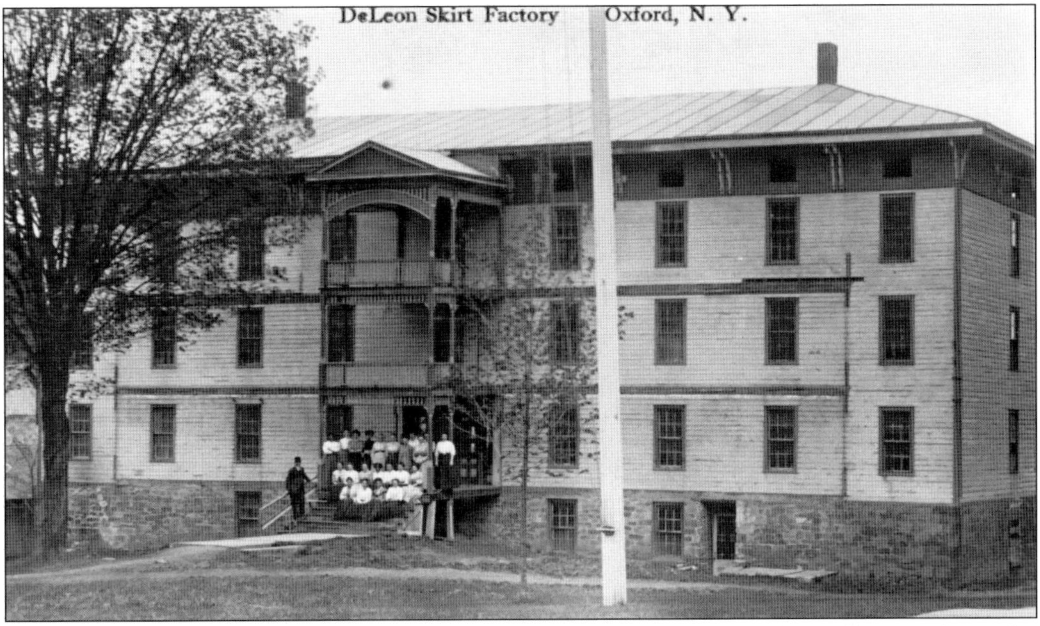

Taken in 1909, several employees from the DeLoen skirt factory pose for a photograph on the front steps of Oxford Academy's boarding hall. The boarding hall used house the Oxford shirt factory. (Courtesy of Anna Stark.)

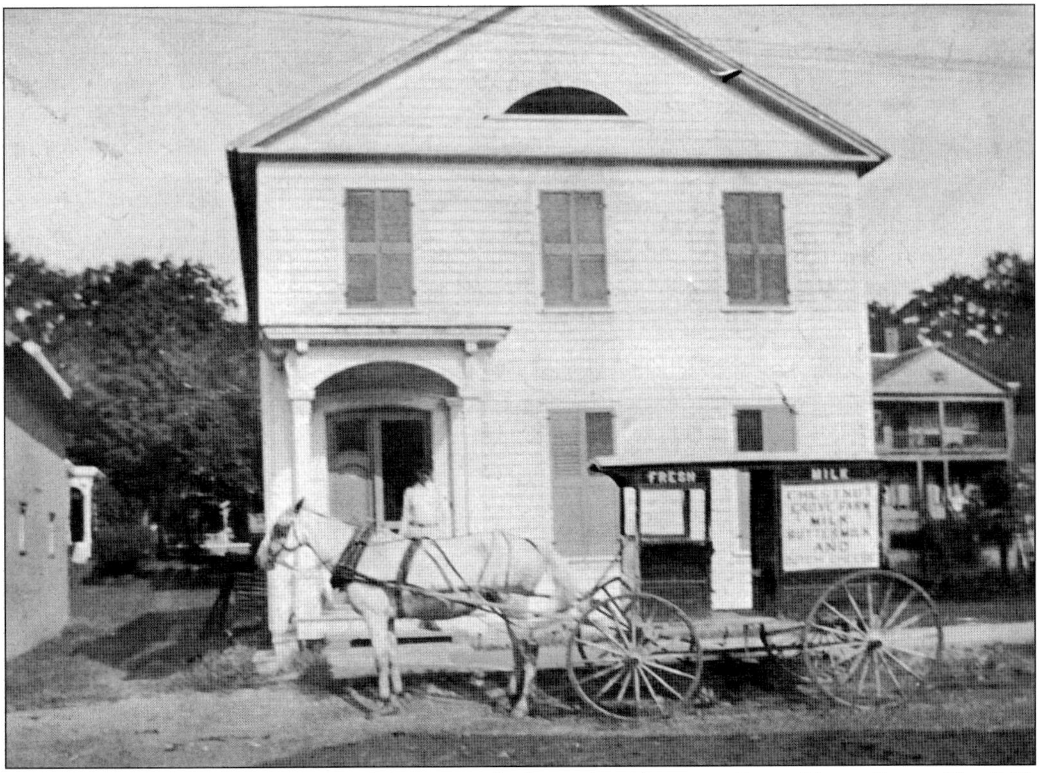

This photograph shows the milk delivery outfit from the Chestnut Grove Farm. Started by E.U. Bartle, it was the earliest company to offer house-to-house milk delivery in Oxford.

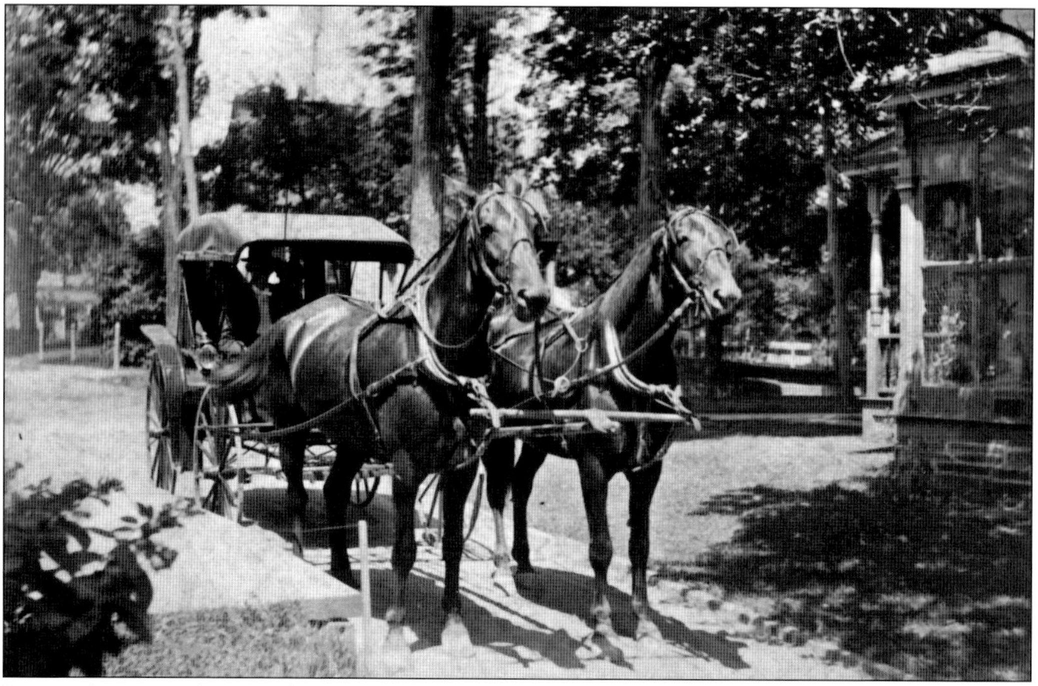

Pictured are members of the Bills and Pettis Undertakers team near their South Washington Street establishment. R.H. Bills was quite an entrepreneur; he was a furniture maker, coffin builder, and undertaker.

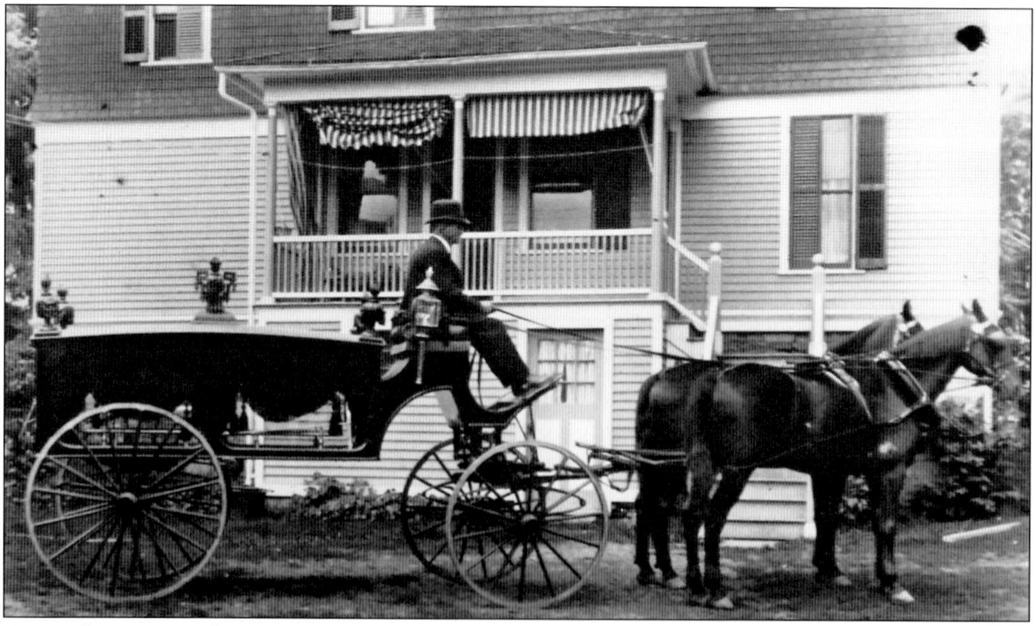

R.H. Bills is seen with a pair of horses and his new hearse at the rear of his furniture and undertaking establishment after Bills bought out Pettis's share of the business. Later on, F.W. Seymour would succeed Bills. Seymour was the first tenant in the new Navy Island Block in November 1917, conducting a furniture and undertaking business. He would later pass it on to Judson Behe and then his son Steve.

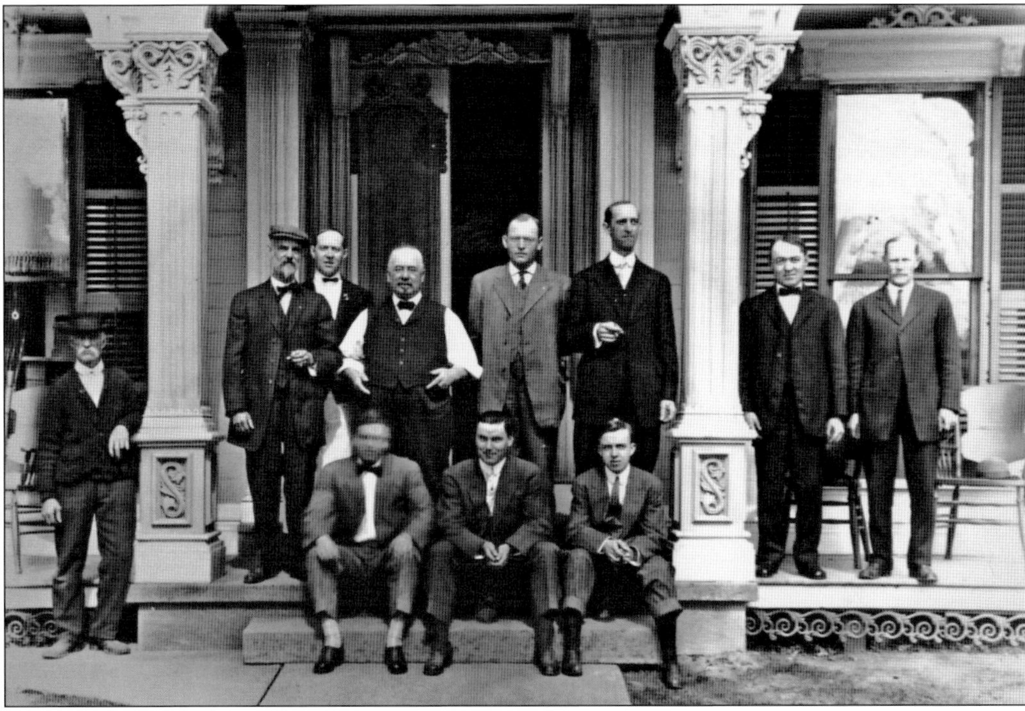

Men pose outside of Robinson's boardinghouse on South Washington Avenue. It is now the residence of Gray and Kate Stevens, who are both retired educators.

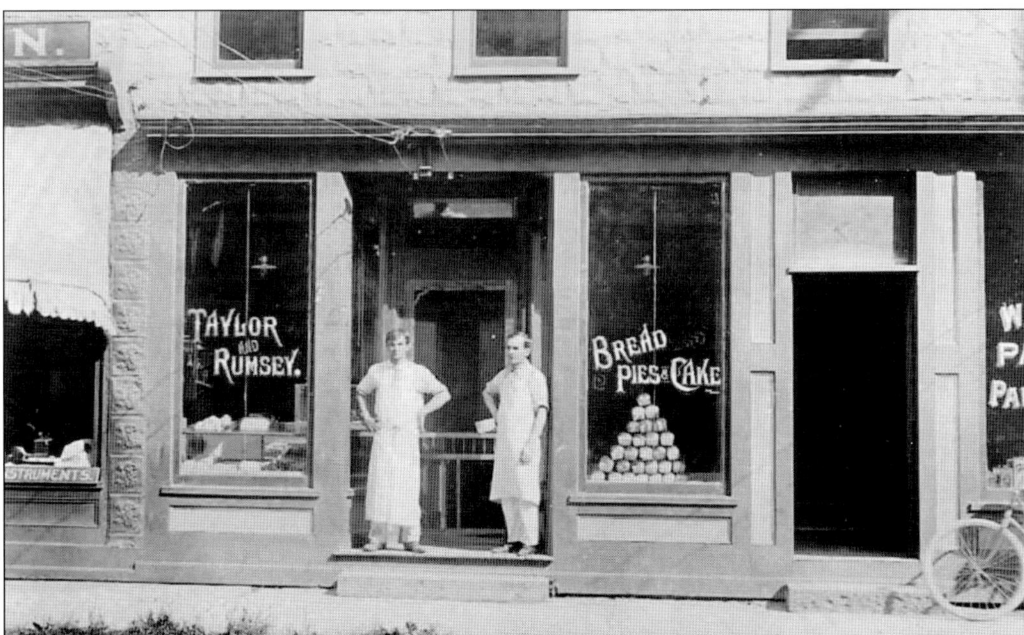

This photograph shows the owners of Taylor and Rumsey Bakery on East Main Street. Advertisements in local papers indicate there were always several grocery or butcher shops, but for many years there was just one bakery—Taylor and Rumsey's.

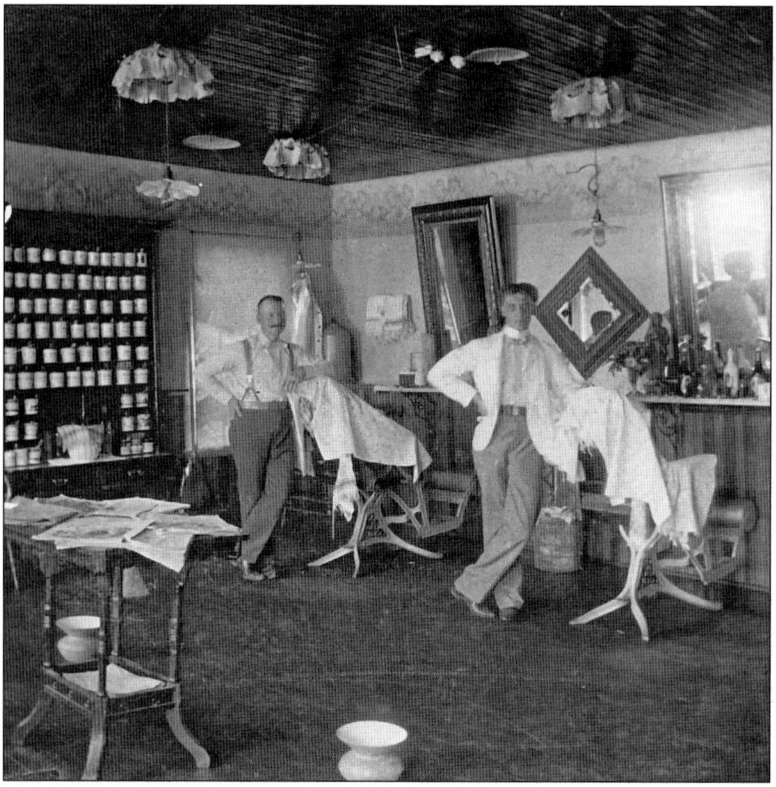

Everitt Lewis and Fred Adams are pictured in their barbershop alongside their customers' shaving mugs and convenient spittoons.

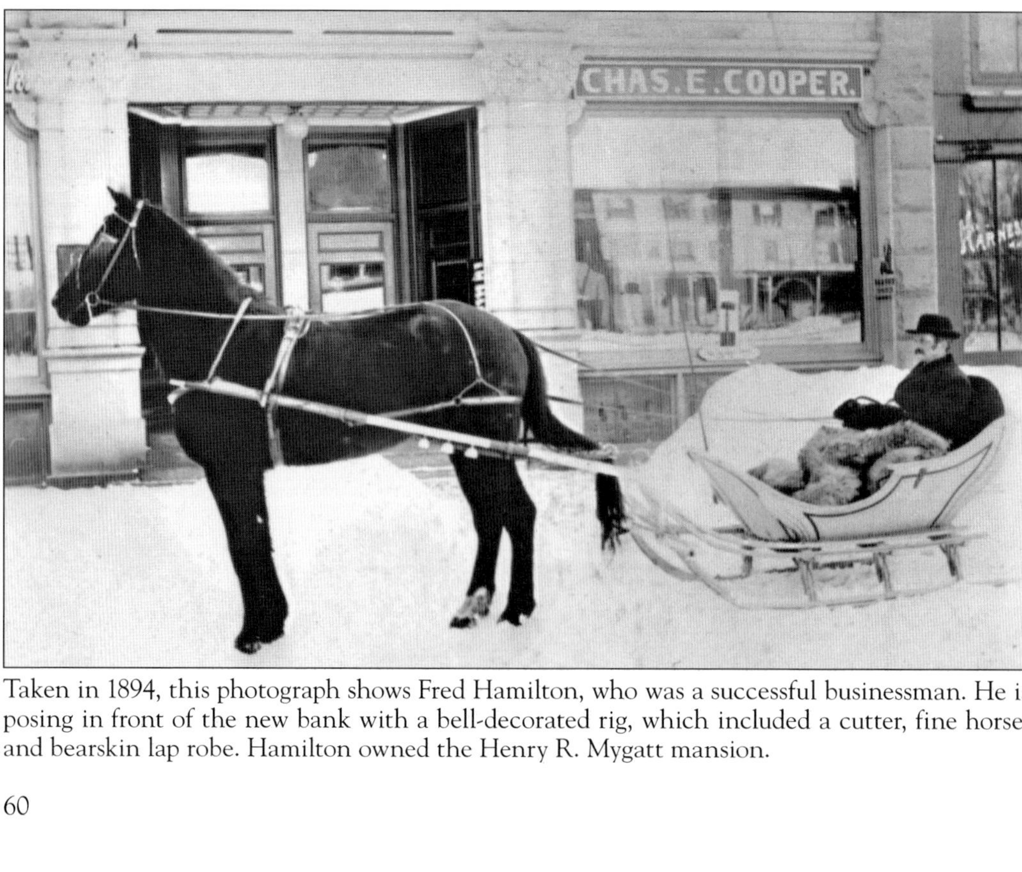

Taken in 1894, this photograph shows Fred Hamilton, who was a successful businessman. He is posing in front of the new bank with a bell-decorated rig, which included a cutter, fine horse, and bearskin lap robe. Hamilton owned the Henry R. Mygatt mansion.

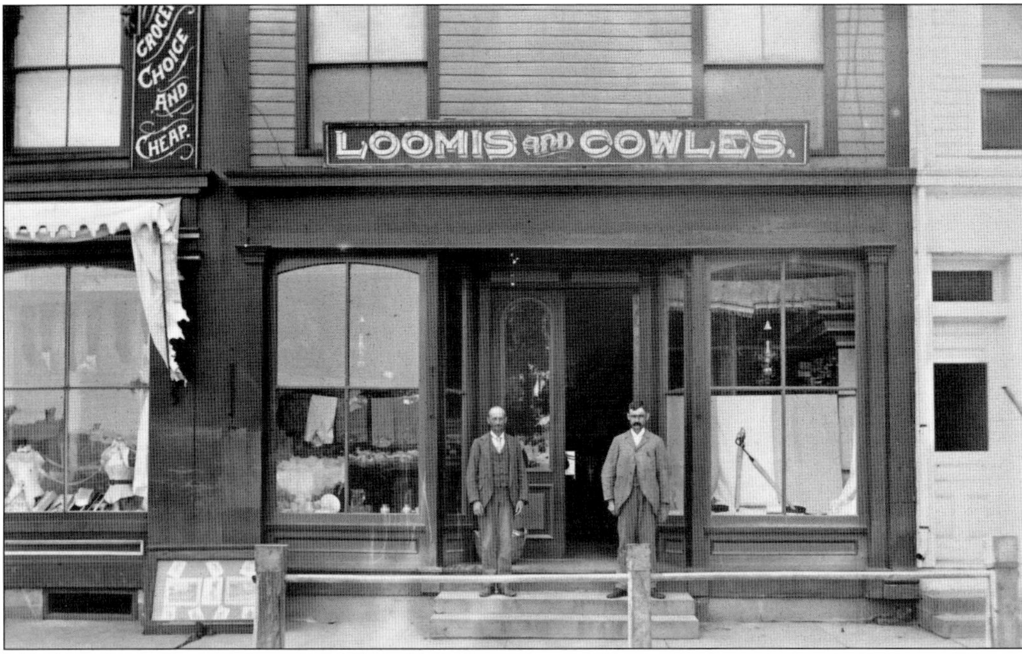

The Loomis and Cowles store stands here with the owners out front. The large sign advertises their slogan that reads, "Groceries, Choice and Cheap."

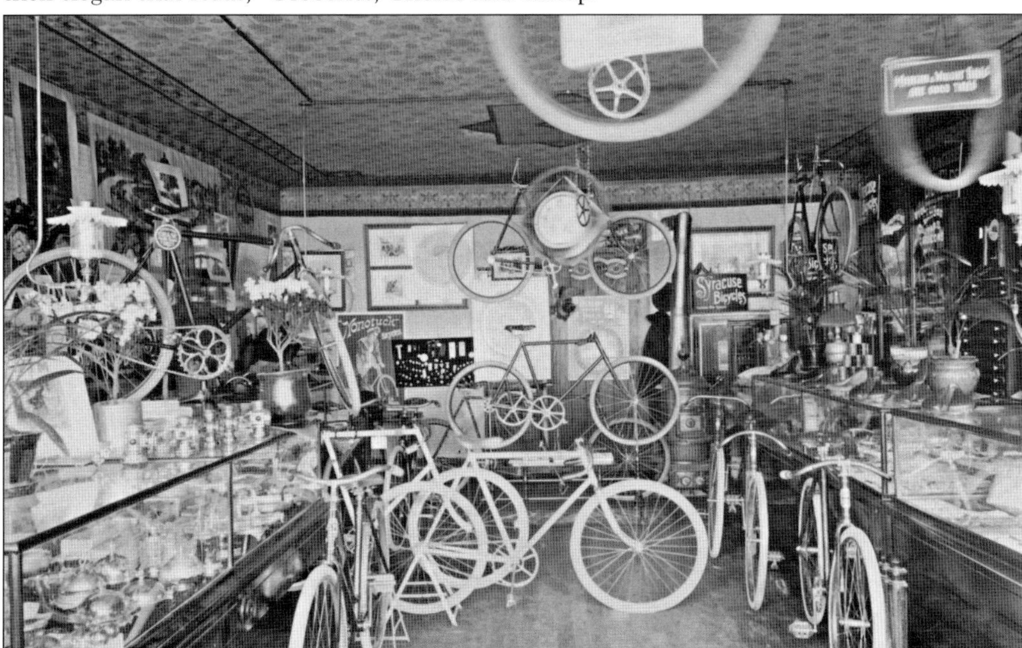

The photograph shows the interior of the Corbin store, which was located on South Canal Street. The store had a variety of goods and featured bicycles from many manufacturers. Bicycling was quite popular from the 1890s up to the period of World War I, which was when automobiles really became popular. During this time, there was a bicycle club and a racing club in Oxford, and members of both kept logs of their mileage.

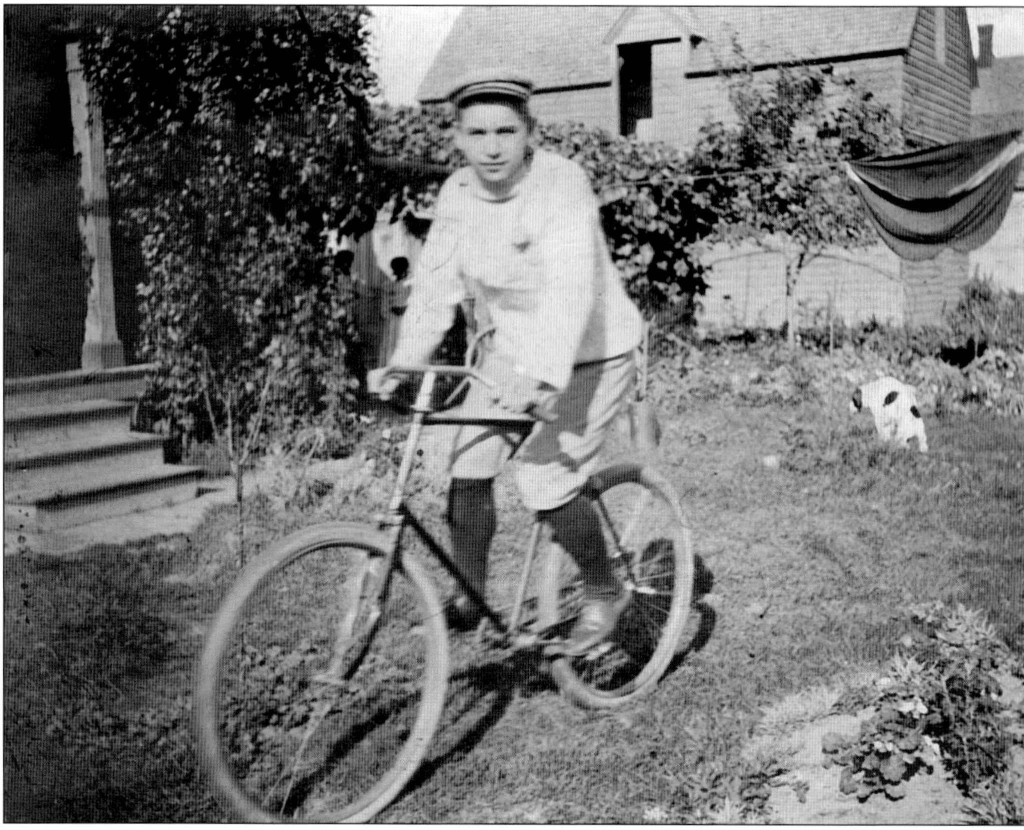

This young man is riding an Oxford bicycle that was probably built in Asa Hyde's machine shop. The boy may be the proud owner but is unidentified. The F.W. Hubbard Cycle Co. may have used part of the ingenious Asa Hyde's machine shop. St. John Morton sold them out of Father's Jewelry Store, and they were sold in the Corbin store as well. They could not compete with national brands.

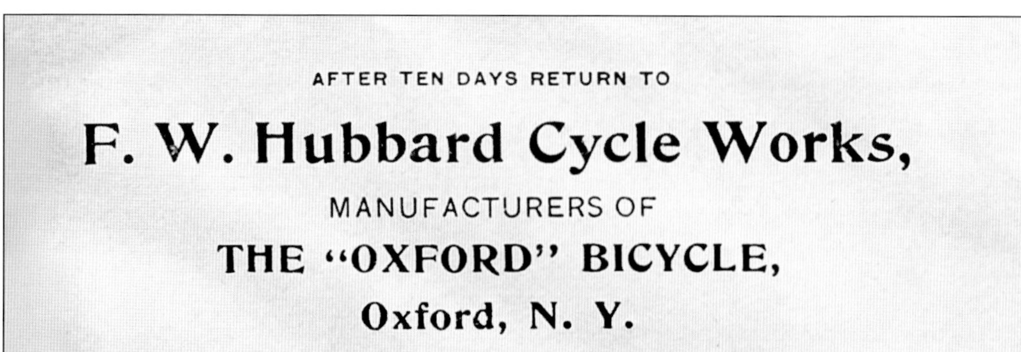

AFTER TEN DAYS RETURN TO

F. W. Hubbard Cycle Works,

MANUFACTURERS OF

THE "OXFORD" BICYCLE,

Oxford, N. Y.

Here is a return-address envelope that was part of F.W. Hubbard Cycle Works's company memorabilia. The company boasted that it built the "Oxford Bicycle."

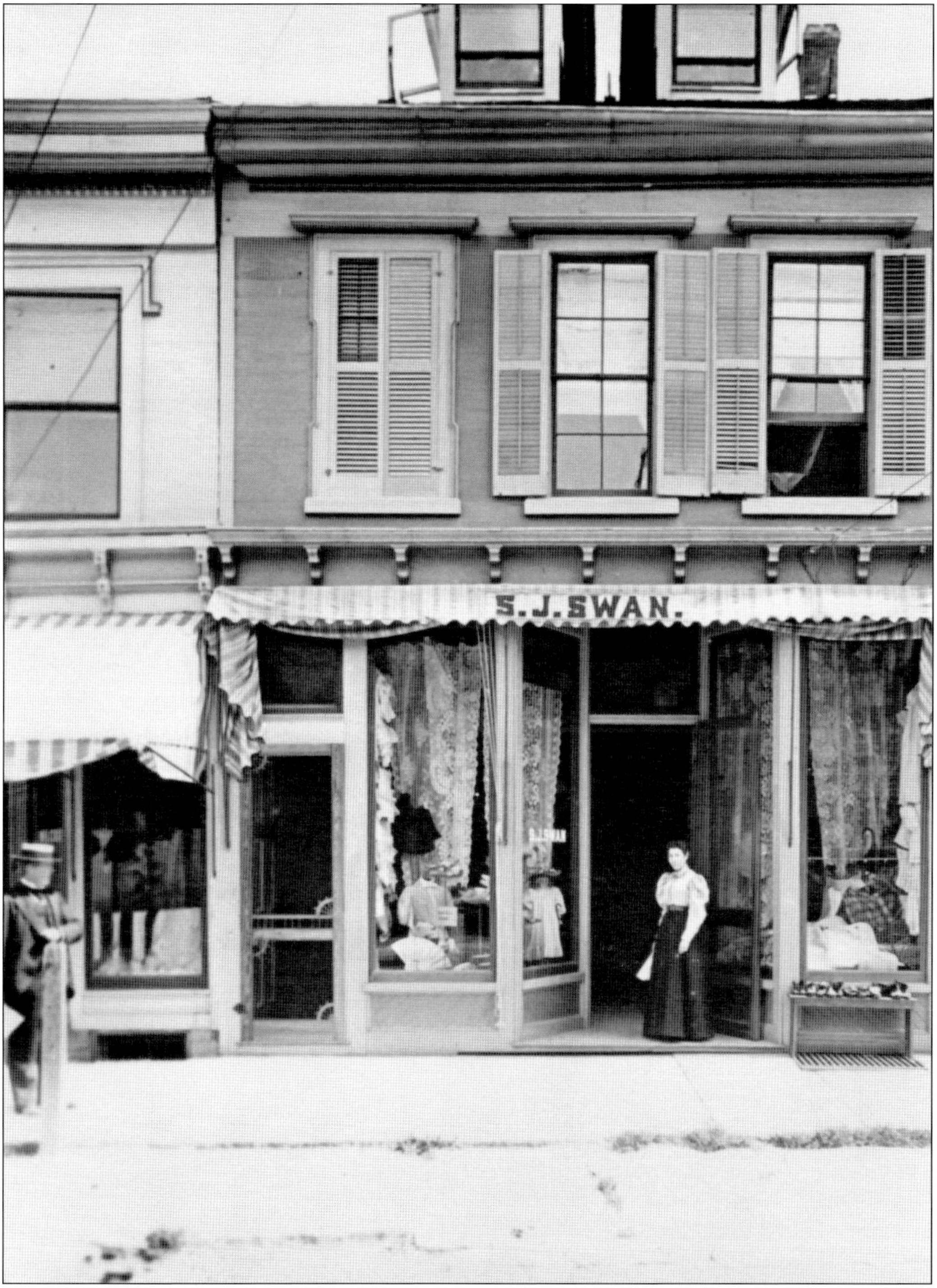

S.J. Swan poses out front of her shop that featured fine women's clothing and children's outfits. She operated the store for 62 years. Early each year, she would close the shop and spend a week in New York City to see the new styles in fashion and then place her season's orders based on the new trends. Loyal customers described her taste as impeccable.

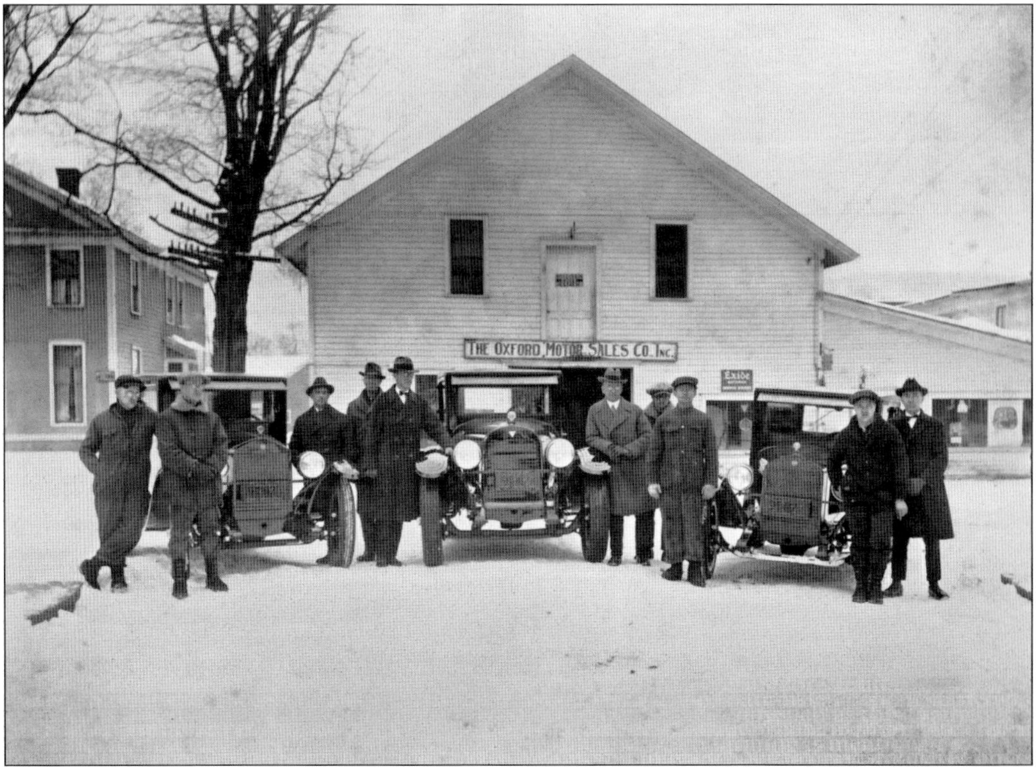

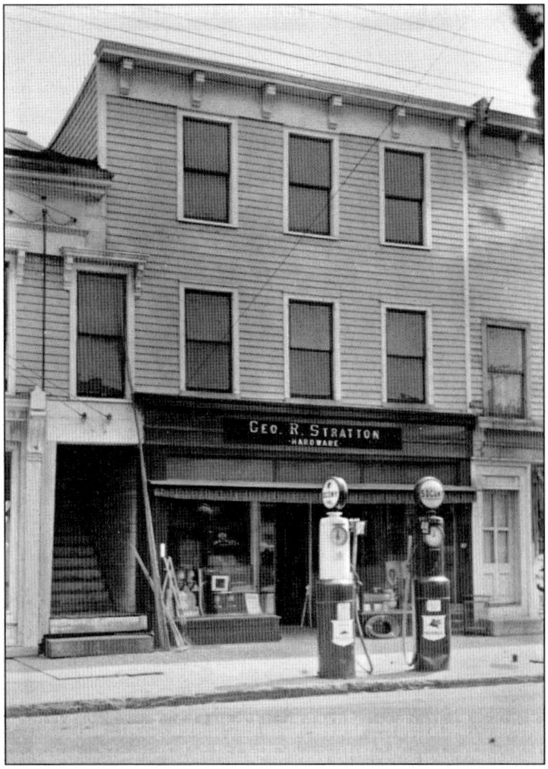

This photograph is of the Oxford Motor Sales Co., Inc., which opened in 1910. The owners are posing with their automobiles and potential customers; mechanic Earnest Lamb is seen on the far left.

The Stratton Hardware store is depicted here with brand-new Socony gas pumps that served the demand from automobiles. Socony gasoline was owned by J.D. Rockefeller, who lived nearby in Richford.

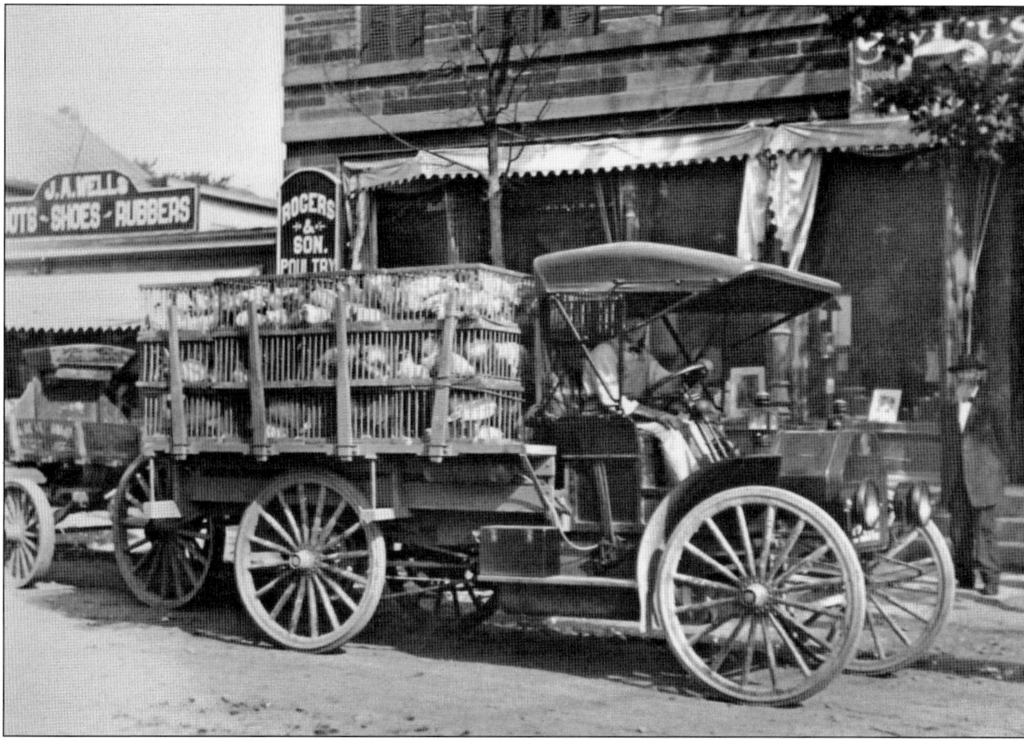

Taken around 1912, this image shows a truck that delivered chickens to the Rogers & Son Poultry store, located on the Tuttle Block.

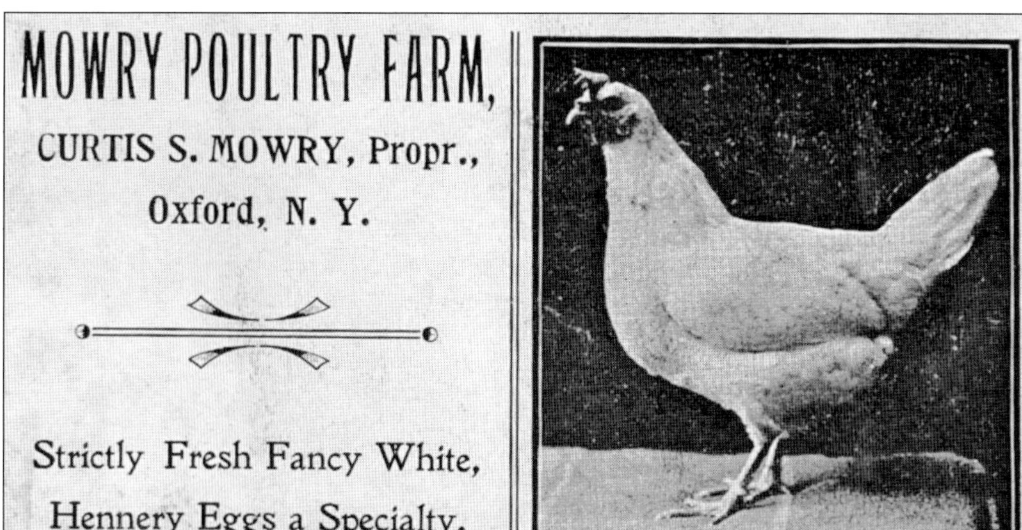

Here is an advertisement of chickens raised by the Mowry Poultry Farm; the chickens in the above photograph may have been raised there. The farm was located one mile north of the village, near the WRC Home. Curtis S. Mowry's wares are listed in this advertisement.

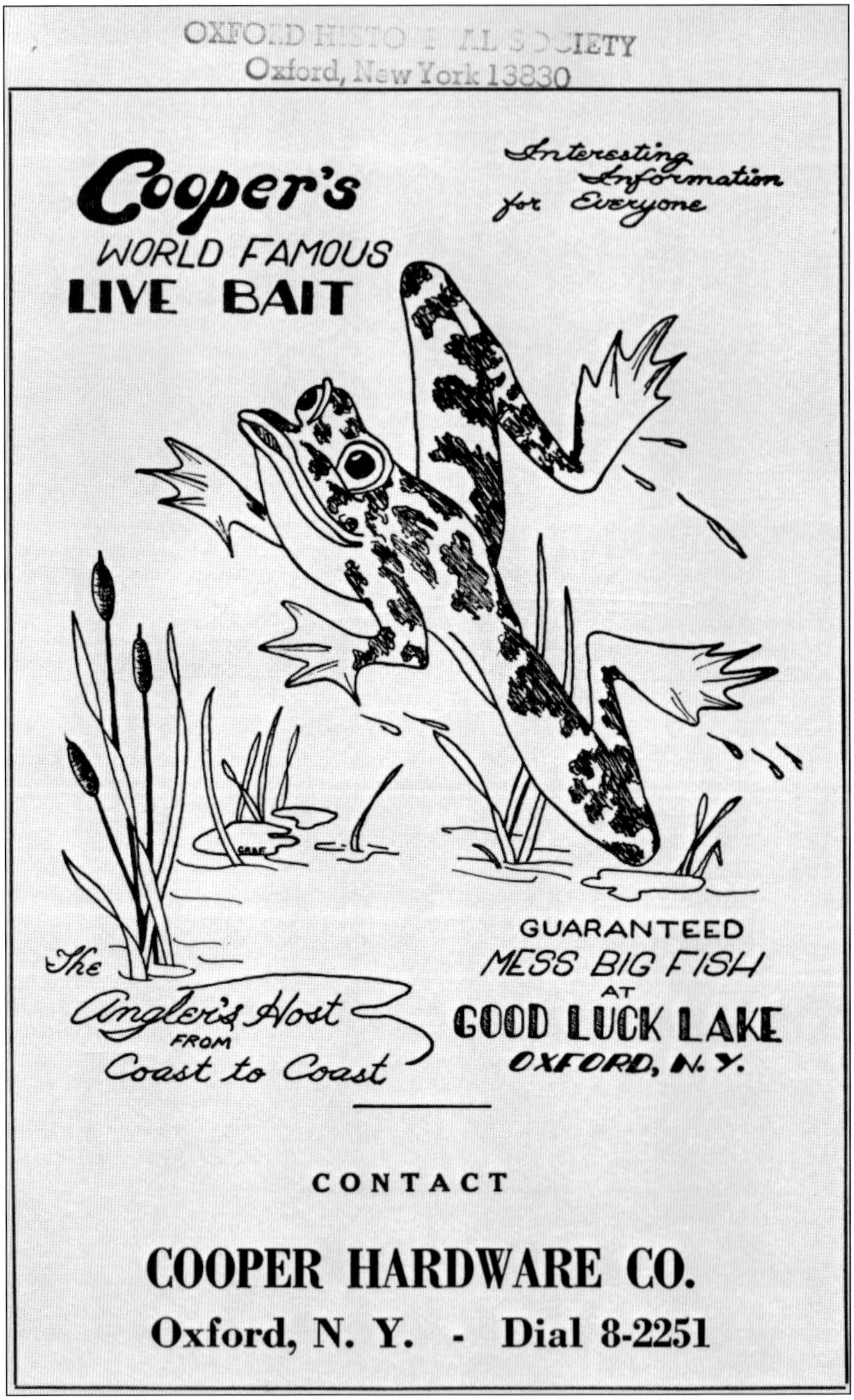

The Cooper Hardware Co. was one of the most enterprising retail stores in Oxford. Mort and Les Cooper started their company by purchasing the Burchard Hardware store on East Main Street. They converted the old front to a sportsman's store, entertainment center, and the usual hardware store. The image shows one of their catalogs, which was printed in bright orange to attract customers.

Many People Travel Many Miles

to

COOPER'S—OXFORD

for

GOOSE YOKES
BOOT JACKS
CUSPIDORS
BED PANS
LAMPS and CHIMNEYS
PIGEON FOUNTAINS
DAHLIA STAKES
COT BEDS
BULL STAFFS
MOLE TRAPS
CIDER BARRELS
WINE KEGS
BOTTLE CAPS and MACHINES
DOG BRITCHES
PAINTED BABY TURTLES
COLLEGE BRED PARAKEETS

TURKEY DUSTERS
POLICE CLUBS
HUNTING ARCHERY
WELDING COMPOUND
DeHORNING SHEARS
HARNESS SNAPS and PARTS
HORSE and PONY SHOES
CAT SCRATCHING POSTS
24-TOOTH HAND RAKES
OLD FASHIONED LANTERNS
STOVE LIFTERS
ICE SPUDS
ICE CREEPERS
TRACTOR UMBRELLAS
GOLD FISH and every known accessory for them

Talk about HANDLES. We have 125 kinds for almost every known tool. Furthermore, you can have them put in by an expert while you wait. You may call back if you desire, or have them mailed.

Round and square furniture knobs, odd sizes of bolts and nuts, large earthen crocks, kitchen gadgets from all over the world, and thousands of unusual items seldom stocked anymore, can be found here. Hundreds of people start out with their neighbors and friends just to see these unusual sights, always returning with a world of satisfaction, plus a most educational visit. Plan your trip soon—we will be looking for you.

This advertisement shows a partial list of goods offered at Cooper Hardware Co. The store's most popular item on the list of attractions was its "world famous indoor fishing pond."

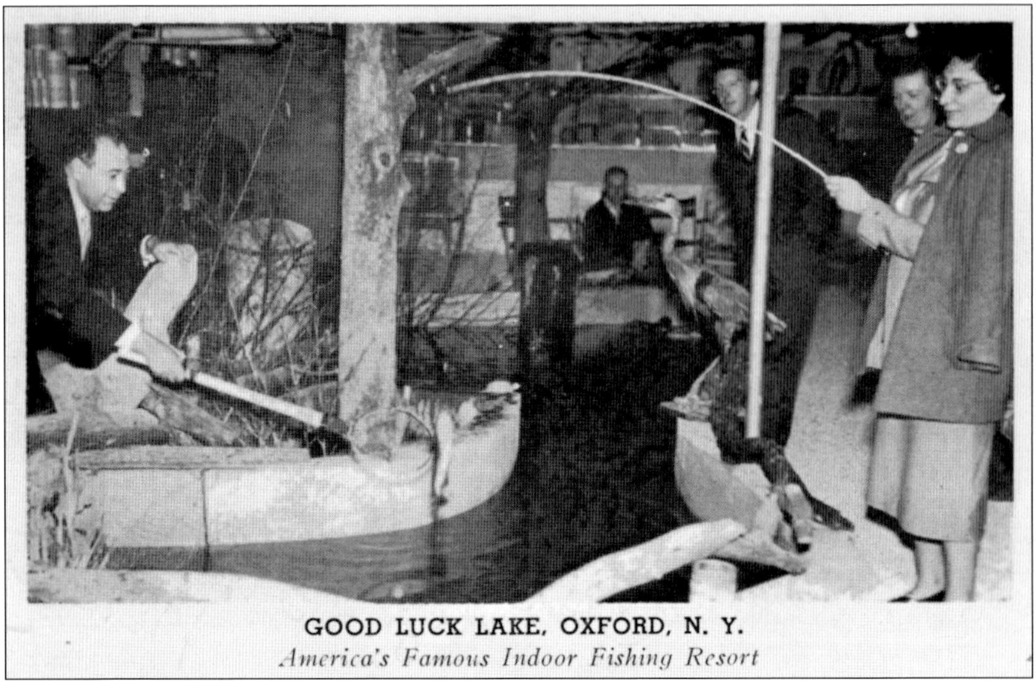

A customer is seen catching a live fish from the fishing pond, which was located in the basement of Cooper Hardware Co.

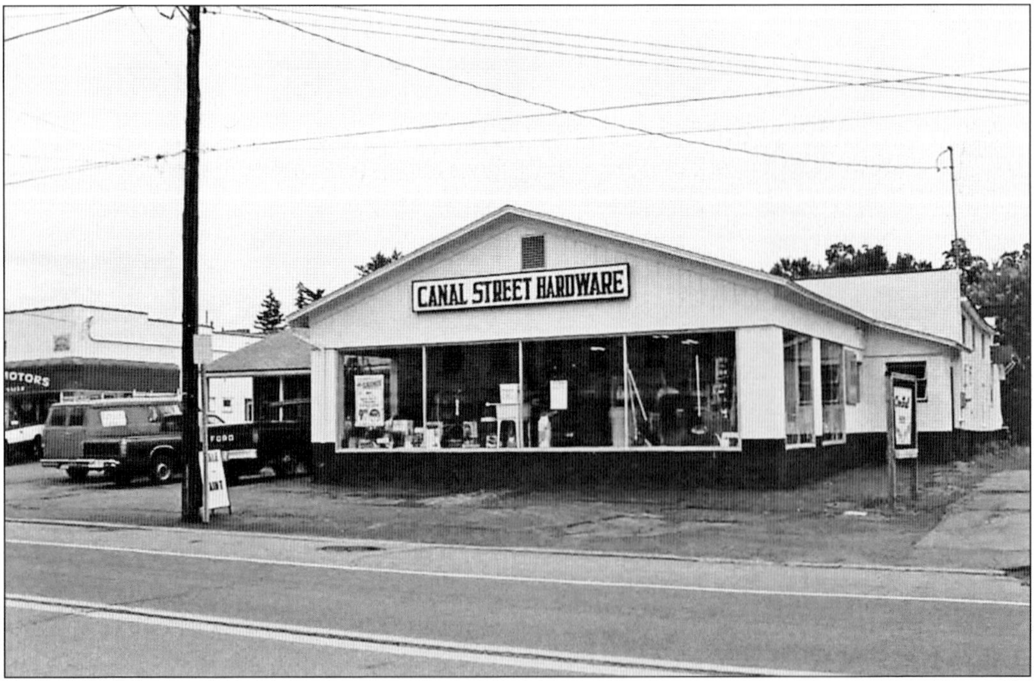

This is the present-day Canal Street Hardware store, which is located around the corner from the defunct Cooper Hardware Co. Canal Street Hardware is one of the few remaining retail stores in Oxford.

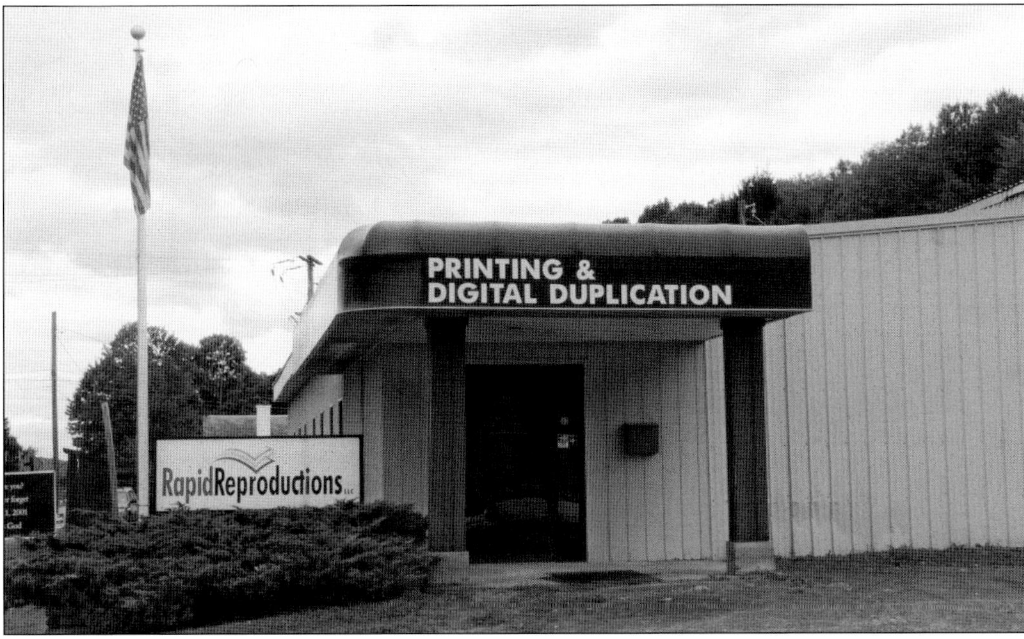

Here is the present-day printing shop owned by LaTourette Rapid Reproductions. This printing and graphic-arts shop employs around 10 people, and its customers are located in 50 states because of its high quality and reliability. A retired Long Island printer, Richard LaTourette and his wife, Jane, established this business in 1977. It operates at the cutting edge of offset and digital printing, earning a national reputation. (Courtesy of Keith Lanfear.)

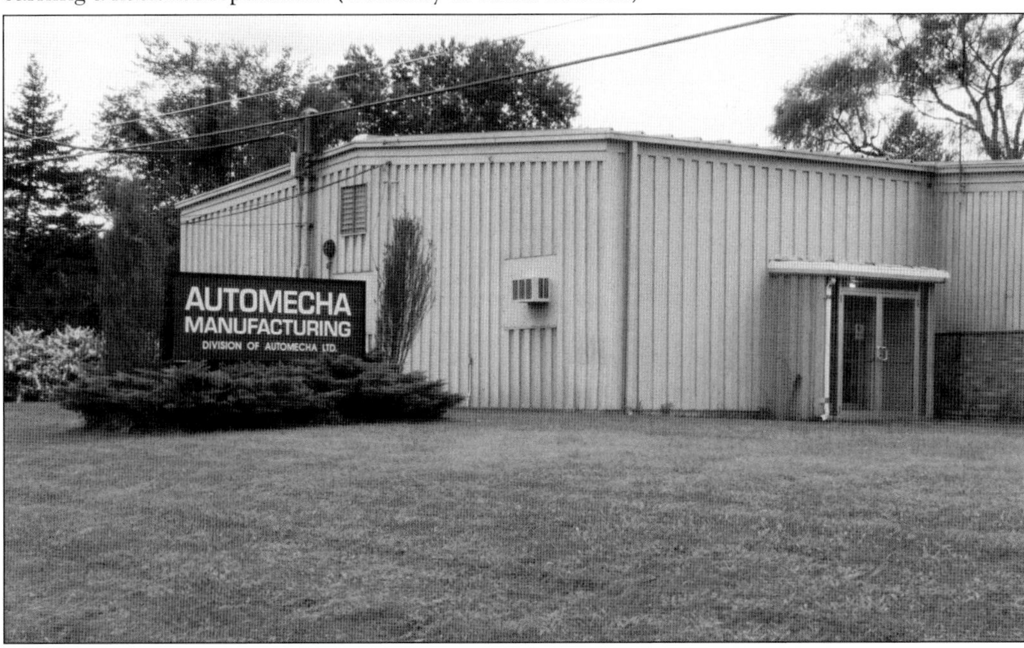

This photograph shows the Automecha Manufacturing shop, which employs around 15 people. The shop sells mail-sorting and addressing machines, plate embossers, and packaging machines. Automecha established its own operations in Oxford when the defunct Cortland Corset Factory put the building on the market in the late 1970s. (Courtesy of Keith Lenfear.)

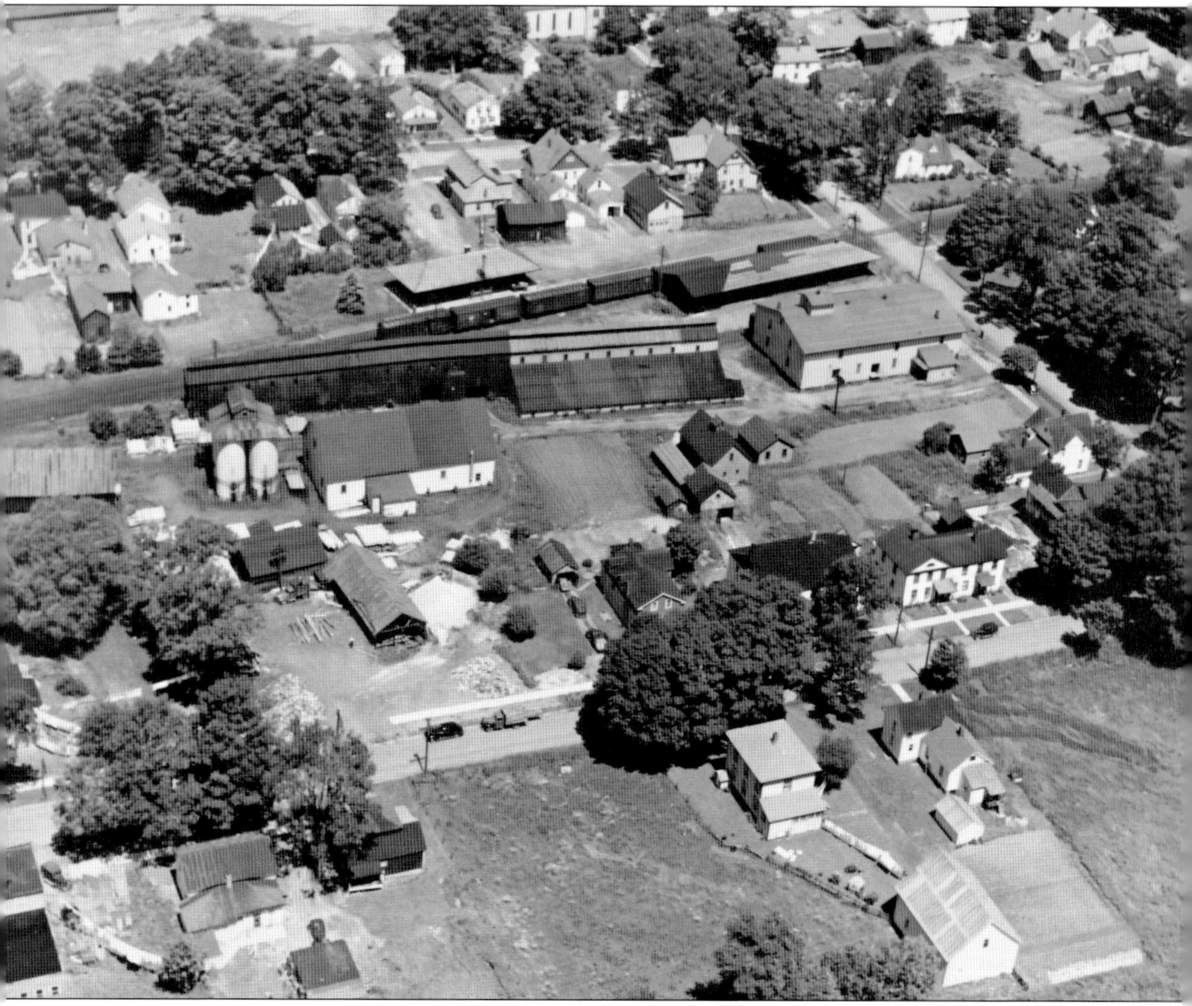

An aerial view captures Oxford's east side and its business facilities in the early 1950s when the area was a busy commercial center. It shows the section that is north and adjacent to the Borden's plant. In the center of the photograph, there is the long coal shed that belonged to Corbin and Fletcher; Borden's was one block to the left. Inside the coal shed, railcars were pushed onto an elevated track and coal unloaded into large bins. The DL&W depot was located across the track. McDowell and Walker's feed mill was located to the right of the coal shed, and the freight depot was next to the feed mill. In the photograph, Greene Street is in the foreground. Until the 1970s, the sawmill was in operation and located near McDowell and Walker's grain silos.

Four

The Academy

No institution in Oxford has affected more people, been of more public concern, or created more loyalty than the Oxford Academy. Today's graduating classes seem to disburse faster and farther than previous generations to college, the military, and careers in distant states and countries—but they come back. For over 200 years, many academy alumni have returned to their beloved school to share fond memories with the current student body.

In 1792, with only a few families in Oxford, Yale graduate Uri Tracy was teaching in a two-story building near Washington Park. By January 1794, he achieved his dream of establishing a New York state charter school for a private academy in Oxford. During that time, the academy was one of only four charter schools that were west of the Hudson River.

The academy attracted students from Oxford and nearby counties. As its reputation grew, it also attracted students from nearby states like Ohio, Indiana, and Kentucky. The Oxford Academy was a coeducational school for many years, and young ladies had their own boarding hall. Many students opted for the classical curriculum, and the academy offered a range of subjects, such as Latin, French, mathematics, astronomy, geography, history, literature, and rhetoric. The Oxford Academy's extensive curriculum prepared its students for college.

For a century, which ended in a gala centennial celebration in 1894, the charter school continued to retain its name and private academy status. In 1895, the school changed its name to the Oxford Academy and Union School. Today's school is now called the Oxford Academy and Central School.

For three centuries, the Oxford Academy has continued its school pride and lifelong traditions.

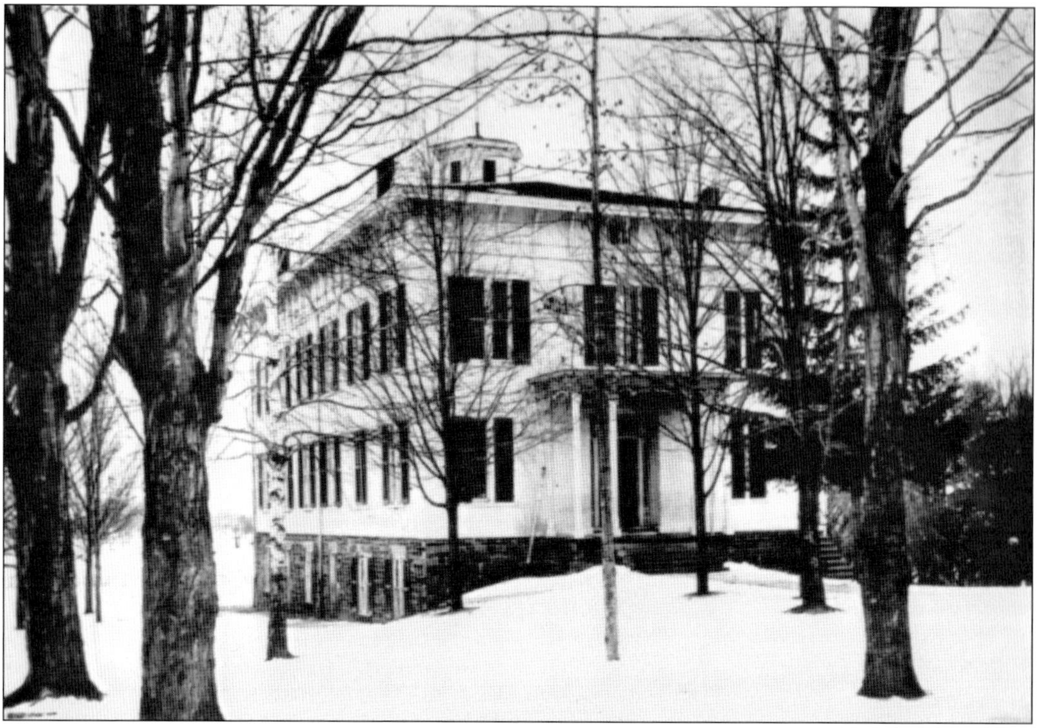

This photograph shows the Oxford Academy's school building, which was located at the head of Fort Hill Park. The two different boarding halls, separated by gender, were situated next to the school building. During that time, Katharine Whitney was the "preceptress" (a dean of women) of Oxford Academy; most 19th-century coed schools had one.

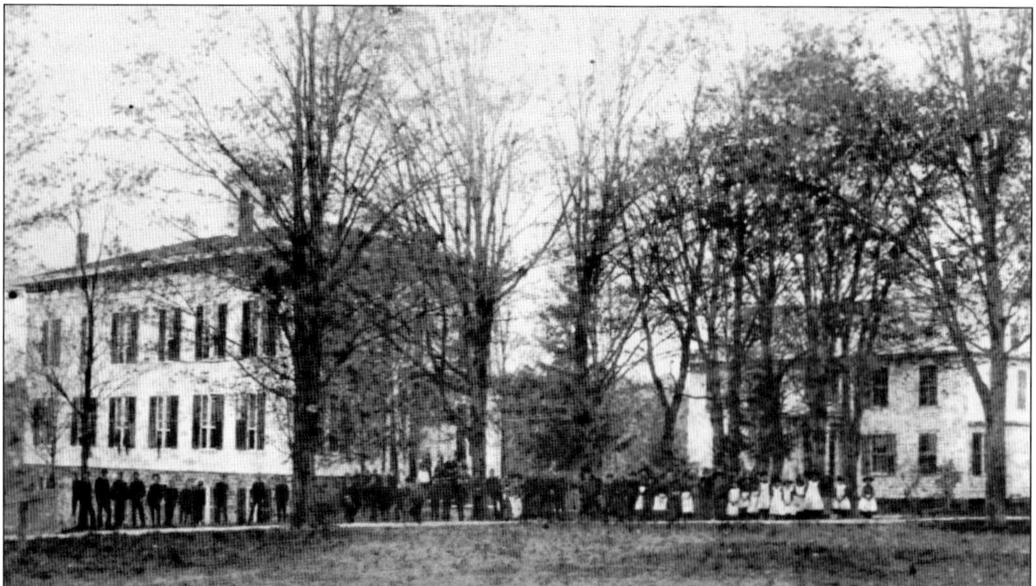

The academy's classroom building and female boarding hall are seen here with students lined up in front. According to the annual catalogs in the Oxford Historical Society's archives, the school's population ranged from 200 to over 300 students.

The class of 1885 poses for the camera. The image portrays the decorum of the times and also the prominence of young ladies at the academy.

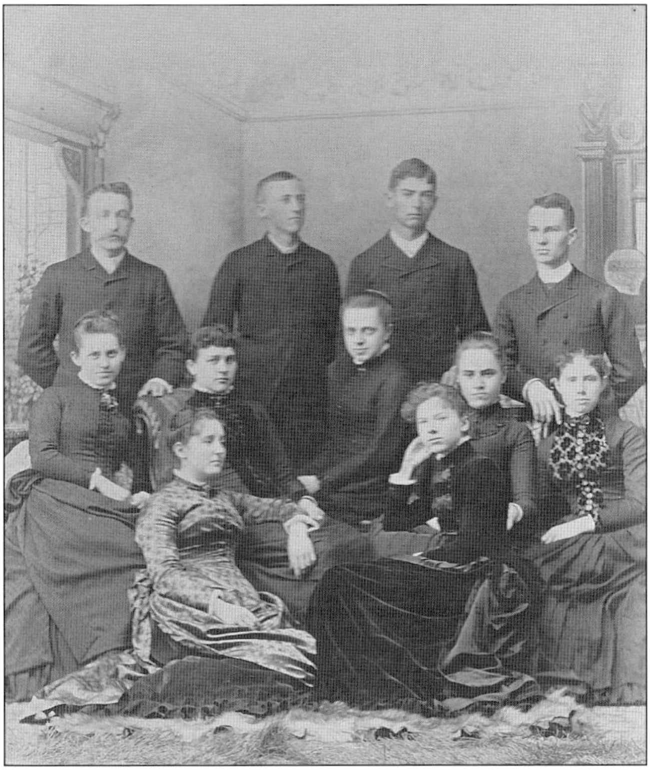

This photograph depicts the class of 1894. These students are part of the last class to graduate the academy before it became a union school. (A union school is a tax-supported public school that is open to students from the surrounding districts in the township at no fee.) Again, the young ladies dominate the scene.

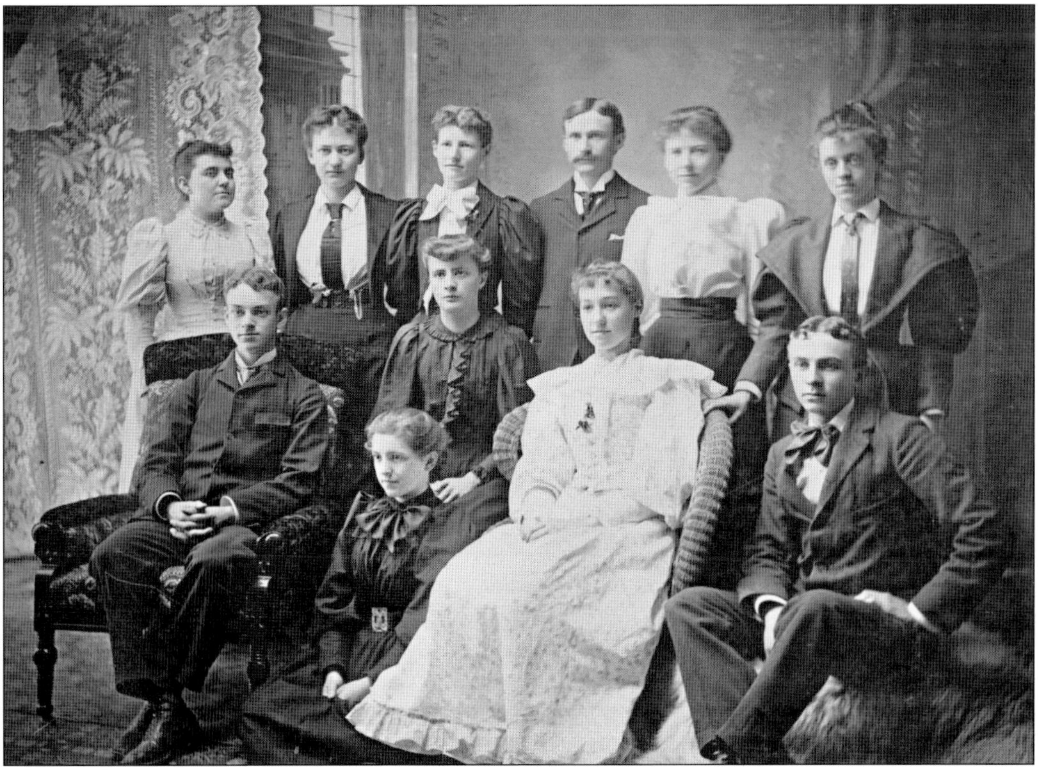

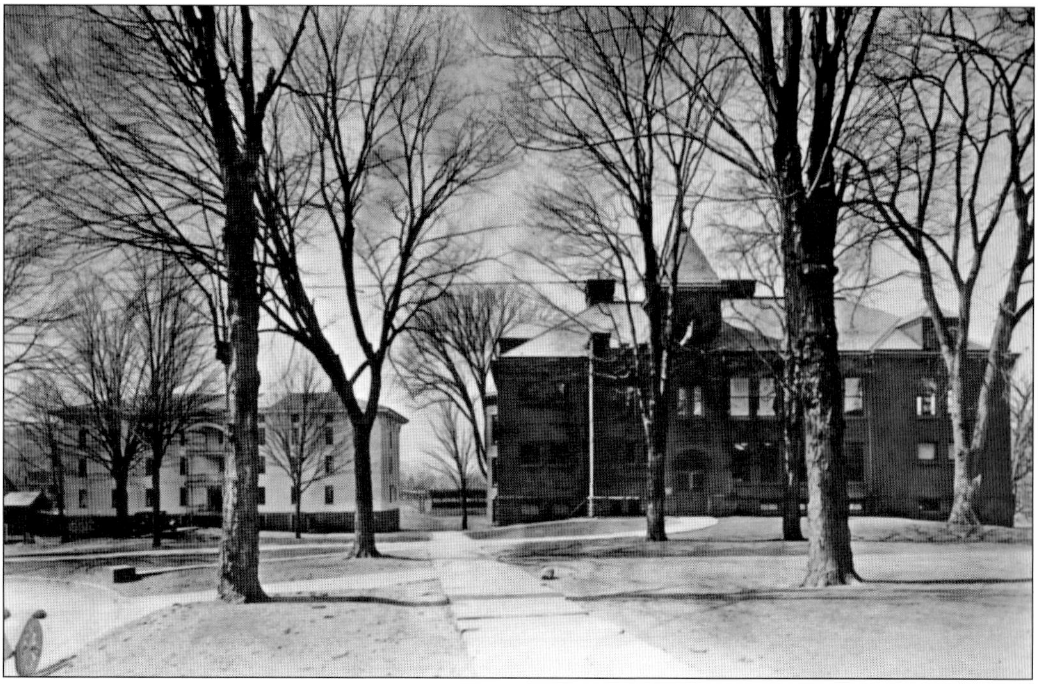

The new union school was built on the site of the old classroom building, which had been moved down to Merchant Street and used as a storage facility. The boarding halls became an apartment complex known as Morton's Flats. Later, the building became a shirt factory, then a skirt factory, and finally, when it was moved to Greene Street, it became an apartment complex that still exists today.

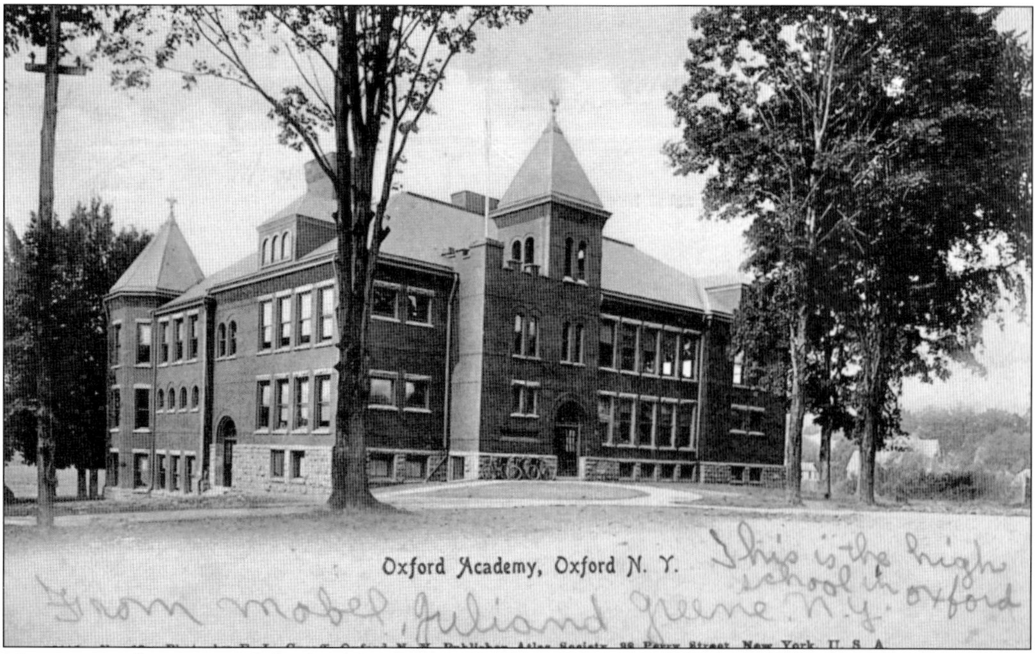

This is another view of the building in 1895. It was torn down in 1929. In 1930, another new school was built, and it is now Oxford Academy's present-day middle school.

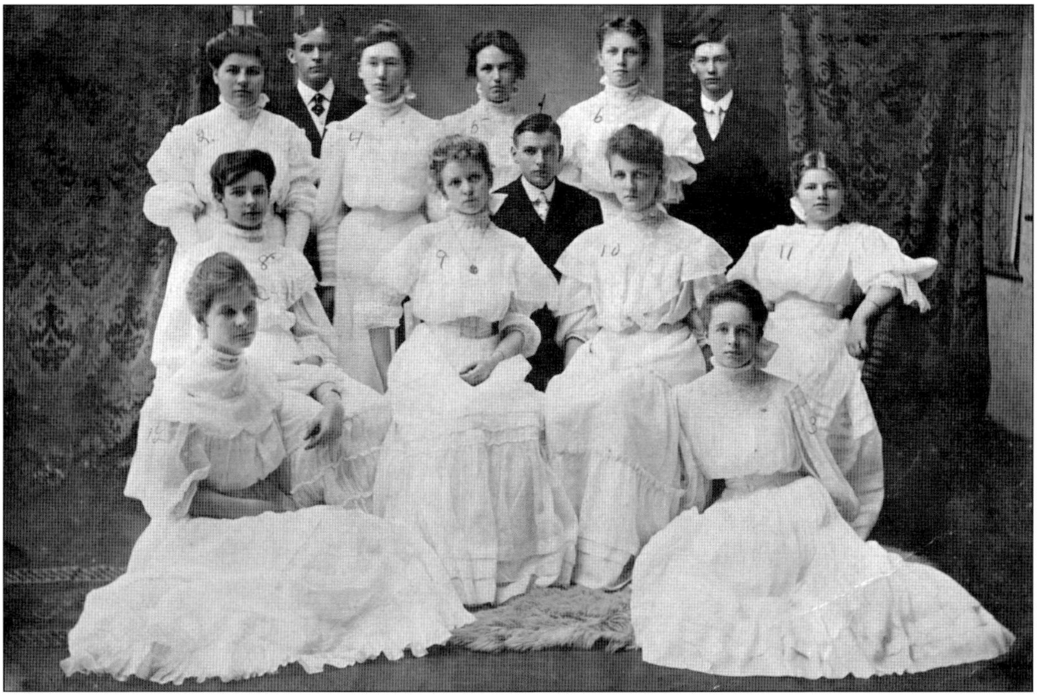

The graduating class of 1905 poses here. In the photograph, the union school is 10 years old and has kept up its high standards; the young women still outnumber the young men. (The names of these graduates and of all the Oxford Academy photographs are in the archives of the Oxford Historical Society.) Listed in no particular order are Roy Carl, Stella Harrington, Frank Dunn, Elizabeth Dodge, Clara Powers, Helen Emerson, Erwin Miles, Evelyn Wands, Nina Dedrick, Ursula VanWagenen, Bertha Kirchner, Mabel Graef, and Mary Jones.

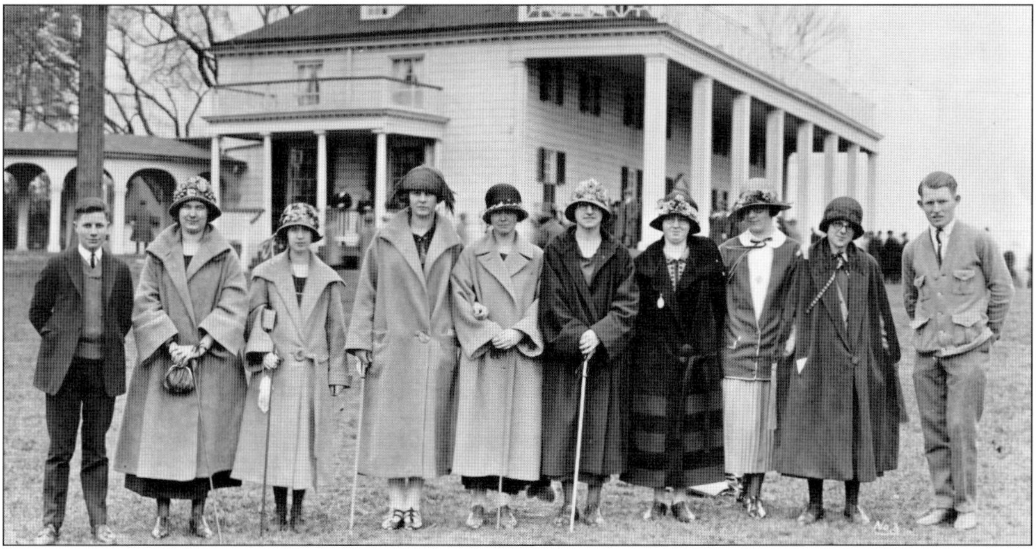

This photograph shows a school trip to Mount Vernon in 1924. Francis Hill, seen on the far right, played on three consecutive undefeated football teams. Pictured from left to right are Lewis Whitney, Mary ? , Edna Miles, Lemira Stratton, Margaret Quinn, Margaret Marshman, Dorothy ? , Grace Hovey, Eleanor Barrows, and Hill.

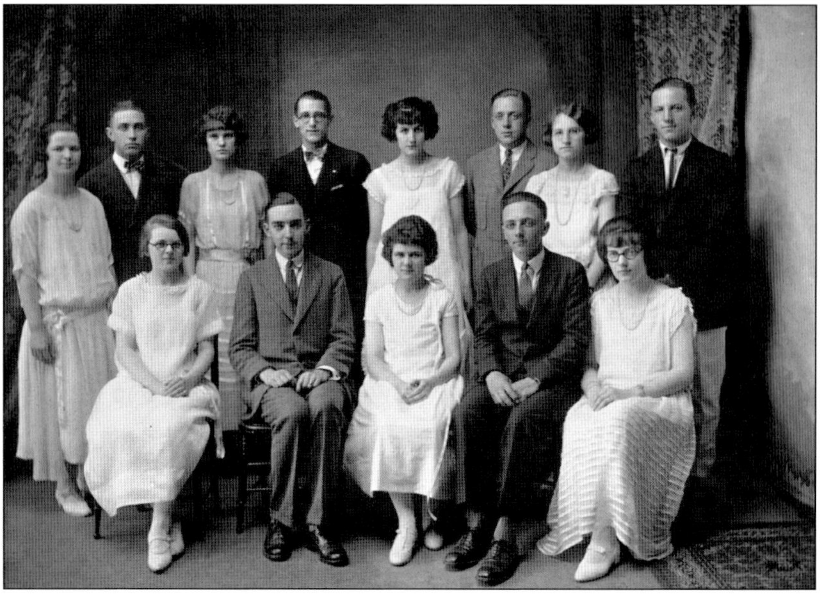

Here is the graduating class of 1924. Pictured from left to right are (first row) Eleanor Barrows, Richard Quinn, Margaret Muler, Russel Muler, and Grace Hovey; (second row) Edna Miles, Frank Root, Louise Boname, Van Estelow, Jennie Barnes, James Dunn, Margaret Marshman, and Arthur Potter.

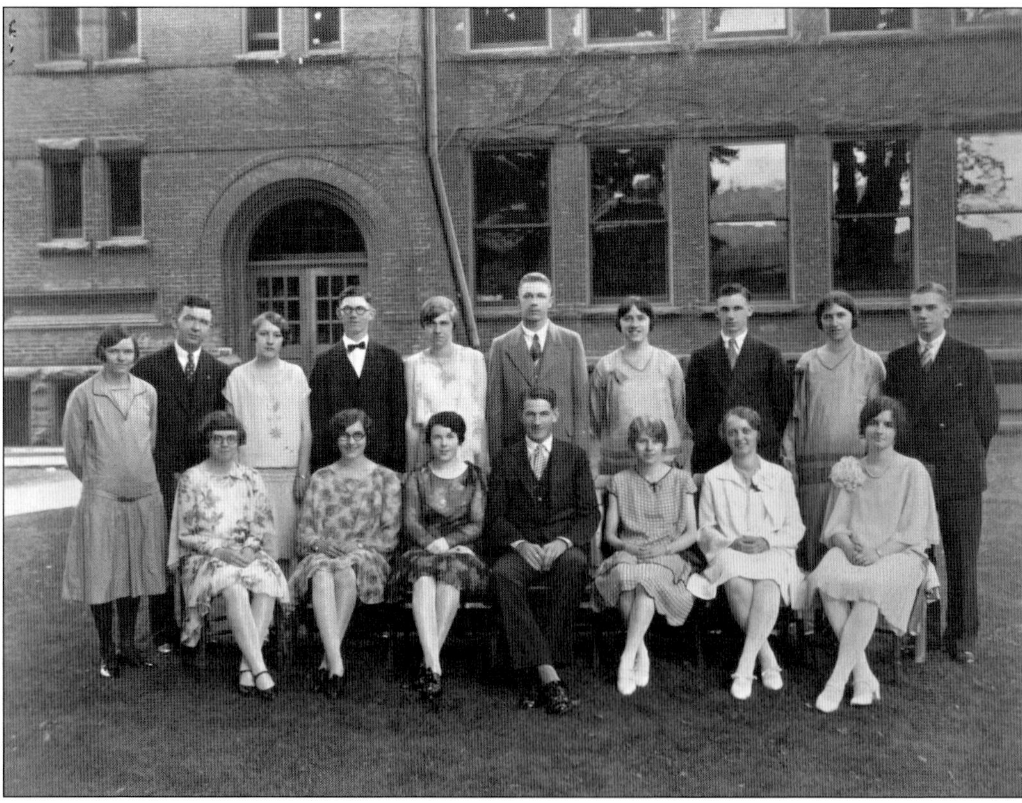

The graduating class of 1928 takes a turn for the camera. From left to right are (first row) Anna Bartle, Doris Beckwith, Dorothy Flanagan, Elmer Coston, Helen Munyon, Charlotte Sherwood, and Elizabeth Hoban; (second row) Marion Smith, Paul Dowd, Doris Sharpe, Maurice Malloy, Elizabeth Race, Herbert Stafford, Doris Barnes, Paul O'Connor, Dorothy Barnes, and Clarence Munyon.

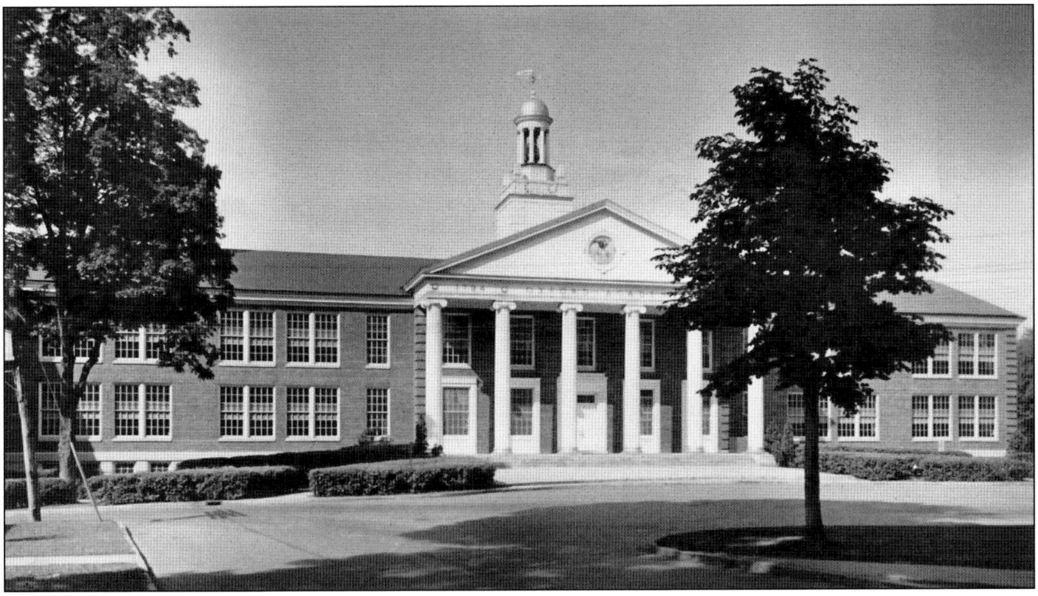

This photograph shows the new school that was built during 1929 to 1930. It housed all grades until 1963, when a new junior and senior high school was completed across the river on South Washington Avenue. The building seen here is now the middle school. Many loyalists consider it the most beautiful school in the county.

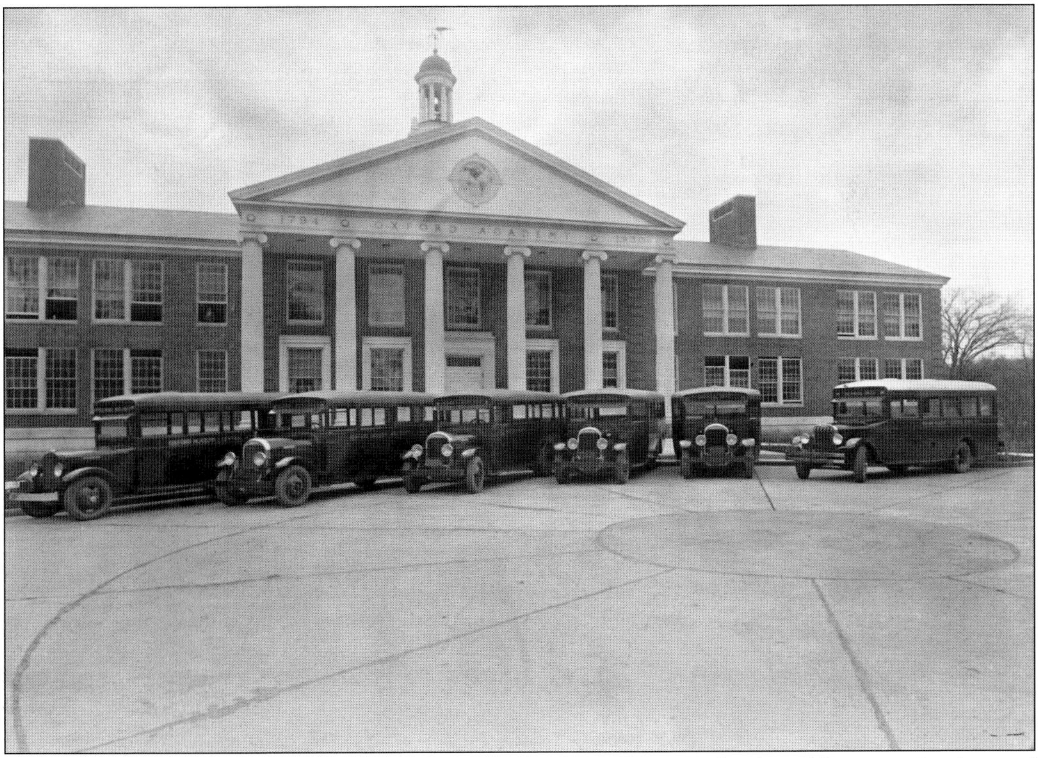

Along with the new school in 1930 came a new fleet of buses, displayed here in the front of the school.

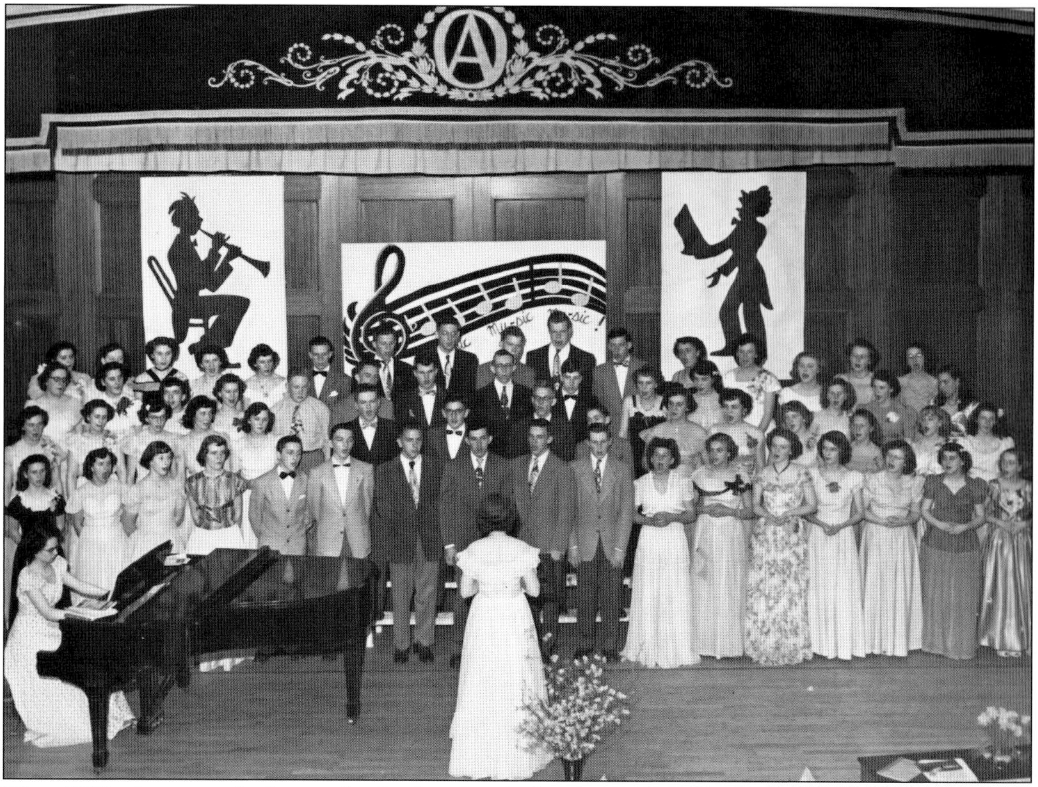

This 1950 photograph shows the high school chorus onstage. Behind the walnut divider is the gymnasium. Beth Carhart Preston is the musical director seen here, and Louise Hann is the accompanist.

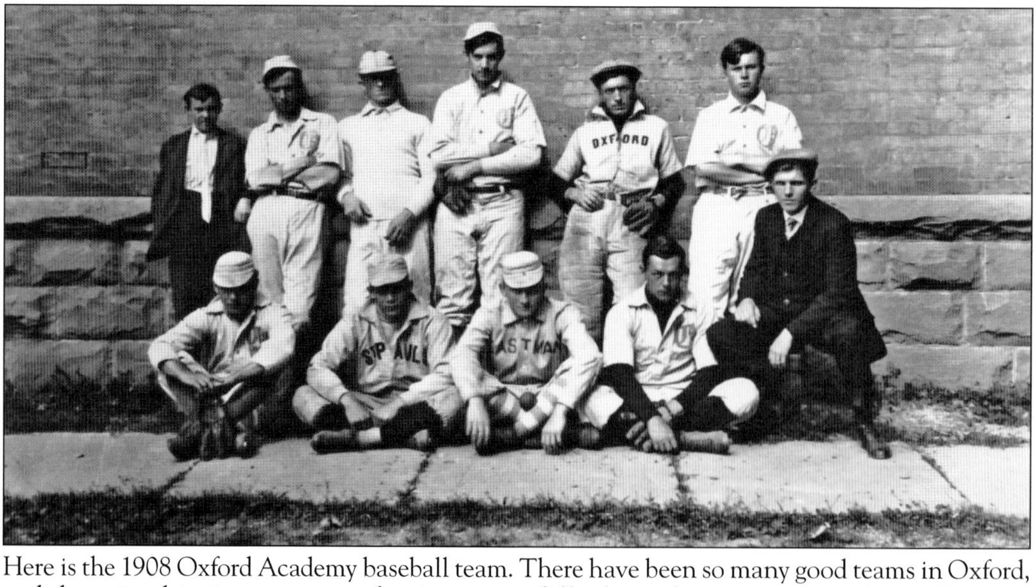

Here is the 1908 Oxford Academy baseball team. There have been so many good teams in Oxford, and championships in every sport, that it was very difficult to select images for inclusion. Pictured in no particular order are Jeff Harris, Ben Lounsberry, Walter Rugg, Morgan Harris, Ed Powers, Al Robinson, M. Morehouse, Eliot Payson, Fred Crumb, Fred Glassel, and Harry Lally.

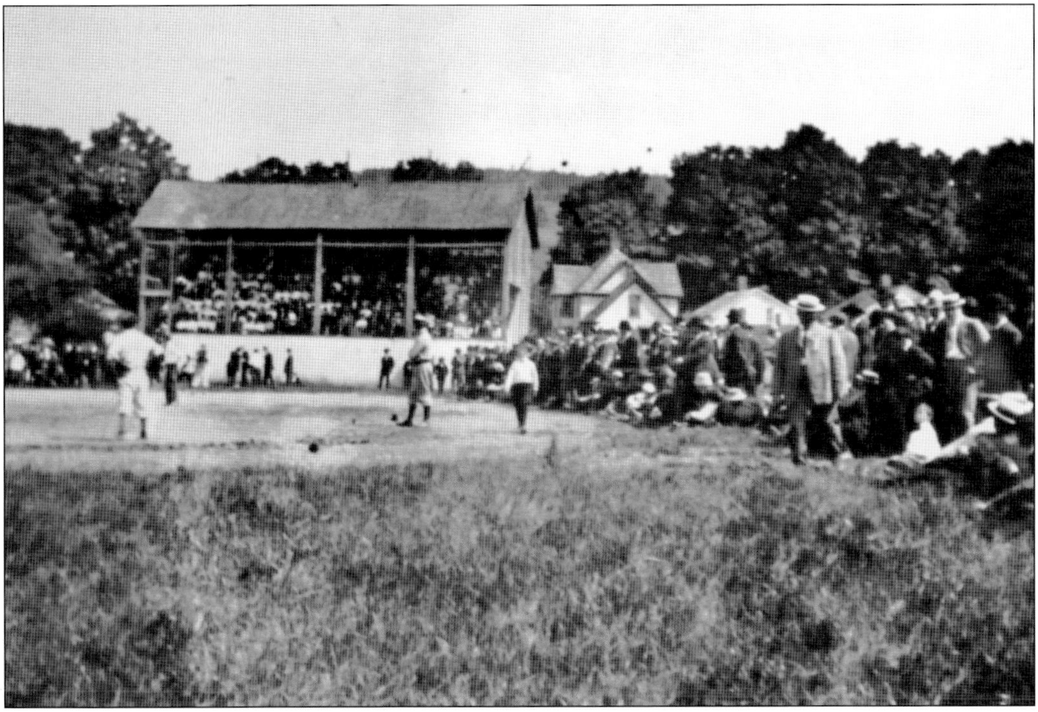

This 1908 photograph depicts a ball game behind the school. Judging by the stands, baseball was a very popular sport in Oxford.

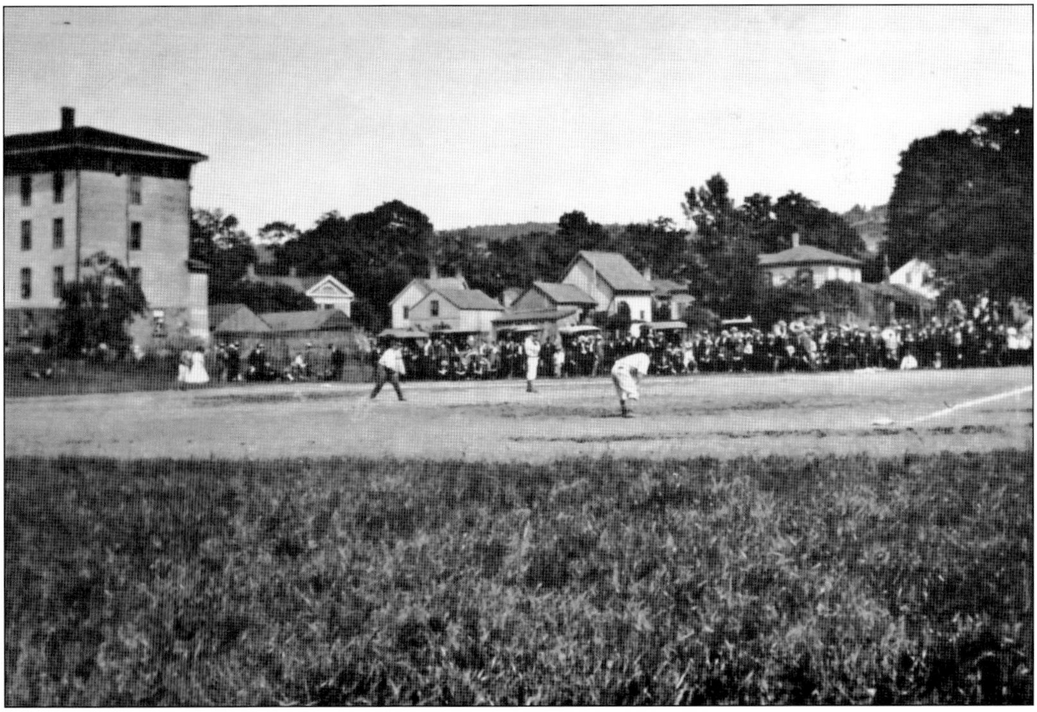

Here is another angle of the 1908 baseball game with the crowd lining the first-base side. It appears to be a big game, maybe even a championship.

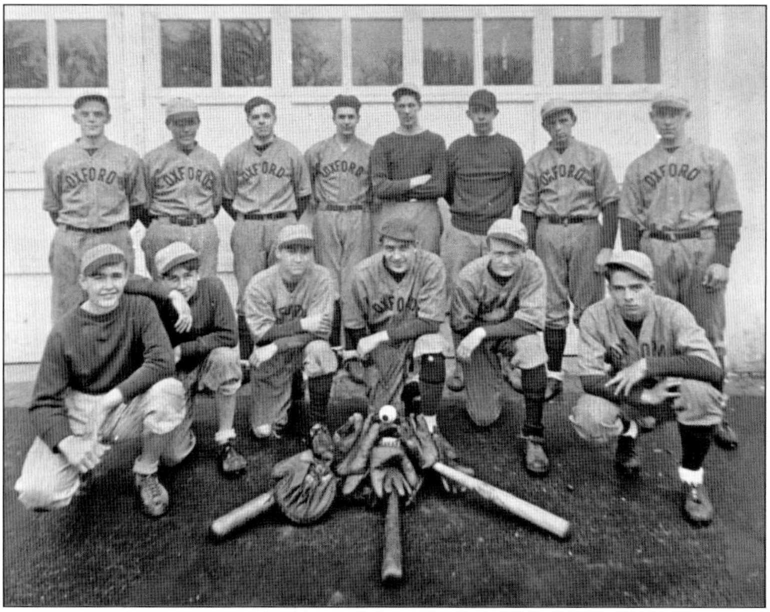

Posing here is either the 1931 or 1932 varsity baseball team. Pictured from left to right are (first row) David Emerson, Carl Leach, Gerald Cooper, Edward Loomis, Clifford McNitt, and Curtis Mowry; (second row) Lynn "Slugger" Loomis, Charles Seiler, Kenneth Dutcher, Kenneth Race, Herdman Sweenburg, Reginald Burdick, coach Robert Wylie, and Lawrence Bates.

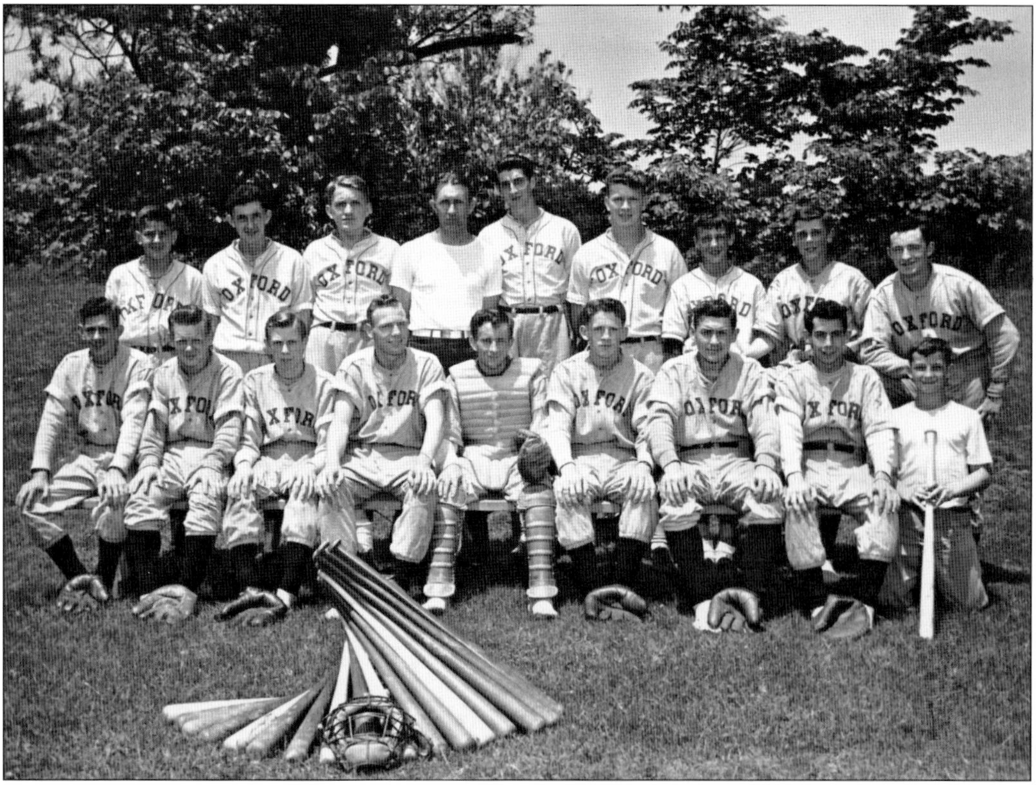

This varsity baseball team won the 1947 Susquenango League championship. Pictured from left to right are (first row) Bill Harvey, Myron Champlin, David Jones, George Lewis, Gerald Cox, Harry Aldrich, Richard Dillenbeck, David Martin, and batboy Donald Rusk; (second row) John Rice, Robert Tansey, Donald Fairchild, coach Andrews, John Witchella, Dwight Bradt, Wendall Barber, George Potter, and Richard Tansey.

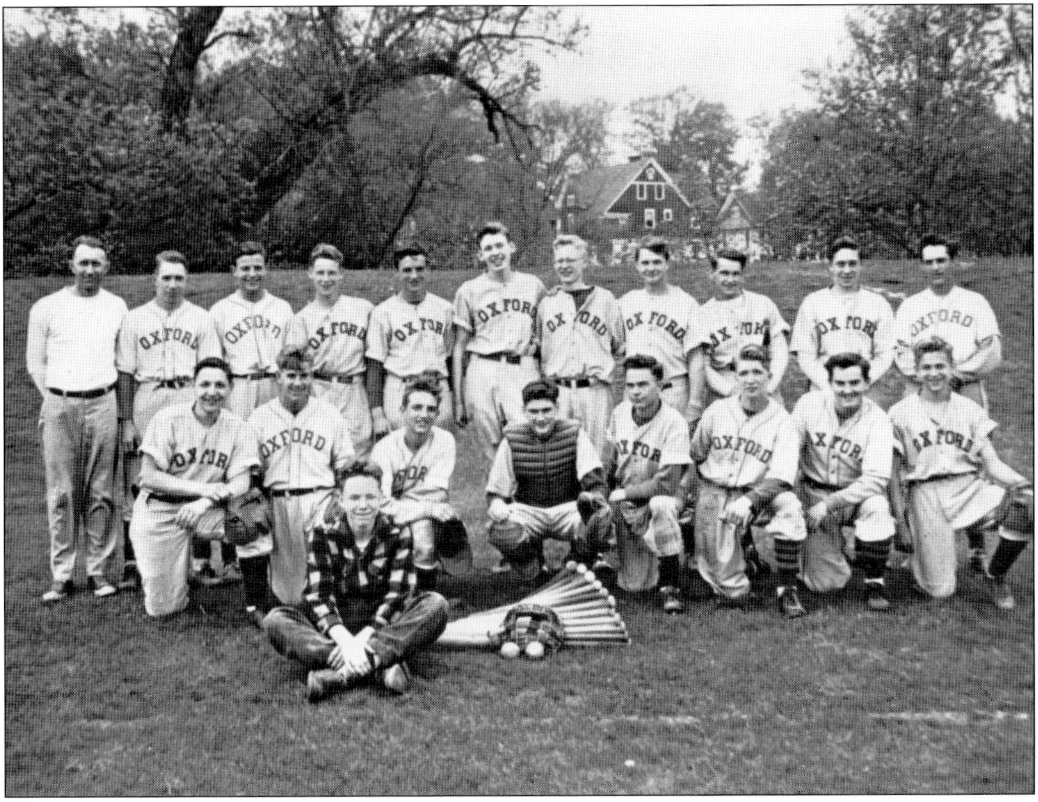

Members of the varsity baseball team are pictured here in 1950. In the front of the group is the student manager Dewey Bonner. Pictured from left to right are (first row) Angelo Paino, Donald Ross, James Potter, Lewis Roberts, Reginald Wackford, Richard Helmke, Gerald Ross, and David Wilcox; (second row) coach Charles Andrews, Robert Hughston, Joseph Laljer, Walter Boname, Wendell Barber, Robert Walden, Robert Harrison, Linn Christian, Durwood Harvey, David Furnare, and William Oliver.

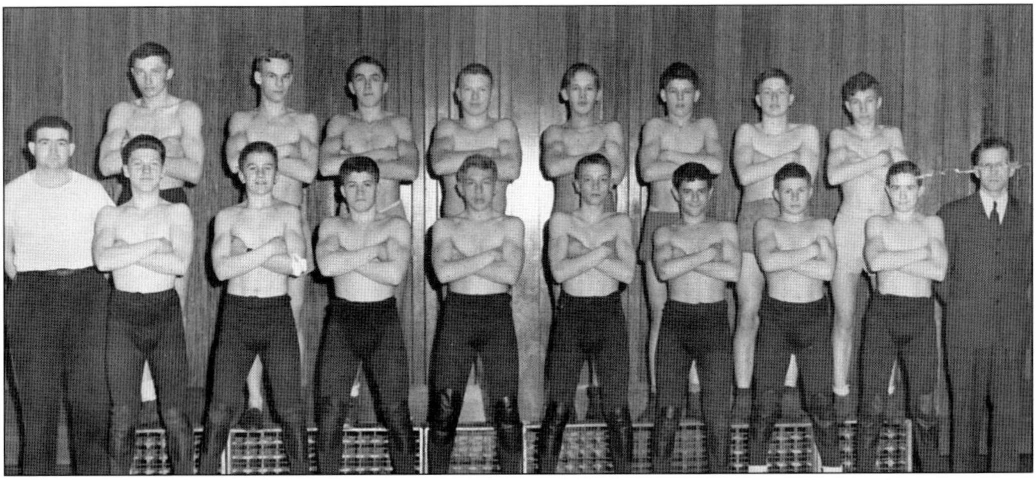

Taken in 1945, this photograph shows members of the school's wrestling team. This team gave another championship title to coach Clyde Cole, who is located on the far right. Team members in the picture are unidentified except for Carl Winner (third from left, first row).

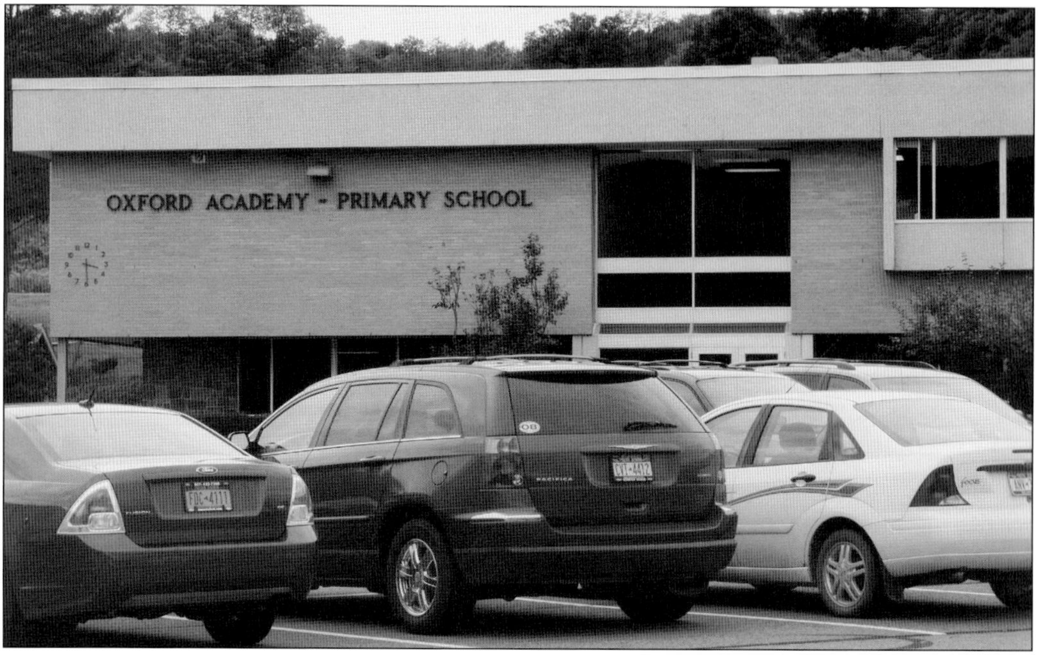

This is the present-day elementary school for preschool, kindergarten, and grades one through four. It is part of a large building that houses the high school at the other end.

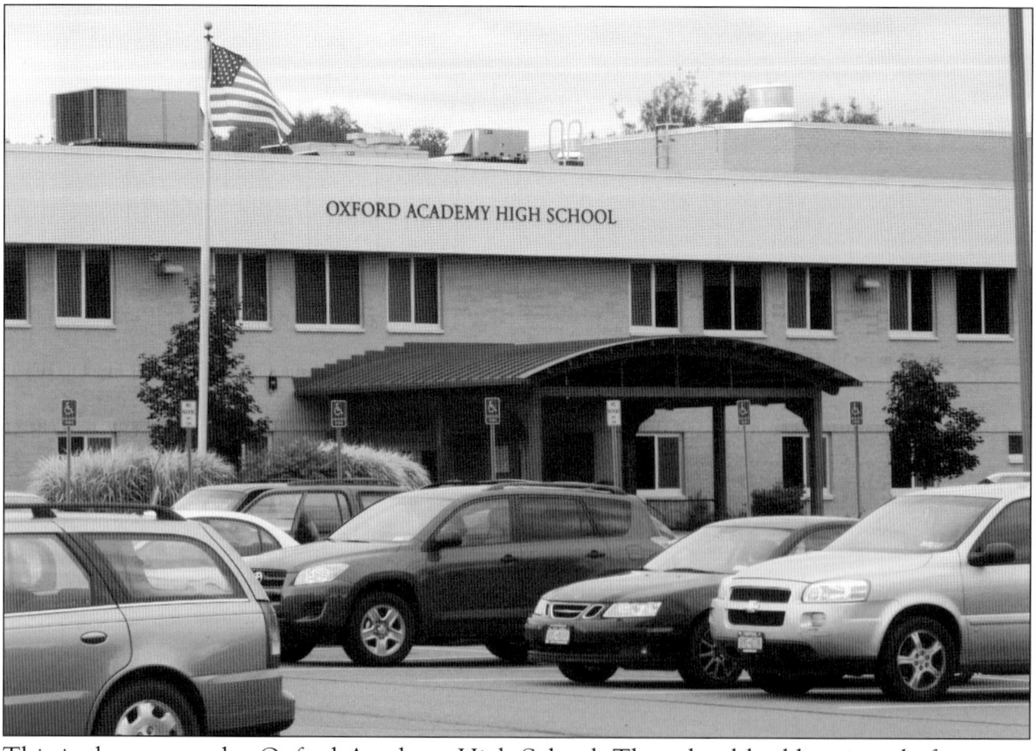

This is the present-day Oxford Academy High School. The school building is only five years old. It has new, state-of-the-art facilities in every department, a beautiful auditorium, and a large gymnasium.

Five

The Oxford Bands

For many years, Oxford Academy has had an excellent musical program and garnered many awards and trophies for its marching band, concert band, and jazz band. However, Oxford's musical repertoire was not always present.

During Oxford Academy's first century of private status, it had no music instruction, no instrument lessons, and no musical ensembles. And 40 years later, the academy still did not have an extensive musical program.

Finally, in 1934, Fred Parsiany became the first of many excellent music instructors hired. As a teacher, Parsiany was strict and stern, but his students loved him. By 1949, both elementary and high school students were enrolled in the music program. There was also a high school band. In the same year, the school's first marching band uniforms were purchased for $1,523.36. Parsiany's last year as a music teacher was 1957.

Richard Herefort came in to replace Parsiany as the new music instructor. He continued the dedication and commitment that built the school's music reputation and its skilled marching band. In 1964, Merritt Russell became the new music instructor for the junior high school, and Herefort and Russell became a good team. In 1971, the school's band was very big, with 112 marching band members, and they were exceptionally good, garnering prizes from Binghamton to Sherburne. In 1977, Herefort retired, and the new music instructor became Francis Wilcox. The school's great reputation continues to this day.

The roots of marching bands date back to the pre–Civil War era and the rise of fire company–marching units. Because of the popularity of marching music and marching bands, Oxford built two band pagodas: one in Washington Park in 1875 and the other in Lafayette Park in 1915. The band tradition continues with annual summer concerts by the Oxford Community Band. Conductor Francis Wilcox leads the contingent.

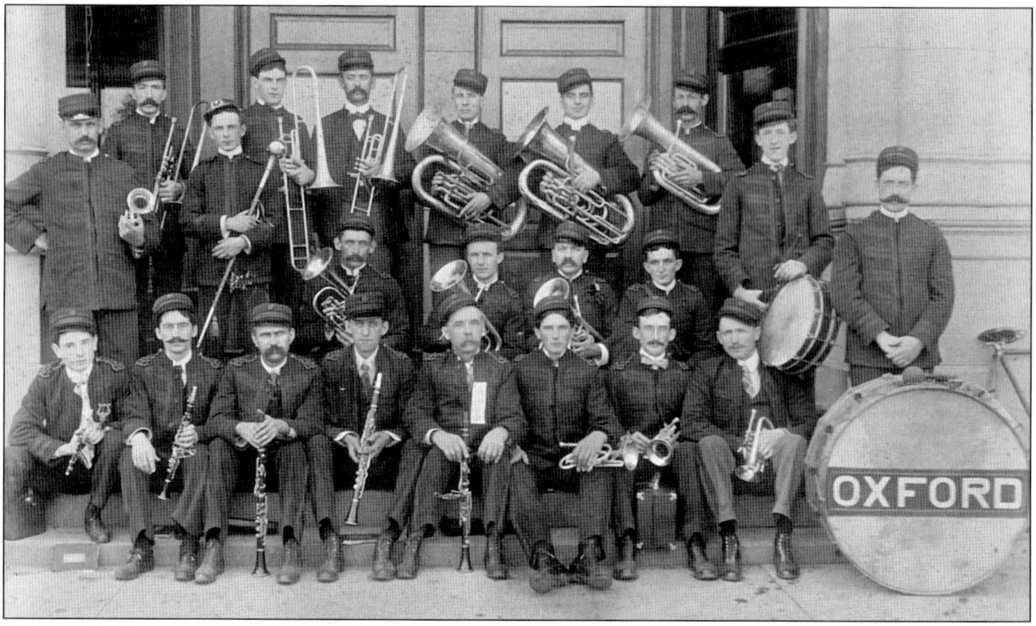

The Oxford Community Band poses on the bank steps in 1890. It provided concerts in the two larger village parks and the Citizen's Opera House and led important local parades. The names of most of the members are listed in the Oxford Historical Depot-Museum. Pictured from left to right are (first row) ? Jones, Ed Walker, Ed Ostrom, John Srveenburgh, Matt Gibbon, ? Dillon, Ed Brown, and ? Sutton; (second row) Ansel Parker, Herb Tew, Ed Miner, and Henry Hunt; (third row) director Gary Biers, Clarence Brown, Chas. Holliger, and Jim Dunn; (fourth row) Ed Eggleston, John Cougan, Norm Birrs, Burr Hurlbert, Ray Brown, and Walt Boname.

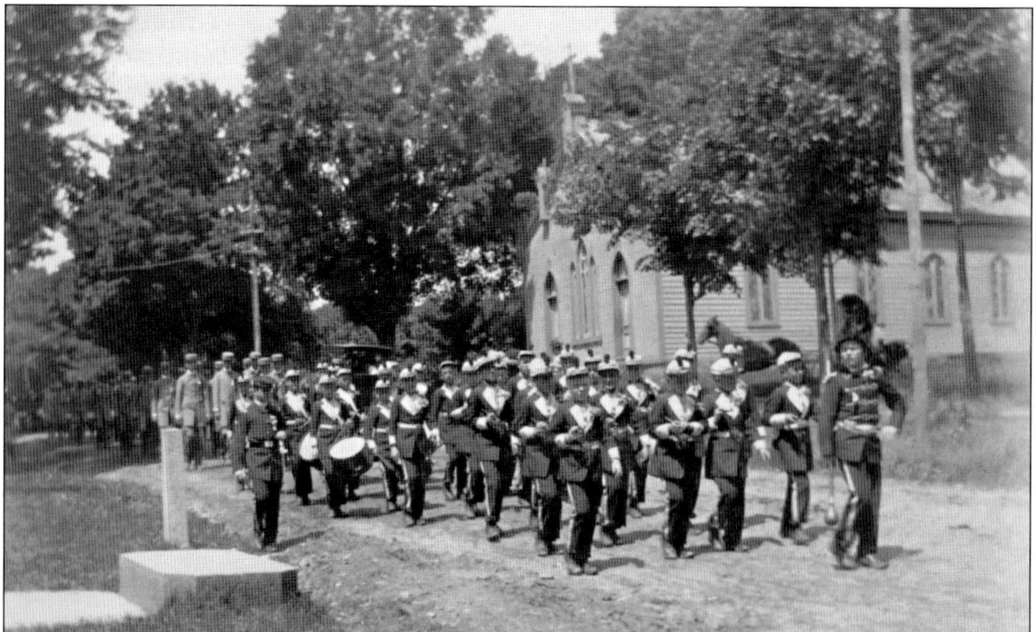

Taken on August 3, 1899, this photograph shows a band heading to the Sappho Hose Company during the Chenango County Firemen's Tournament.

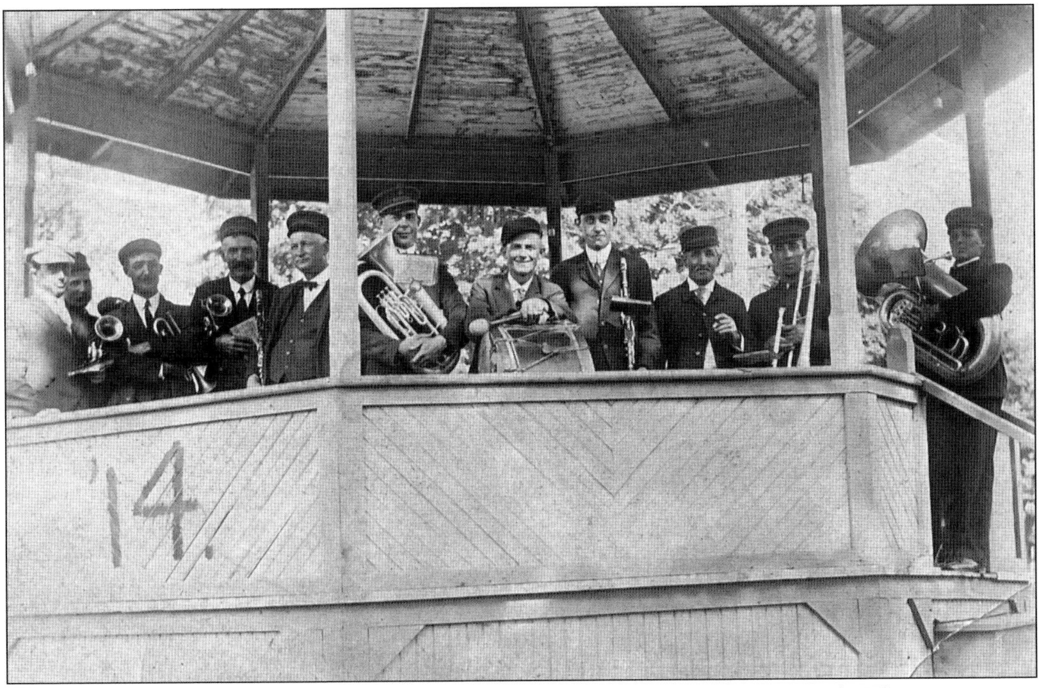

A band pauses for an image in the pagoda that was built in Washington Park. The picture was taken in 1914 when the pagoda was only 30 years old.

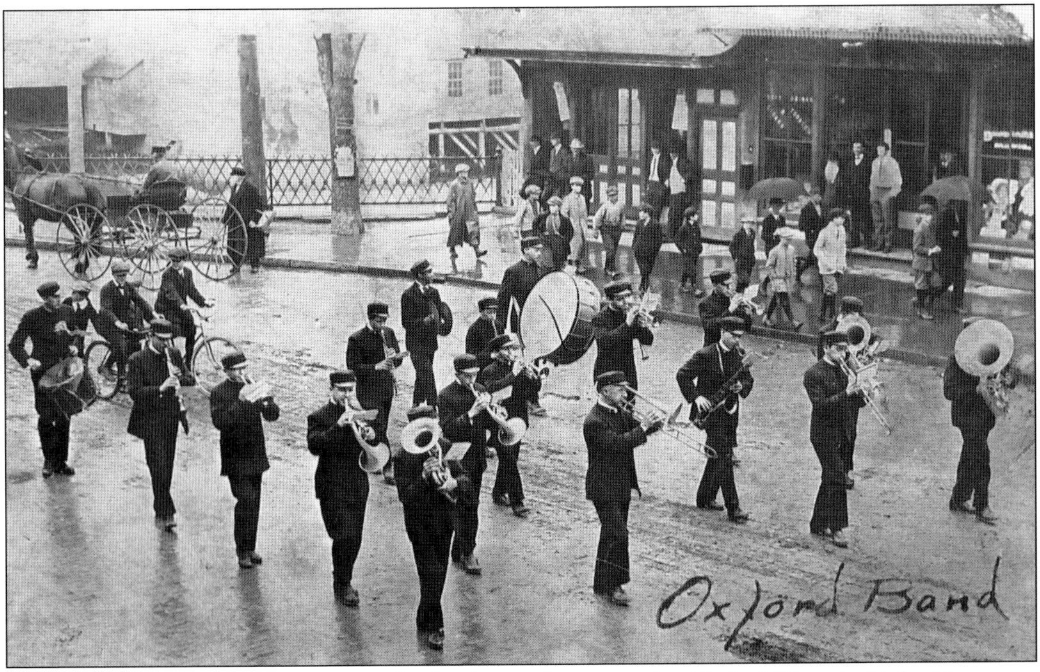

The band is seen in 1908 crossing the bridge and passing the Oxford Electric Light Company during the Old Home Parade. Three well-dressed bicyclists trail the marching band.

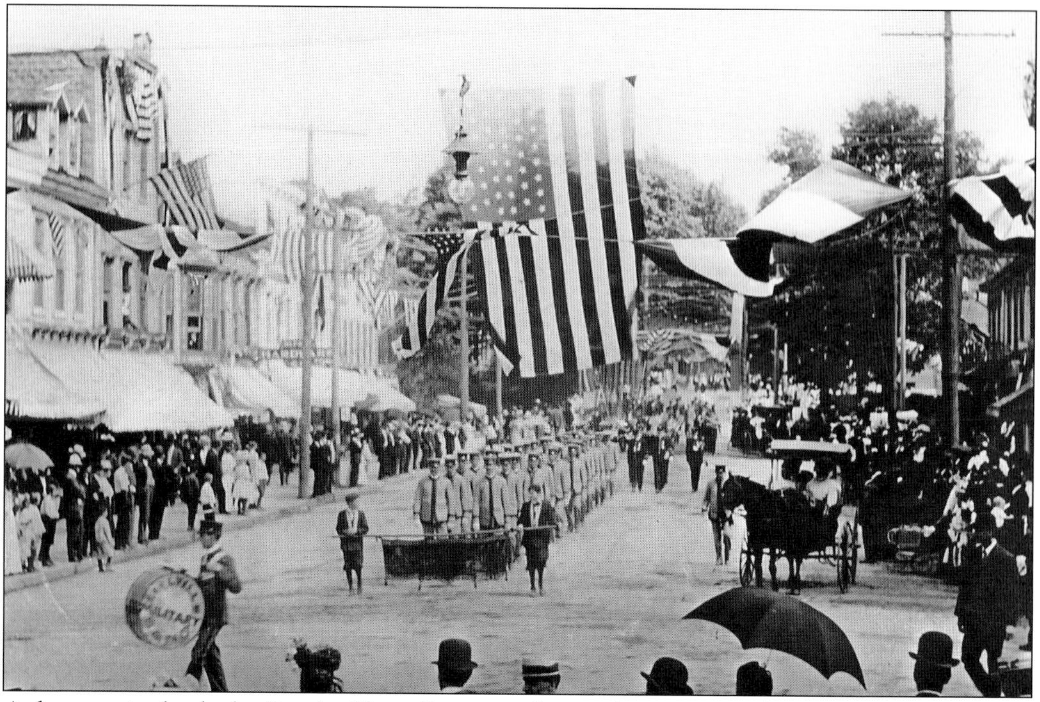

A drum major leads the Sappho Hose Company during the 1908 parade.

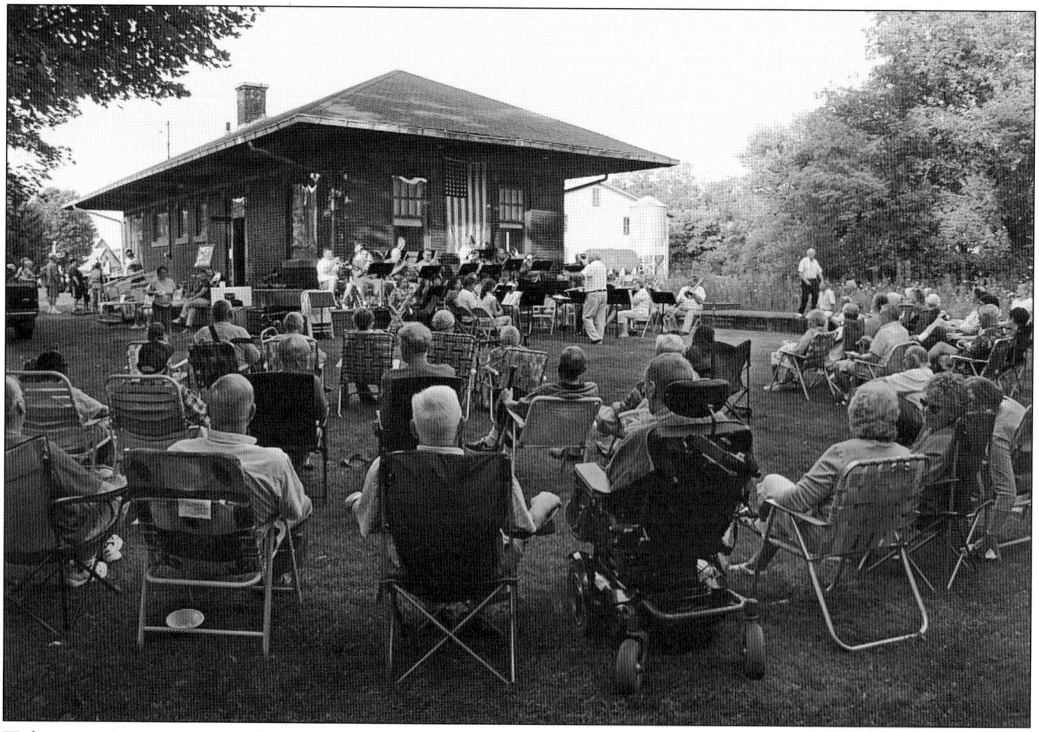

Taken in August 2010, this photograph shows members of the Oxford Community Band. It plays a series of concerts around the village each summer. Members are seen on the rear deck of the Oxford Historical Depot-Museum, while a large crowd enjoys the event.

Six

FIREMAN, SAVE MY HOUSE!

In September 1799, there was a big fire that burned the new school before it was ever used. There was nothing to stop it that night—no organization, no equipment, and no water supply.

That grave situation is a far cry from today's Oxford Fire Department and its modern station, five engines, pumpers, rescue vehicle, and high-ladder truck. The crew is highly trained and has a four-minute response time. It has equipment and material to combat any type of fire in the Oxford district or nearby communities. The fire department has two ambulances staffed with emergency medical technicians, a river rescue boat, and a jaws-of-life for automobile and small-space rescues. Also, the Oxford Fire Department is composed of firefighters who are all volunteers. As such, the fire department is one of the most respected organizations in Oxford.

A few years after the big fire in 1799, a fire company was formed with little equipment in 1810. One of its leather buckets survived and is on display at the Oxford Historical Depot-Museum. The early fire department did not even have a fire bell until 1818, which was when the St. Paul's church bell rung whenever there were fires. In April 1845, a Niagara hand engine was purchased, and later the Niagara Hose Company formed. However, the fire company's equipment did not extinguish the fire on the Clarke Block in February 1858. There was more improvement when the hand-pumper "Lady Washington" was purchased in 1858, and a new company was formed a year later called the Lady Washington Hose Company.

There were many fire companies that formed in the late 19th century, including the Sappho Hose Company in 1873 and later the Steamer Company. In 1878, the Hook and Ladder Company formed, and in 1898 the Independent Hose Company started. The fire companies shared the Fort Hill Building, and they all eventually merged together soon after World War II. The new building, with its state-of-the-art equipment, has been the company's crowning achievement.

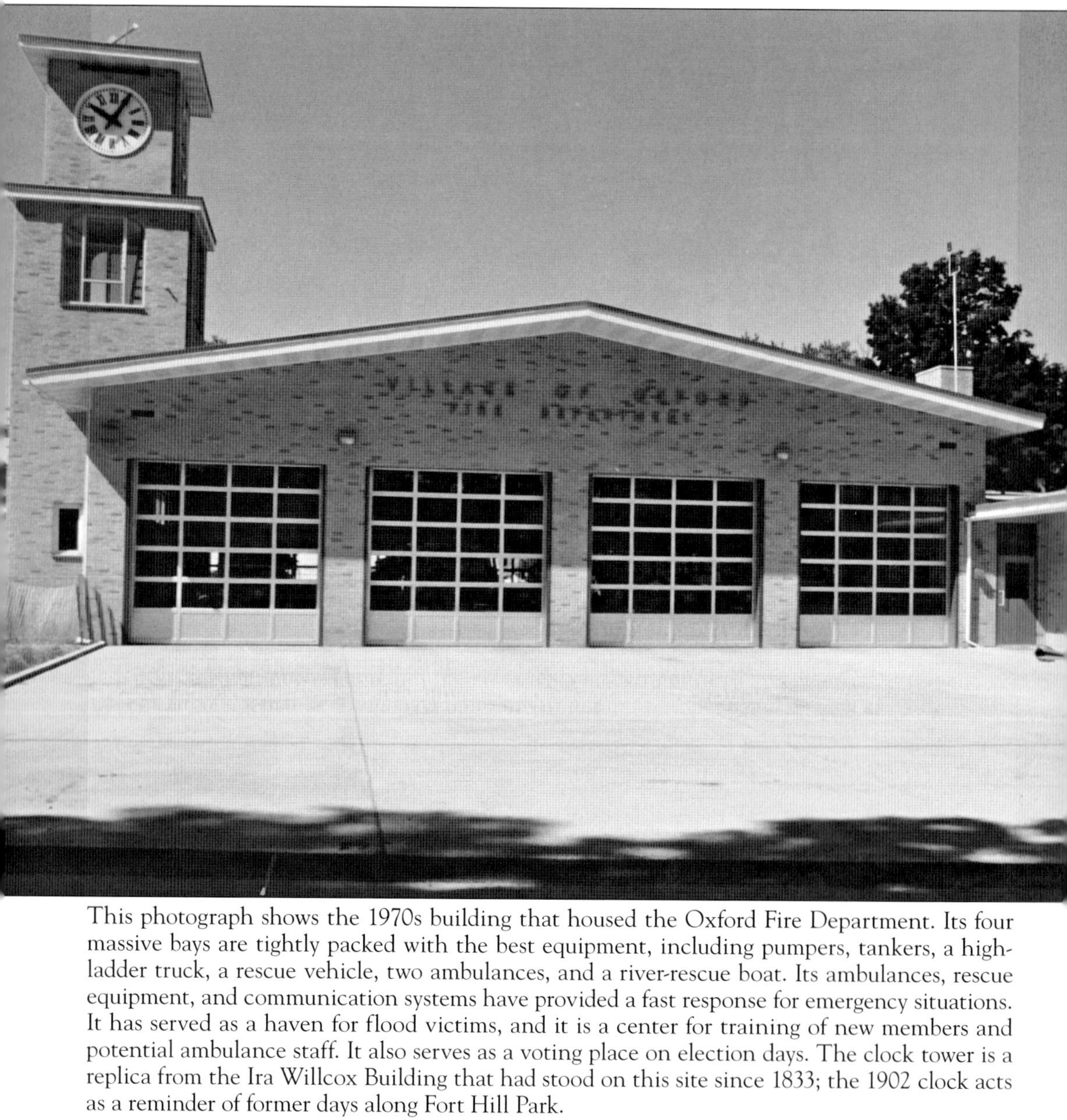

This photograph shows the 1970s building that housed the Oxford Fire Department. Its four massive bays are tightly packed with the best equipment, including pumpers, tankers, a high-ladder truck, a rescue vehicle, two ambulances, and a river-rescue boat. Its ambulances, rescue equipment, and communication systems have provided a fast response for emergency situations. It has served as a haven for flood victims, and it is a center for training of new members and potential ambulance staff. It also serves as a voting place on election days. The clock tower is a replica from the Ira Willcox Building that had stood on this site since 1833; the 1902 clock acts as a reminder of former days along Fort Hill Park.

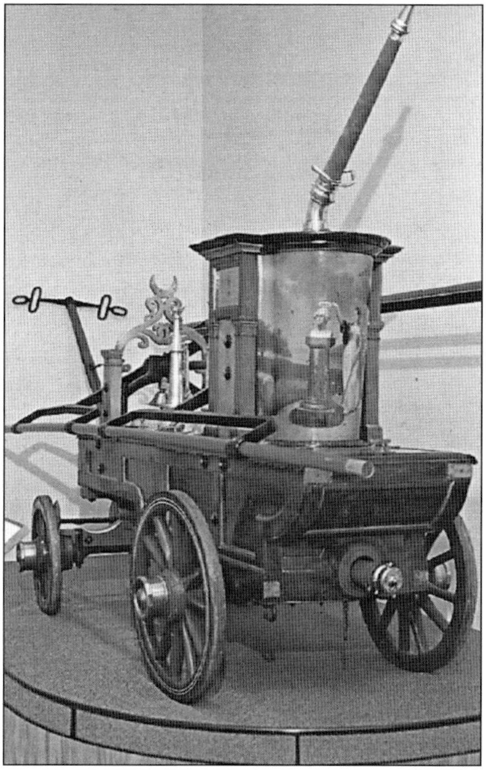

Here is the "Martha Washington" engine that replaced the Lady Washington engine, which was purchased in 1858. It is on permanent display in the Adirondack Museum in Blue Mountain Lake, New York.

This is the oldest known picture of the Sappho Hose Company, taken possibly in 1873 when the company was formed. The firemen are posing on Lafayette Park with their hand-drawn hose cart. The paper lanterns on the ground and suspended around the park indicate a day of celebration. All the buildings are still present, but the bluestone curbs have been replaced.

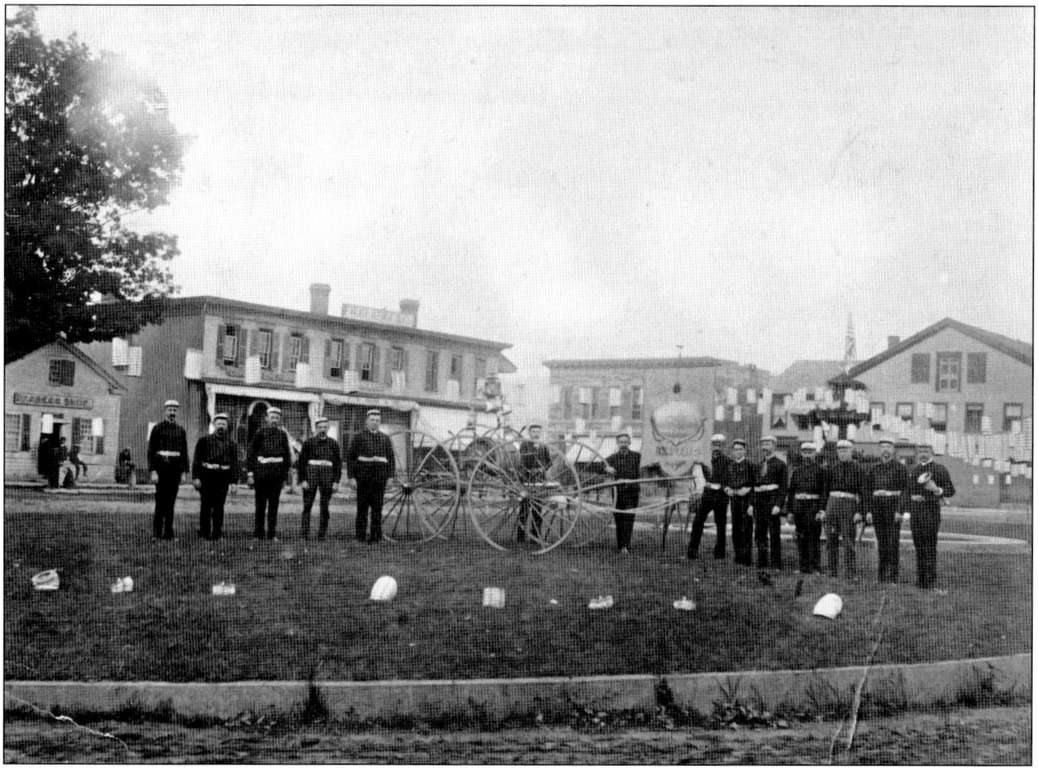

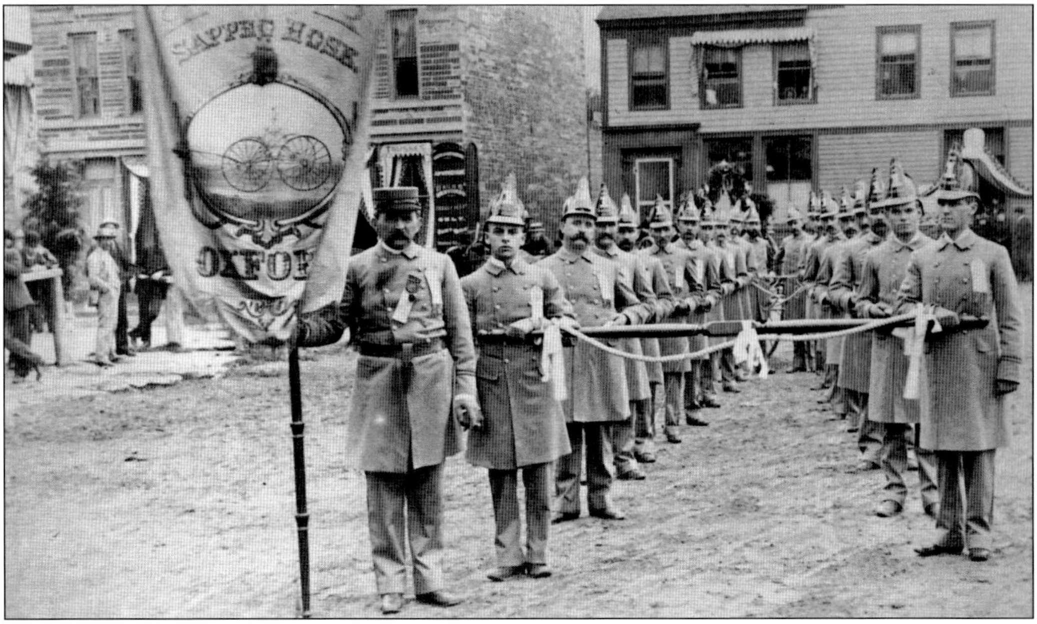

Taken on September 15, 1891, this photograph shows the Sappho Hose Company members posing in their new uniforms on the street near the Tuttle Block. They are standing at attention on the right, while several onlookers are in the background on the corner of Canal and State Streets. This is the location of the present-day Stadium Sports Bar and Grill.

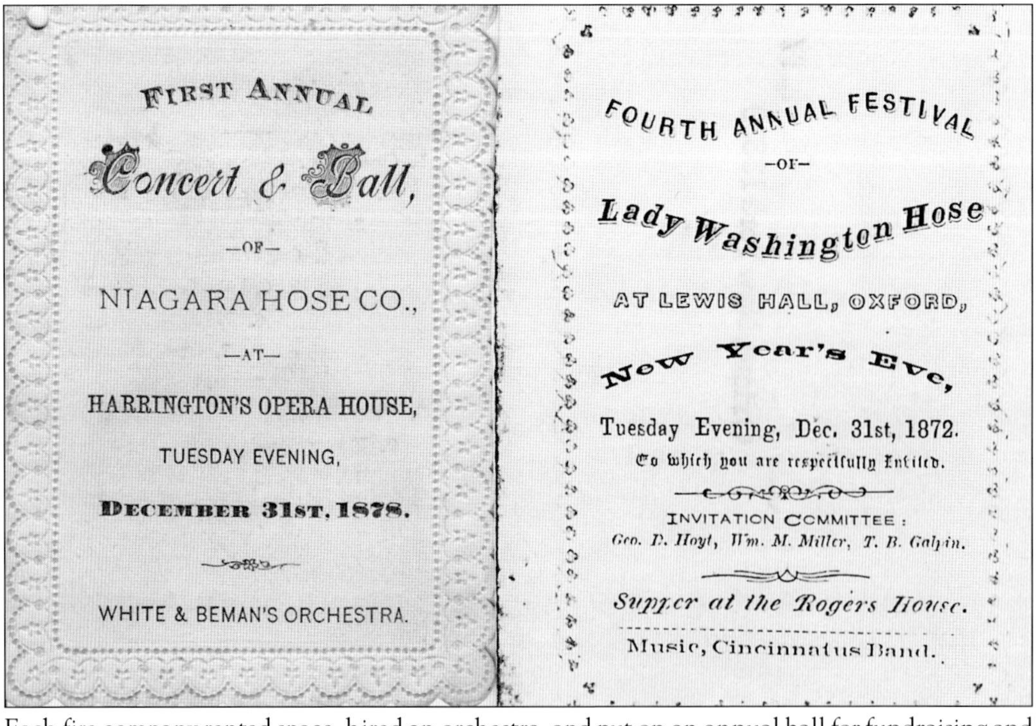

FIRST ANNUAL

Concert & Ball,

—OF—

NIAGARA HOSE CO.,

—AT—

HARRINGTON'S OPERA HOUSE,

TUESDAY EVENING,

DECEMBER 31ST, 1878.

WHITE & BEMAN'S ORCHESTRA.

FOURTH ANNUAL FESTIVAL

—OF—

Lady Washington Hose

AT LEWIS HALL, OXFORD,

New Year's Eve,

Tuesday Evening, Dec. 31st, 1872.

To which you are respectfully Invited.

INVITATION COMMITTEE :

Geo. P. Hoyt, Wm. M. Miller, T. B. Galpin.

Supper at the Rogers House.

Music, Cincinnatus Band.

Each fire company rented space, hired an orchestra, and put on an annual ball for fundraising and socializing. There was a competition between the fire companies to see whose ball was grander. This photograph shows two of several invitations that have been preserved.

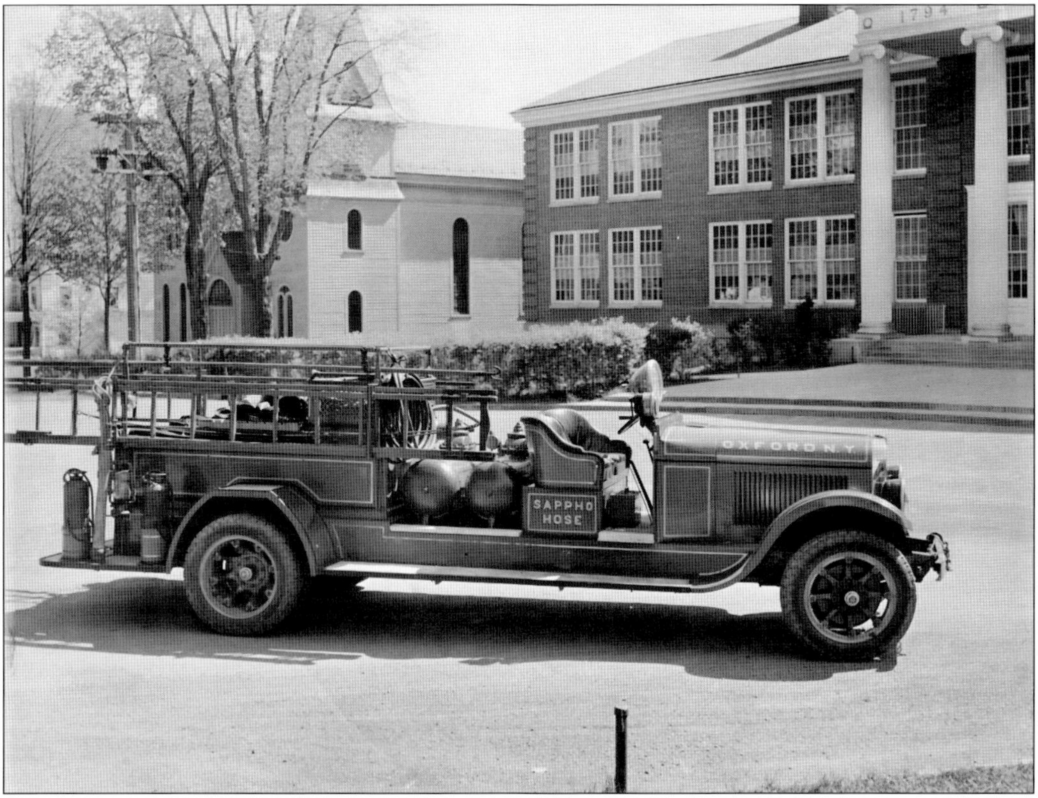

The new Sappho Hose Company fire truck, the company's only piece of equipment in 1932, is on display here. It was considered a pretty good truck for its time because of its searchlight, ladders, portable extinguishers, and pressure tanks.

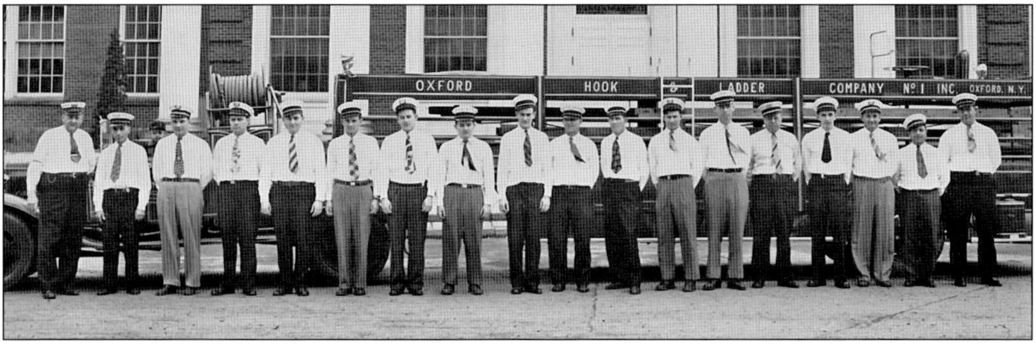

This 1938 photograph shows the new Oxford Hook & Ladder Company. Many of the firemen were also members of Sappho Hose Company or independent fire companies.

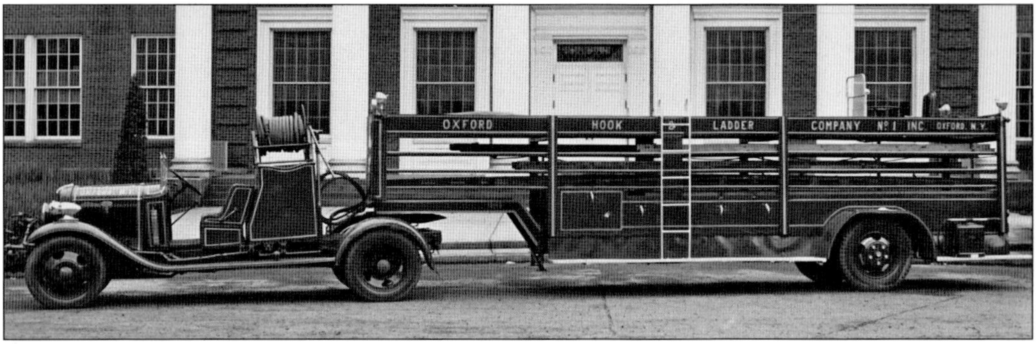

This is the Oxford Hook & Ladder Company truck. The company had a tradition that dates back to 1878. Harold Gray built the truck with much help from high school boys; it was molded from an old truck, and they added new lines. It was taken to fire conventions, where it won several first prizes.

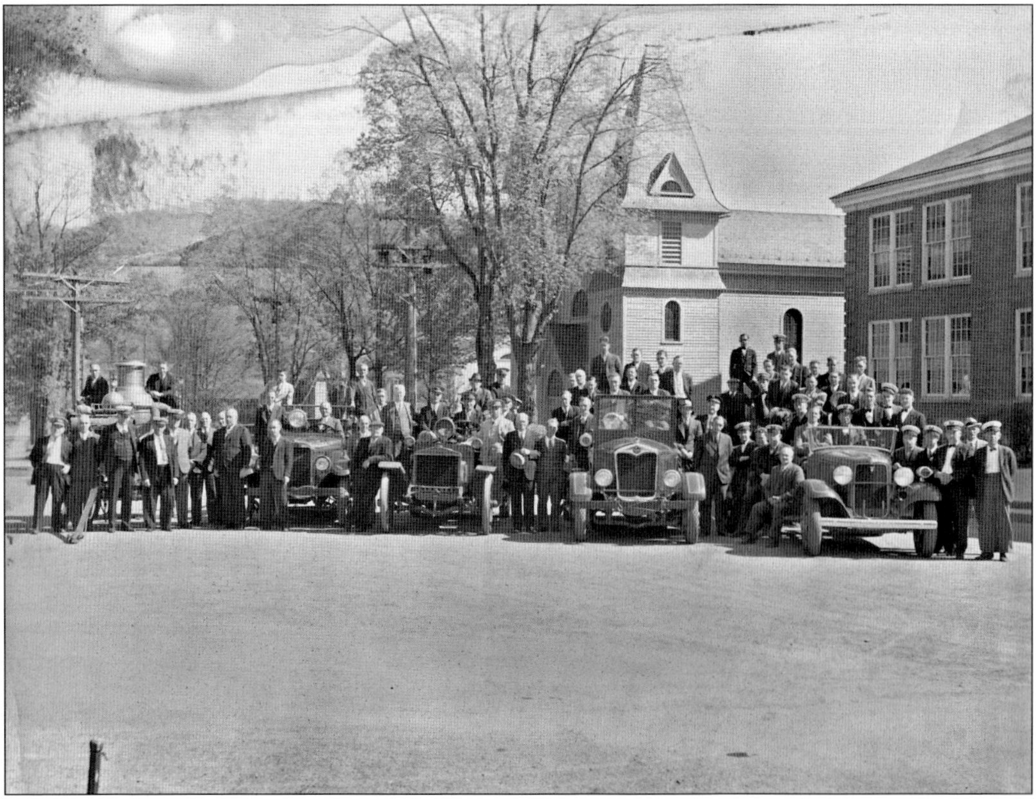

All four fire companies are posing with their equipment in front of the school and the Methodist church in 1938. The steamer was kept as a relic until it was sold to a Syracuse museum for needed cash. Ironically, the Methodist church burned to the ground in 1964.

This is Vivian Frair's membership certificate and a copy of the bylaws and regulations of the Ladies' Auxiliary, which is known today as the Auxiliary. There once was a devastating fire far from the village in January 1979. It was -25 degrees Fahrenheit, and the fire happened at 3:30 a.m., yet the Auxiliary helped others at the scene delivering hot coffee, doughnuts, and warm towels.

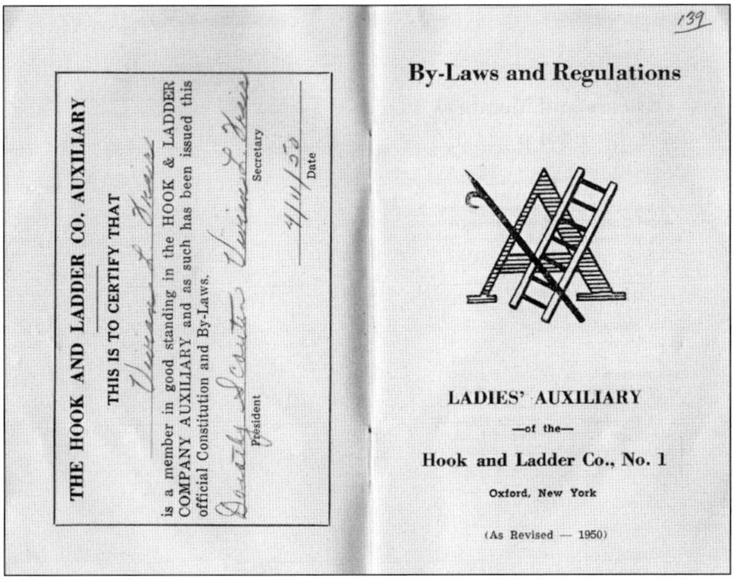

THE HOOK AND LADDER CO. AUXILIARY

THIS IS TO CERTIFY THAT

is a member in good standing in the HOOK & LADDER COMPANY AUXILIARY and as such has been issued this official Constitution and By-Laws.

President

Secretary

4/11/50

Date

139

By-Laws and Regulations

LADIES' AUXILIARY

—of the—

Hook and Ladder Co., No. 1

Oxford, New York

(As Revised — 1950)

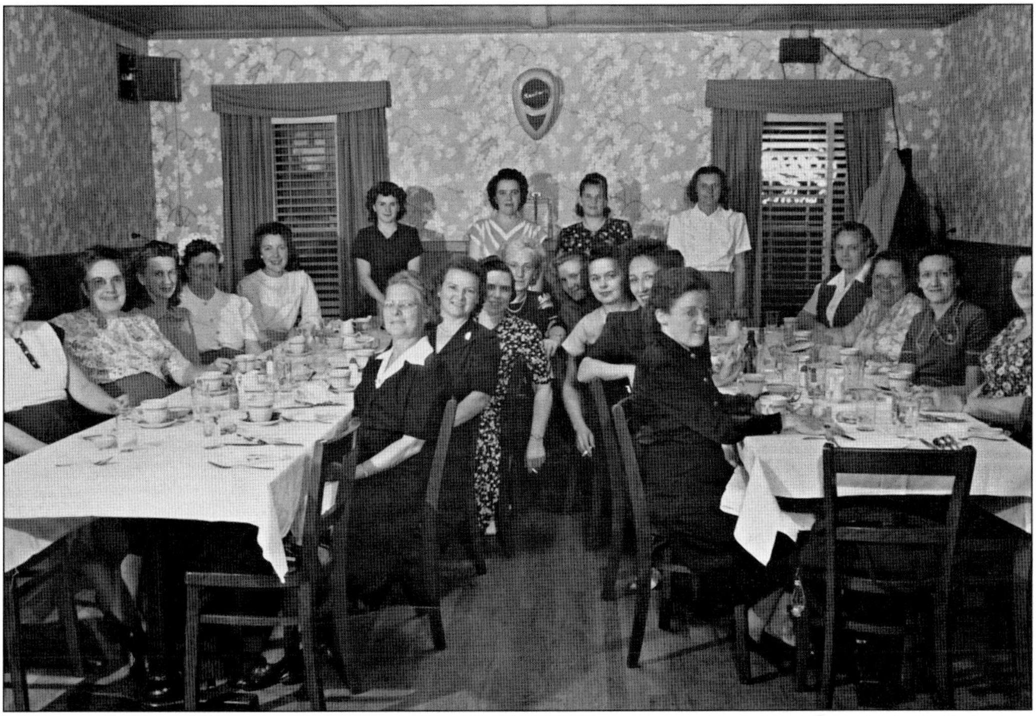

Taken in 1948, this photograph shows members of the Auxiliary at their annual banquet at Fred's Inn. Pictured here among the group are Nancy Biviano, Florence Seeley, Maron Covell, Dorothy Seanter, Sally Murphy, Marie Ross, Martha Rood, Pauline Gilday, Frieda Potter, Louise Hemstrought, Regina Keating, Amanda Leonard, Frances Hemstrought, Jean Weaver, Lillian Gray, and Mildred Marshman.

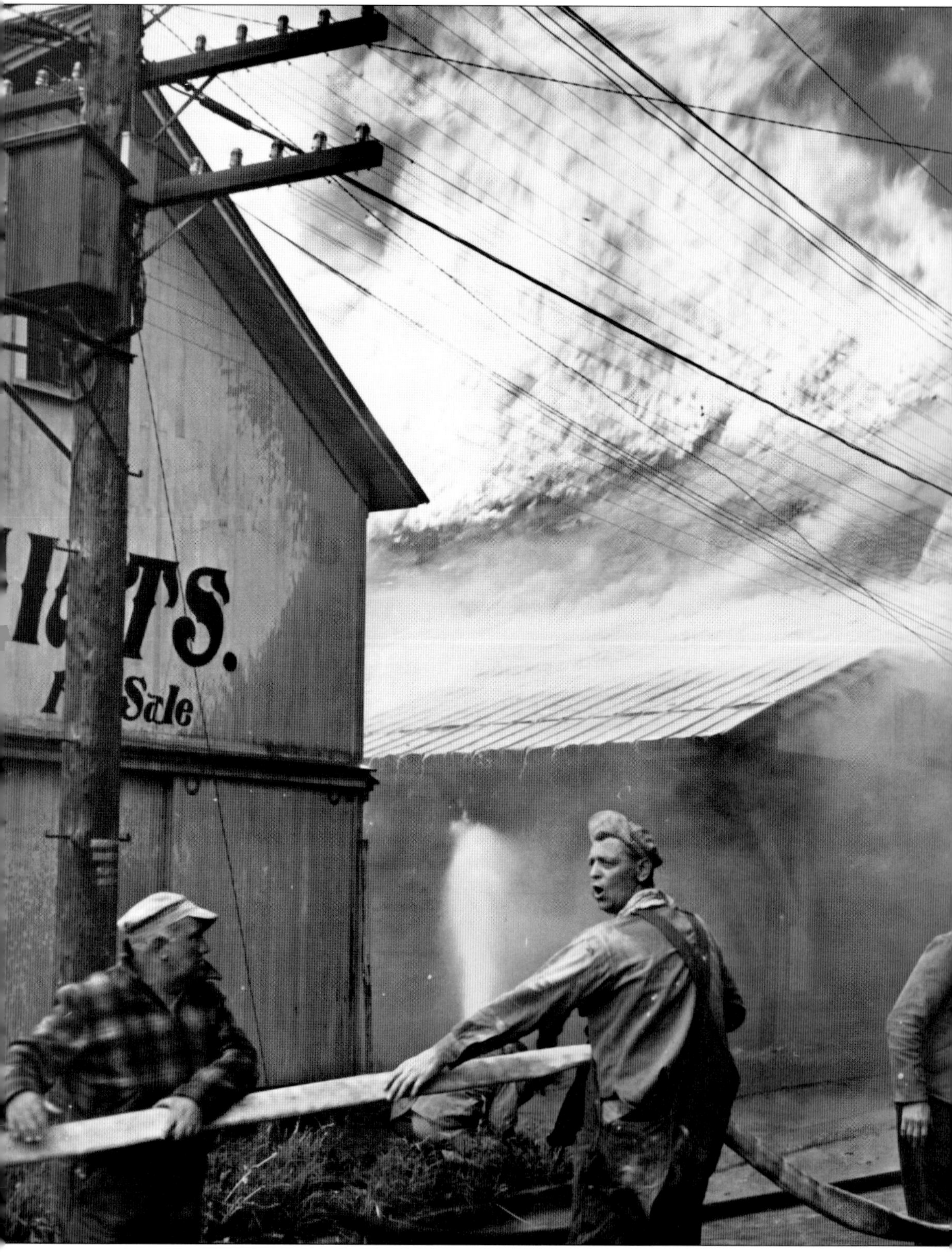
Sale

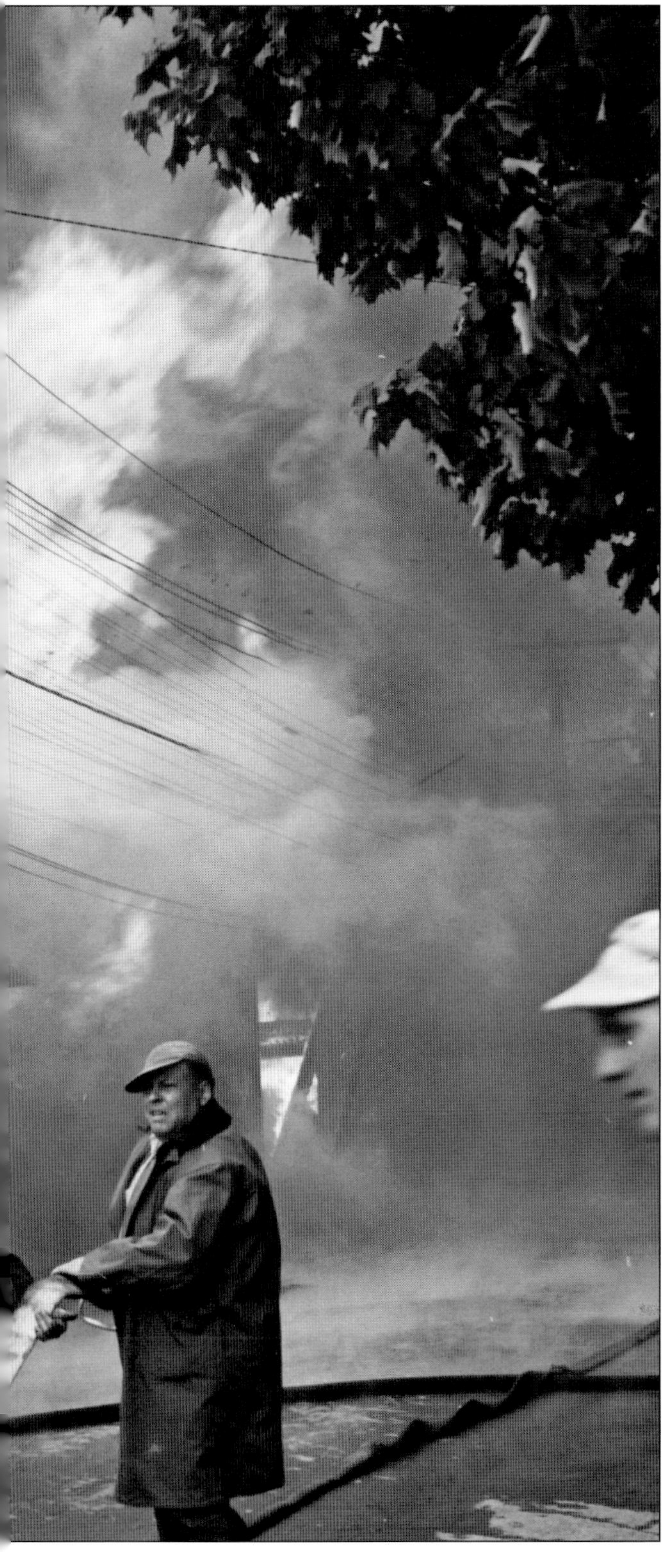

This is the Church's Lumber Company fire on May 26, 1949. Firemen are just arriving on the scene, pulling out empty hoses to hook up to hydrants. The business burned to the ground, but nearby homes and the adjacent Victory Market were saved. Previous to this, whole blocks and hallowed buildings had burned down during blazes. There have been devastating fires in Oxford over the years: at St. James Hotel in 1914, at the basket factory in 1922 and 1928, at the Ontario & Western (O&W) Railway depot in 1931, at the *Oxford Review-Times* and Merithew Block in 1947, at the opera house in 1929, and at the Chapin Block in 1960. There have been no out-of-control blazes since the new fire station was built.

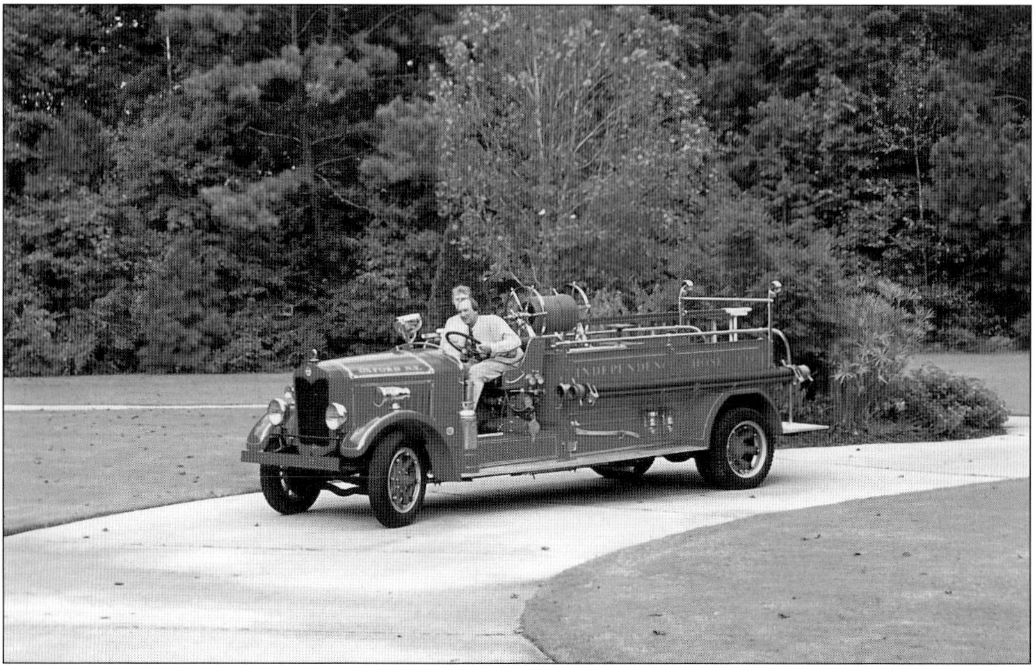

This photograph depicts the Buffalo-Selden truck, which was originally built in 1929, fully restored. Keith Kilgore restored the truck in the early 1900s, and it is still running today.

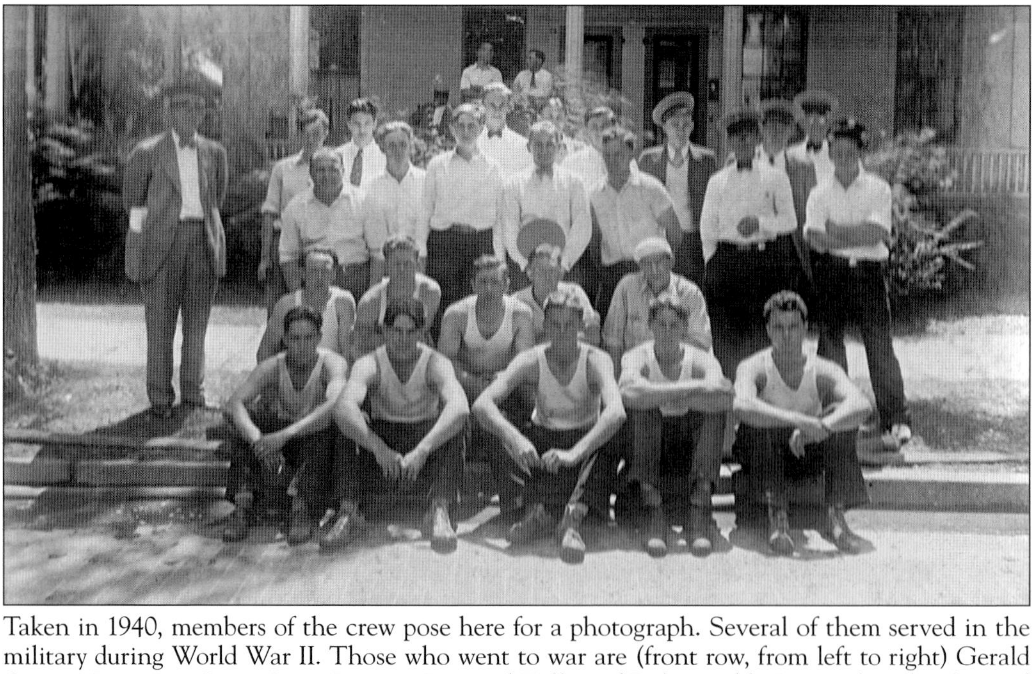

Taken in 1940, members of the crew pose here for a photograph. Several of them served in the military during World War II. Those who went to war are (front row, from left to right) Gerald Cooper, Lawrence Bates, Lynn Loomis, Leonard Tefft, and Robert Eddy. Levi Whittaker (second row) served in the war as well. Others identified in the picture are (second row, from left to right) two unidentified, Levi, Silas Whittaker, and Joe Walling; (third row, from left to right) Julian Moore, Jack Whittaker, two unidentified, Lawrence Bliven, and two unidentified; (fourth row, from left to right) unidentified, Ken Race, Paul Crandall, unidentified, Bob Wylie, and three unidentified.

Here is the honor roll of firemen that was kept during World War II recognizing all Oxford firemen who served in the military.

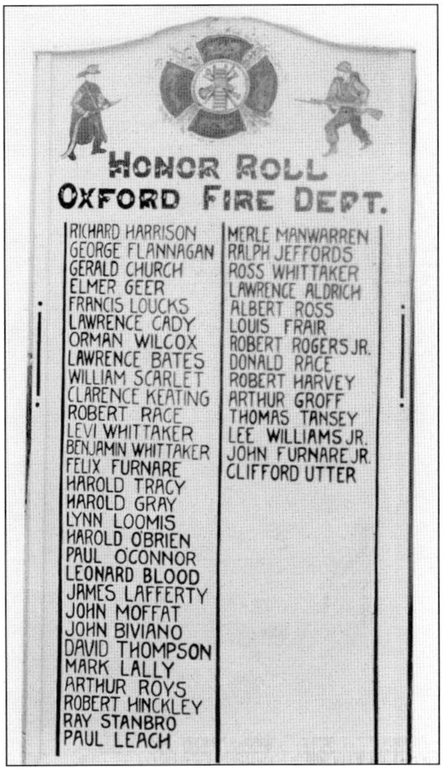

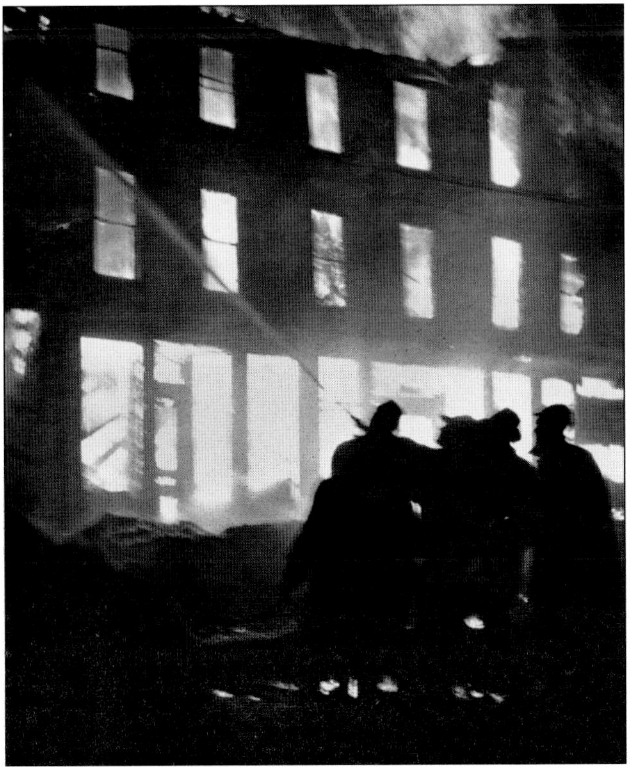

This image shows the fire at the *Oxford Review-Times*, which happened on March 4, 1947. The fire destroyed the whole block. In less than a year, the paper was back in business.

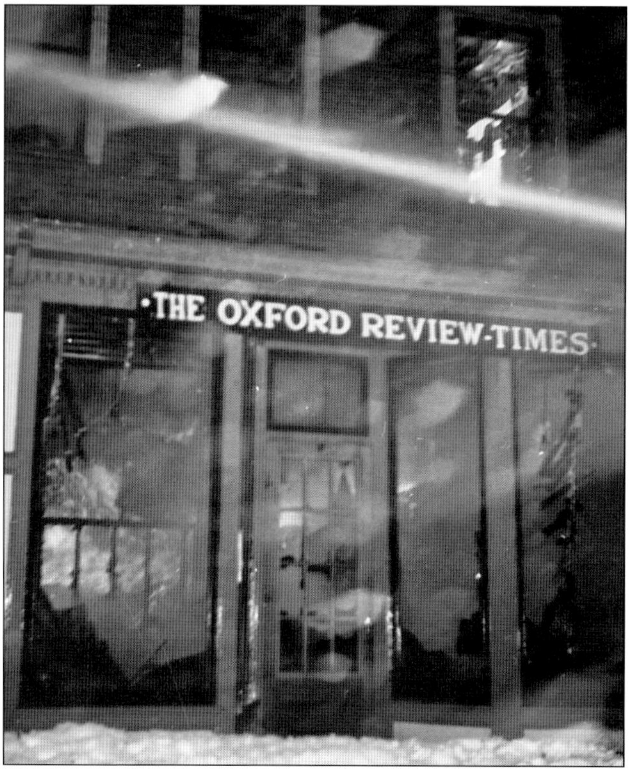

Here is another view of the fire at the local newspaper on a cold night in March 1947.

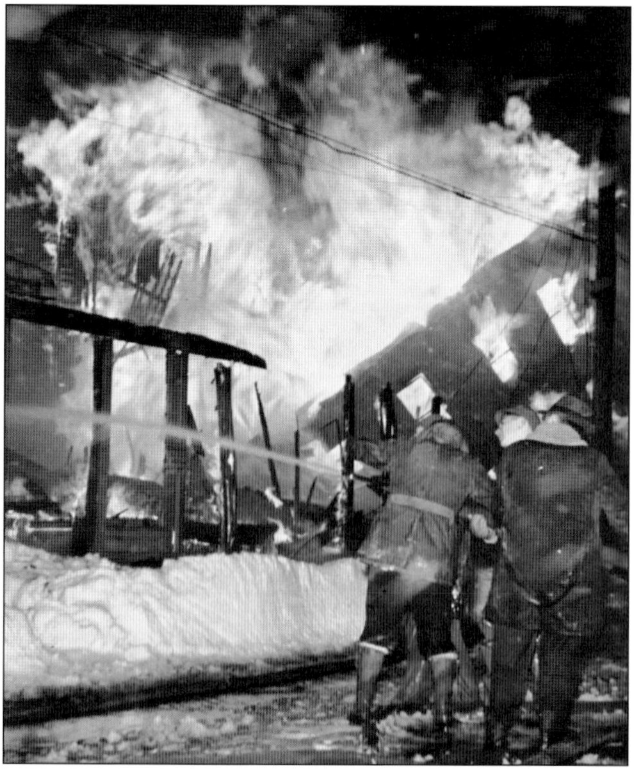

The March 1947 blaze was fought to the end in ice and snow. The rear of the building is seen here just before it crumbled.

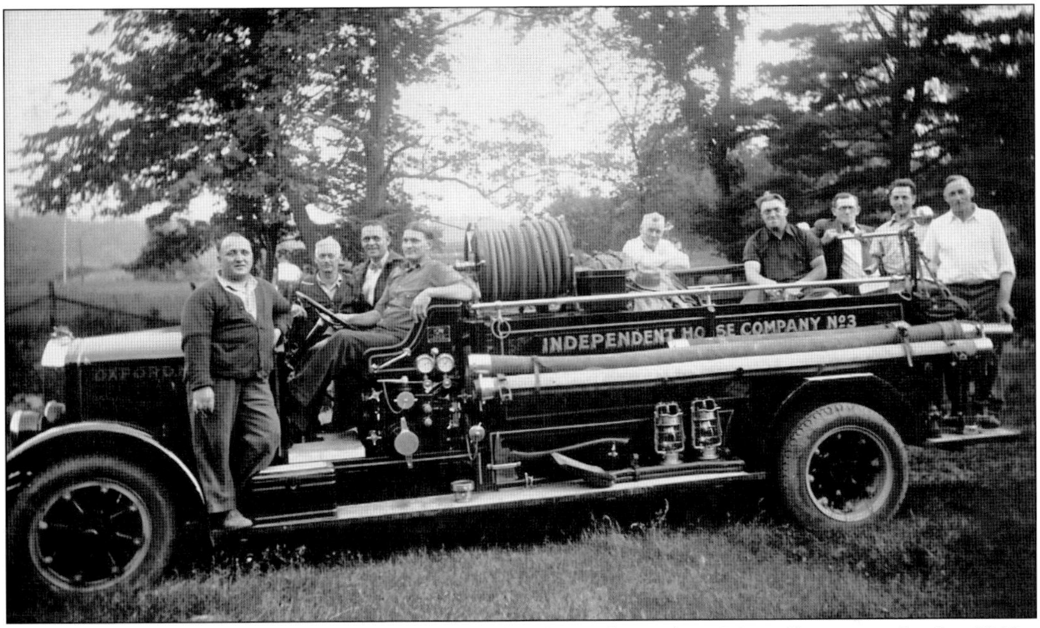

This is a 1929 Buffalo-Selden truck purchased by the Independent Hose Company. In the 1960s, it was sold to the Selden family and shown in parades in Memphis, Tennessee. In the mid-1970s, Don Tidwell of Haleyville, Alabama, purchased the truck. In 2004, Keith Kilgore found it rusting from age and neglect. Kilgore bought the vehicle, had it restored, and even used it in his daughter's wedding in 2009.

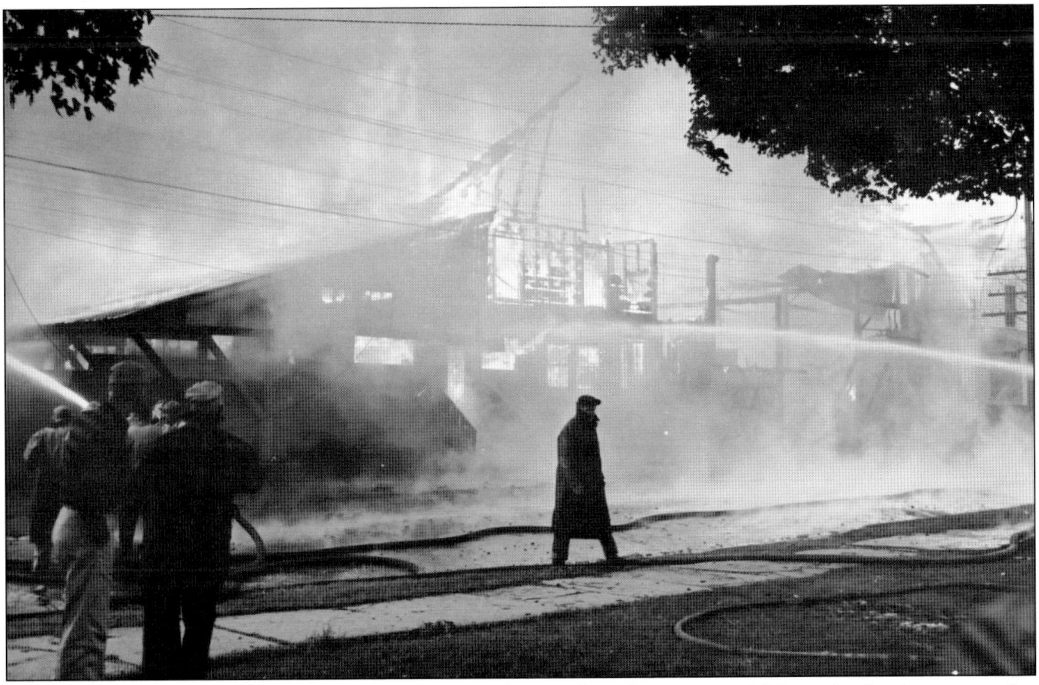

Here is another view of the fire at the Church Lumber Company. Although the house to the right was scorched, it did not burn down because of the fire company's hard work. The whole neighborhood was threatened that night.

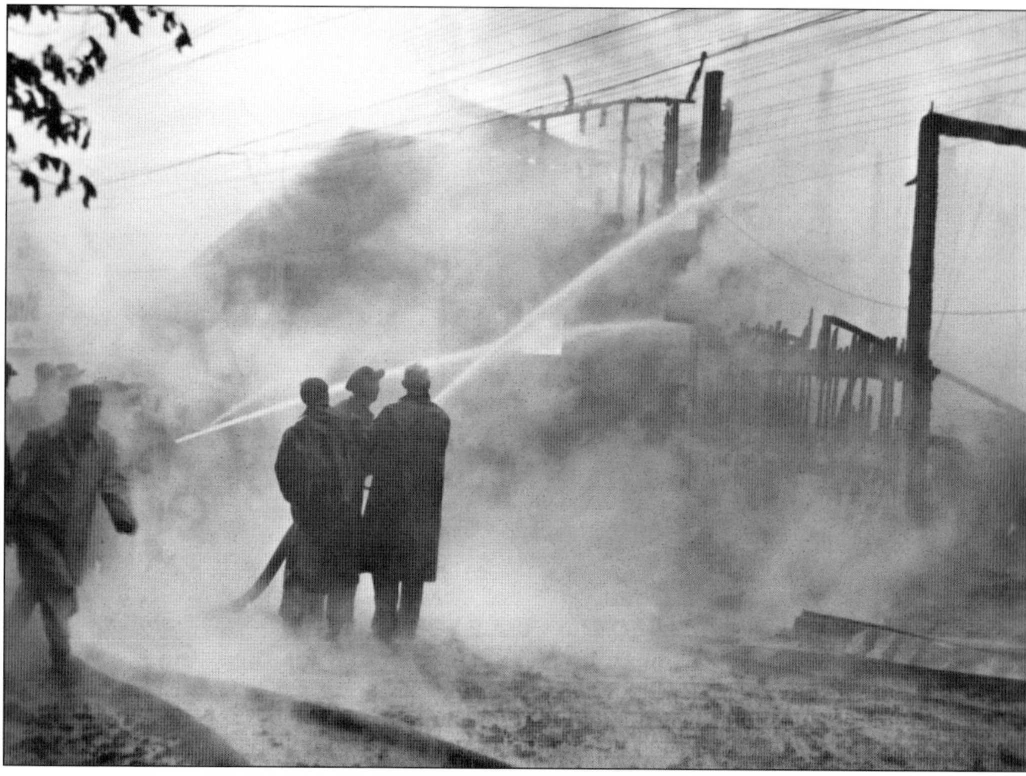

This is the final view of Church Lumber Company as it was being hosed down. The later stages of a big fire, when buildings are crumbling, are more dangerous than the early on.

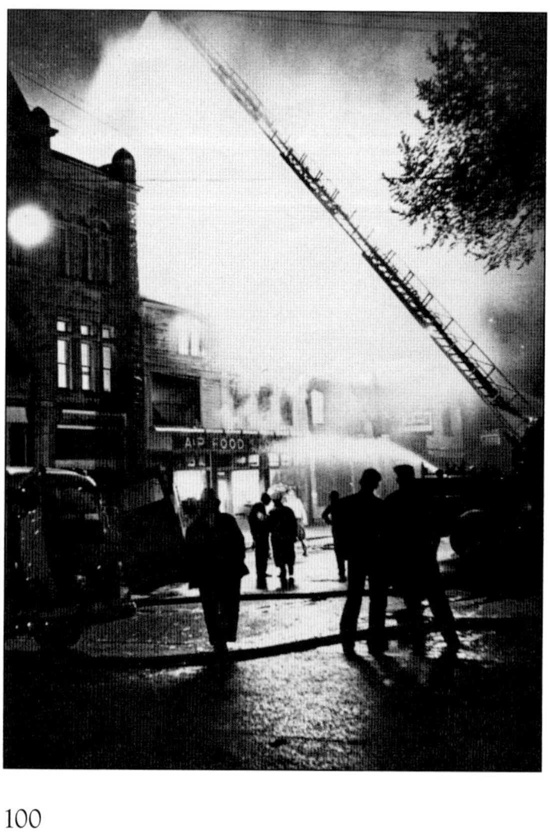

The Chapin Block fire that happened in May 1960 is captured here by the camera. The fire wiped out the whole block, including the pharmacy, apartments, and the A&P store. The blaze would have destroyed the historic bank building on the left, but fortunately the firemen stopped it in time.

Seven

The New York State Veterans' Home

The New York Veterans' Home in Oxford, also known as the "Vets," has a history that goes back to 1897. Like all institutions, it has changed over time. In its early years, the resident population was mainly Civil War veterans and their wives. These members had a comfortable home for their retirement years, and mostly women succeeded that generation. These were the widows, sisters, and daughters of the veterans from the Civil War and Spanish-American War and later the descendants of World War I veterans.

It was known as the Women's Relief Corps (WRC) Home at that time. The WRC had been the Auxiliary to the Grand Army of the Republic (GAR), which was an organization for Civil War veterans. It was the WRC that had successfully appealed to the New York State Legislature and received the funds to build the Vets.

The New York Veterans' Home was composed of five buildings and later a hospital in 1953. The 60-acre campus has served its residents for over 70 years. An influx of World War II veterans, mostly males, brought about the building of a large one-story facility in 1981, and the old buildings were razed. From that point it was called the New York State Veterans' Home. Recently, a new multistory complex has been constructed to replace the structure built in 1981.

The Vets is now billed as a nursing home and offers medical, nursing, psychosocial, and rehabilitative services for eligible veterans. It has a capacity for 242 residents and a staff of 350 to 400 employees. It is located on the same beautiful campus as the former buildings and has spectacular views of the valley. The Vets certainly provides the best possible care for the area's veterans.

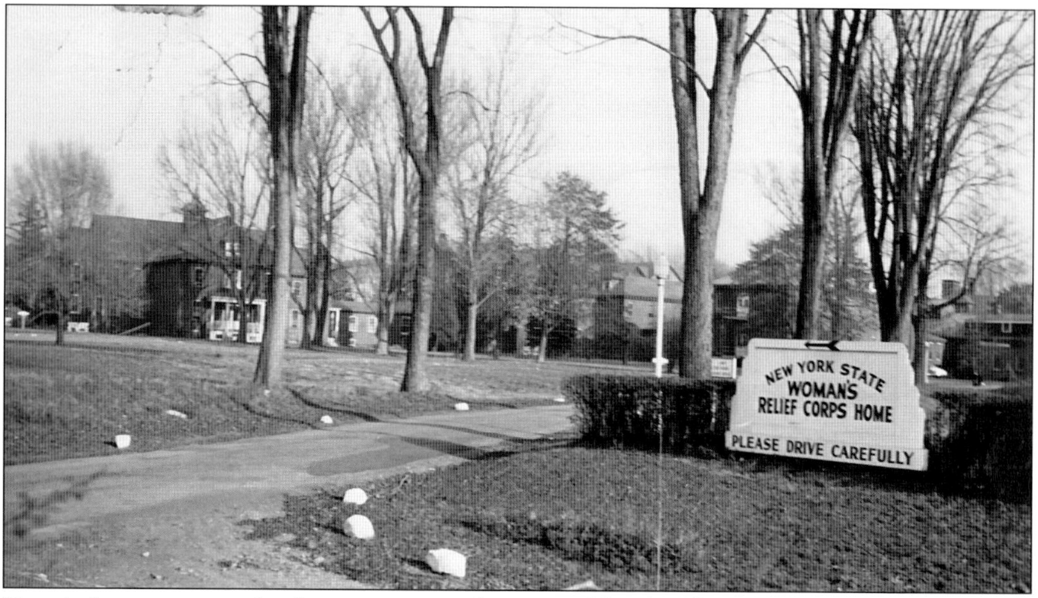

Here is the entrance and welcoming sign to the original five-building New York Veterans' Home. (Courtesy of Sarah Seaman.)

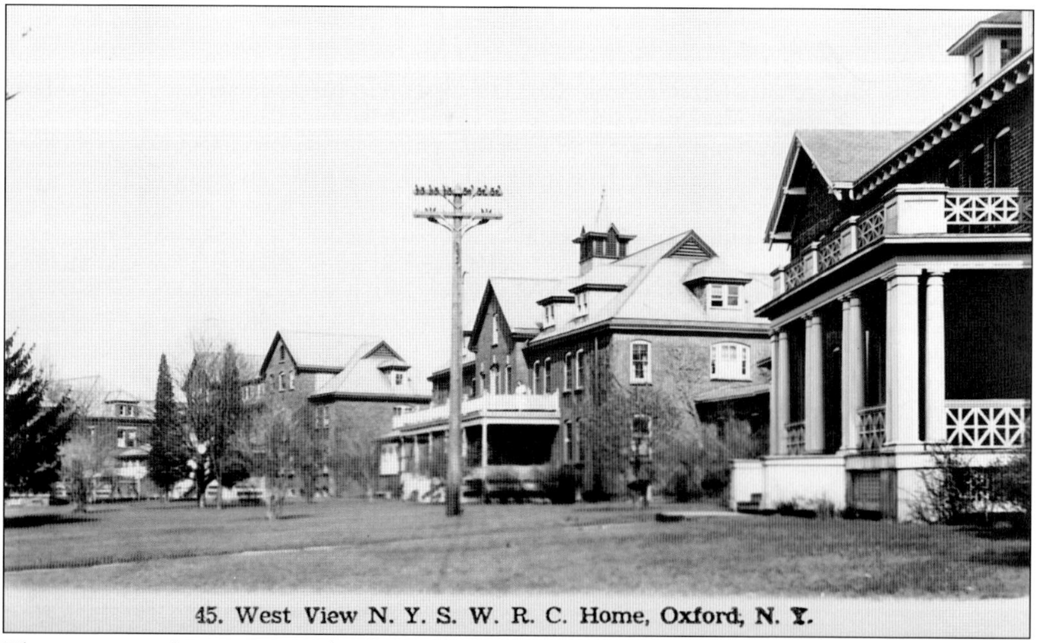

This is a row of cottages on the original campus. They faced the Chenango Valley and had gorgeous sunset views. (Courtesy of Anna Stark.)

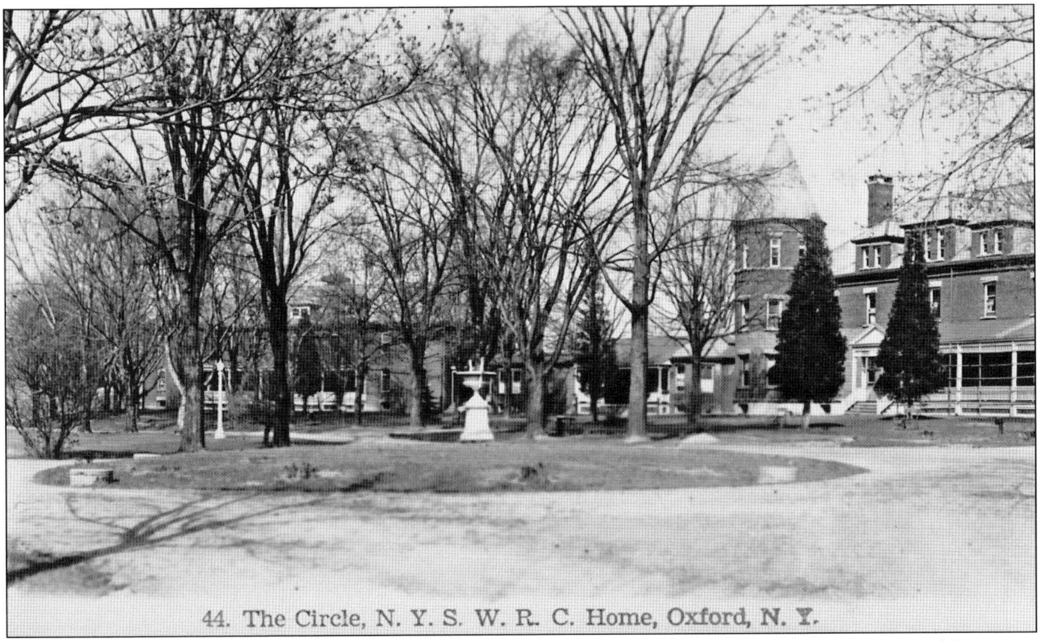

The circular drive known as "The Circle" and the administration building are seen here. (Courtesy of Sarah Seaman.)

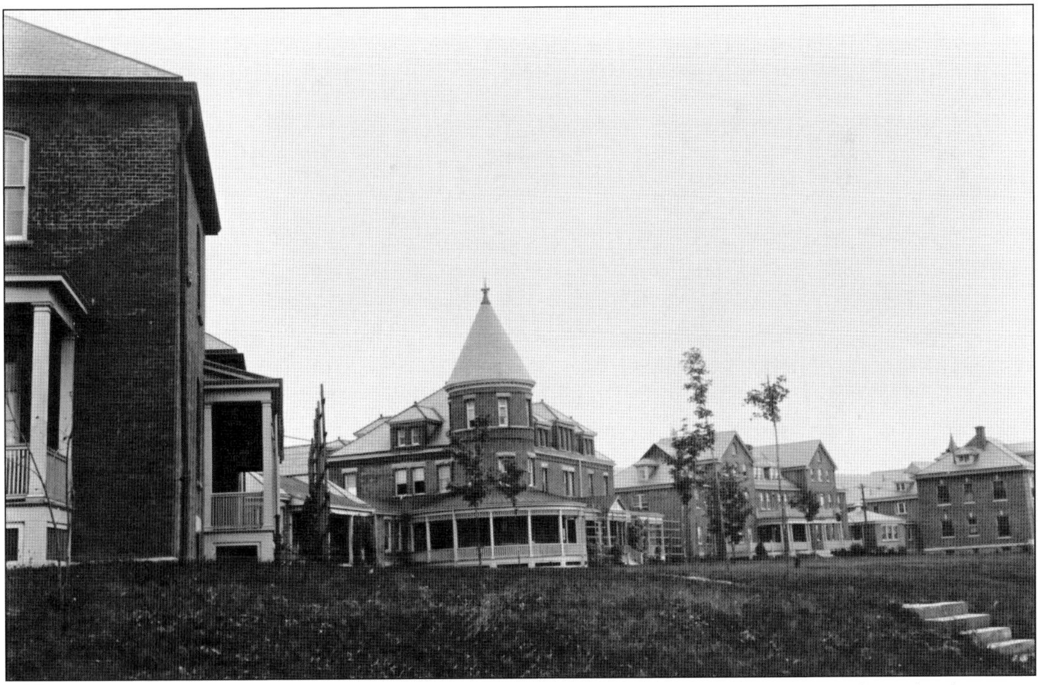

This photograph shows another view of the western fronts of the cottages. Residents had private rooms in Cottages A, B, C, and D. Meals were served in a community dining room. It was a comfortable life, and there was a familial atmosphere in each of the cottages.

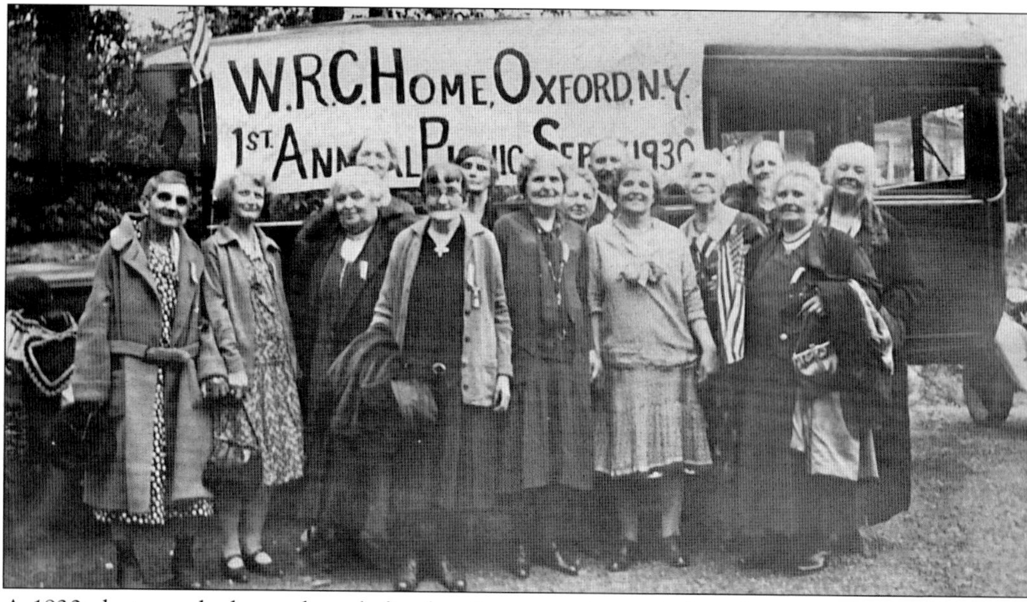

A 1930 photograph shows these ladies heading to a picnic. Before the new structure was built in 1981, it was common for individuals or groups to go off-campus to attend a school concert or spend some time with nearby relatives.

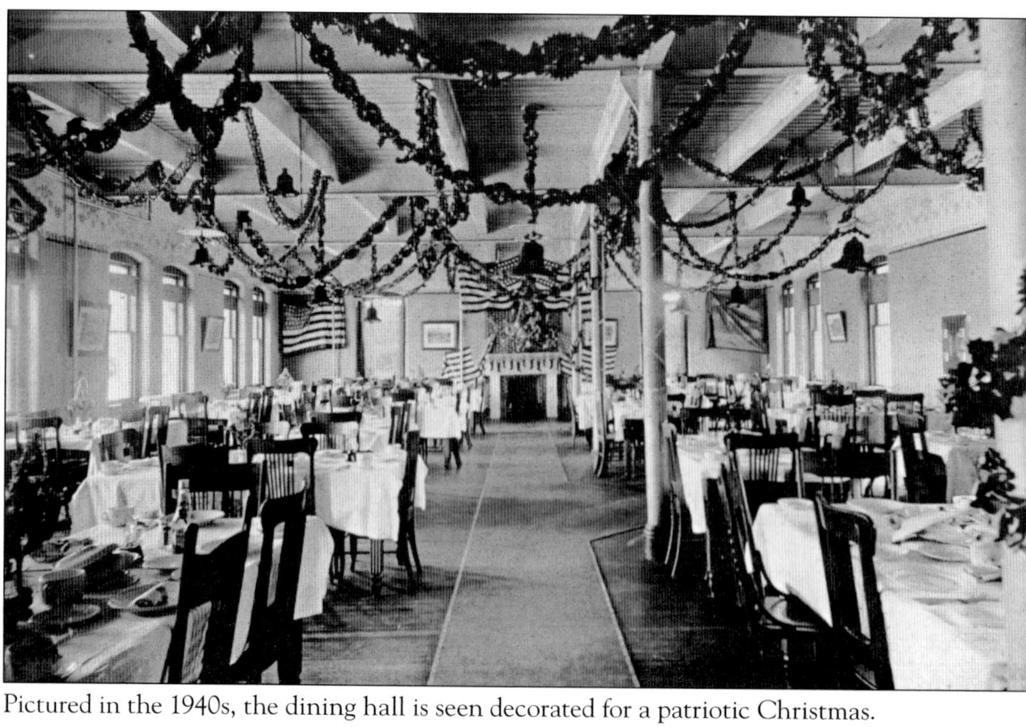

Pictured in the 1940s, the dining hall is seen decorated for a patriotic Christmas.

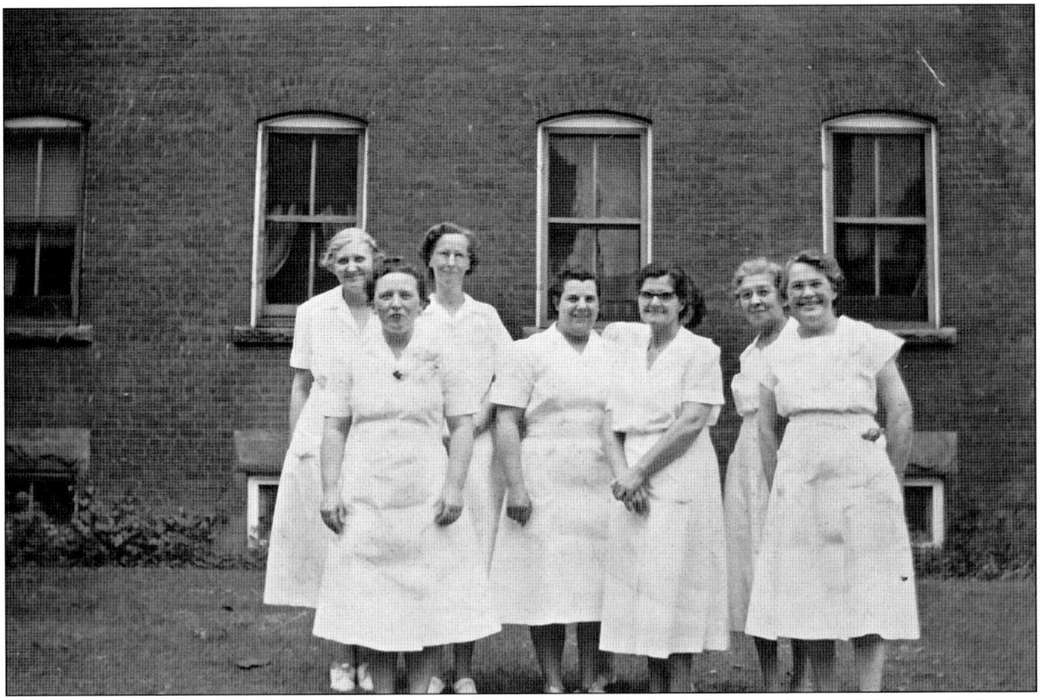

Members of the dining hall staff pose outside in 1950. From left to right are Harriet Bullock, Gladis Mowry, Lucille Dutcher, Edna Baldwin, Naomi Tefft, Mary Keeley, Nell Rice, and Clare Cooper. (Courtesy of Sarah Seaman.)

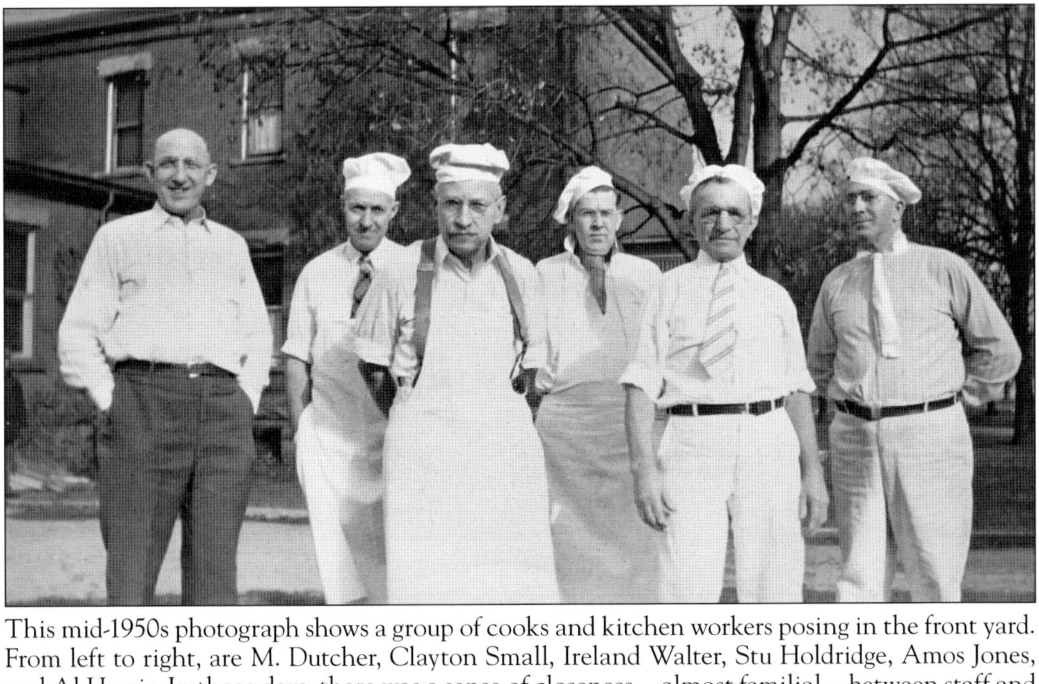

This mid-1950s photograph shows a group of cooks and kitchen workers posing in the front yard. From left to right, are M. Dutcher, Clayton Small, Ireland Walter, Stu Holdridge, Amos Jones, and Al Harris. In those days, there was a sense of closeness—almost familial—between staff and residents. This extended to the community, because almost all employees lived in the village. (Courtesy of Sarah Seaman.)

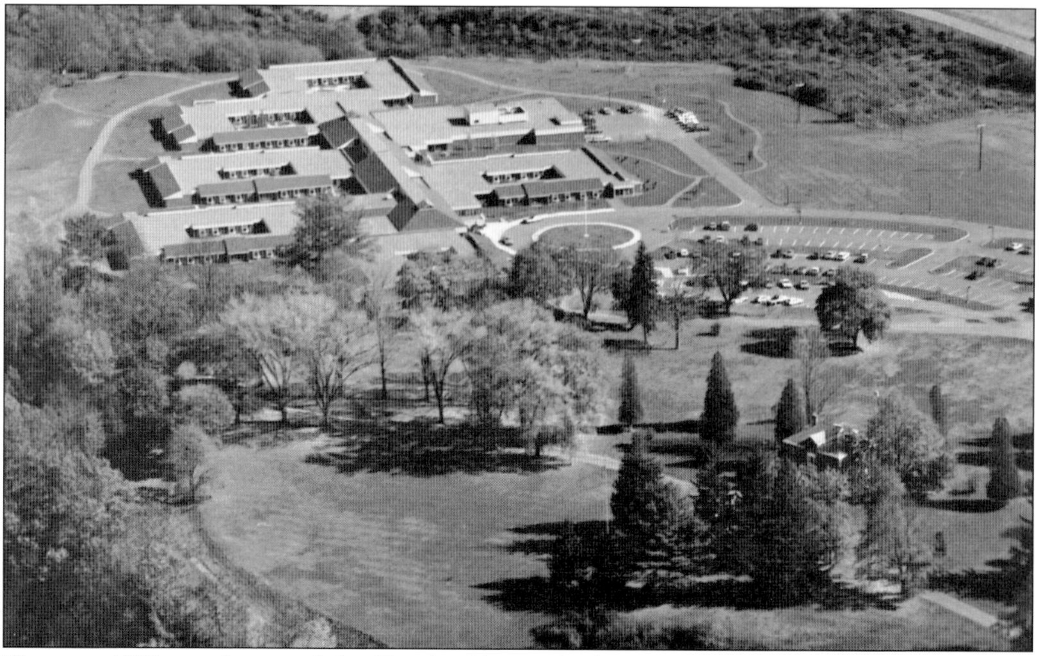

This is a 1981 aerial view of the Vets building, which was entirely connected on one floor. Since another facility has been built and all residents have been moved out, the building may be torn down.

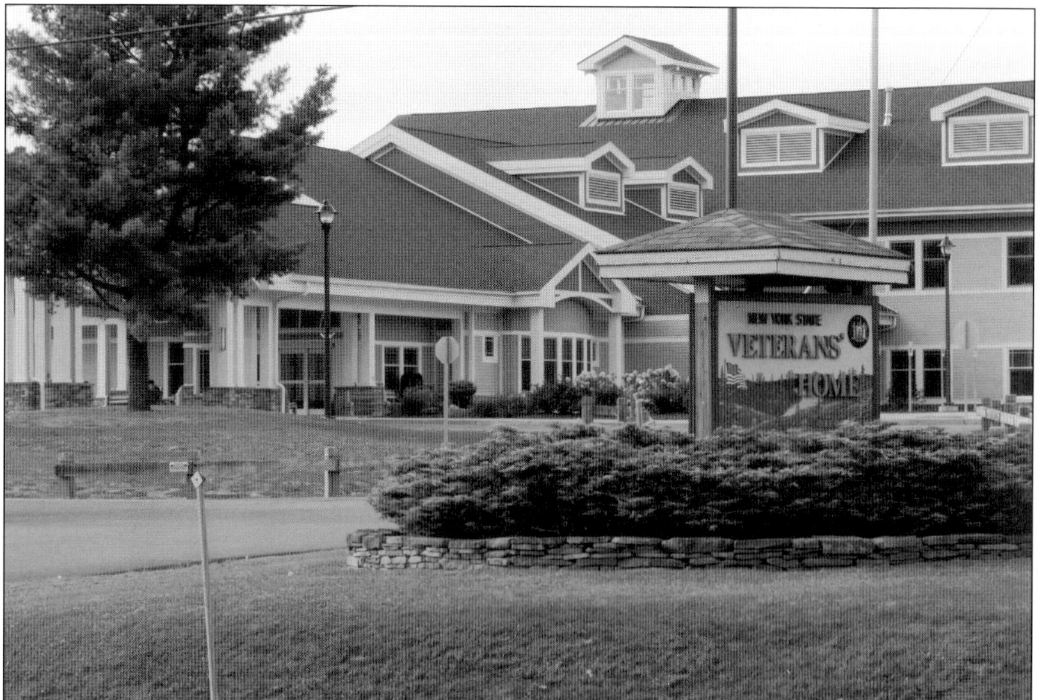

Here is the new building, which features many state-of-the-art facilities that are necessary for the care of the older residents.

Eight

Architecture and the Changing Scene

Although Oxford is a small town, it has an abundance of attractive buildings. Charlotte Stafford's two pamphlets, "A Walking Tour of the East Side" and "A Walking Tour of the West Side," show the town's artistic charm and its architecture styles, including Federal, Greek Revival, Queen Anne, Gothic and Neo-Gothic, Romanesque, and even two octagon houses. Most of Oxford's colorful architecture is located in the National Historic District.

The houses are complemented by the three parks: Fort Hill Park at the geographic center, Washington Park on the east side, and Lafayette Park on the west side. Although the parks are not large in size, they offer a beautiful grassy view, as there are shrubs, trees, flowers, benches, and pedestrian paths in each one.

The variety of trees around the village adds much to the local beauty. Oxford is considered a "Tree City," and it is listed on the National Arbor Day Foundation. The local Tree Board, led by John Godfrey, maintains a survey of village trees, provides tree plantings, and gives away hundreds of seedlings each year on Arbor Day. Finally, the dramatic flower plantings and hanging baskets provided by the Oxford Garden Club brighten up the village.

The village scene is not static, and there have been major changes throughout the years.

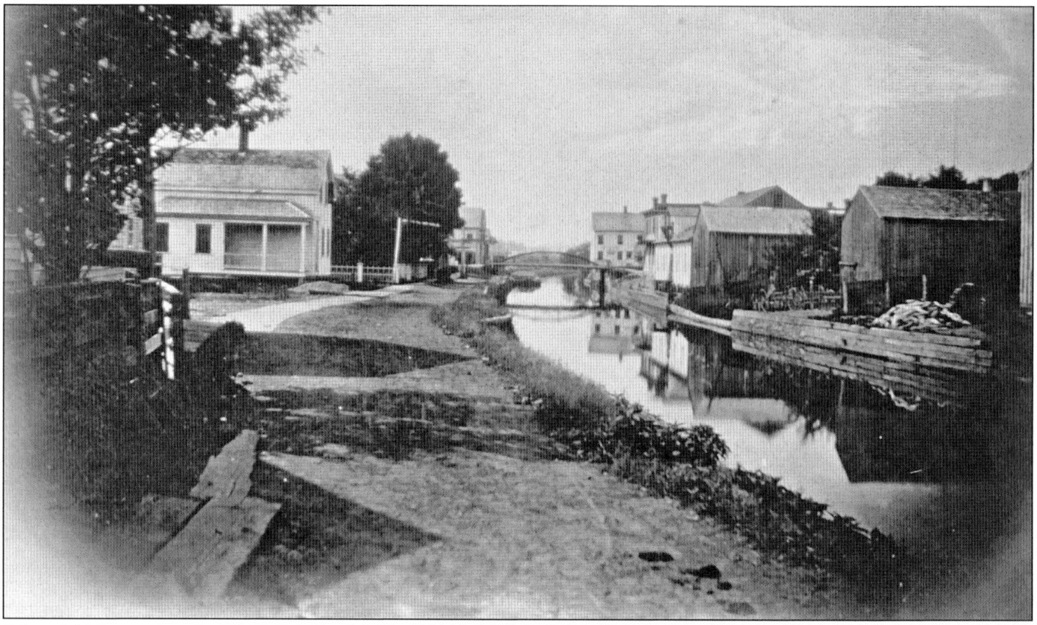

The Chenango Canal opened in 1837. It was a major transportation route through Oxford until it closed in 1873. This photograph shows a southern view of Canal Street along the towpath to the canal bridge in the center of town. Most of the buildings are still standing. New York State Route 12 later replaced the canal.

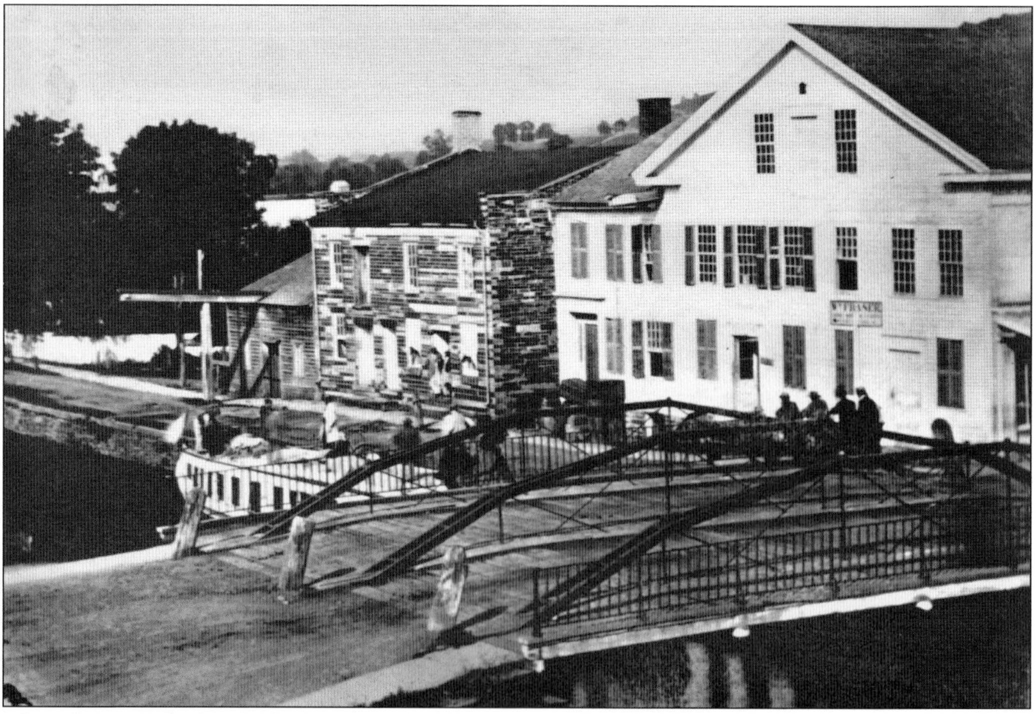

This photograph shows the canal bridge, the packet boat *Lillie*, and the Tuttle Block. The stone building was made from bluestone from a southern quarry in Oxford. The block between the canal and the river became known as Navy Island.

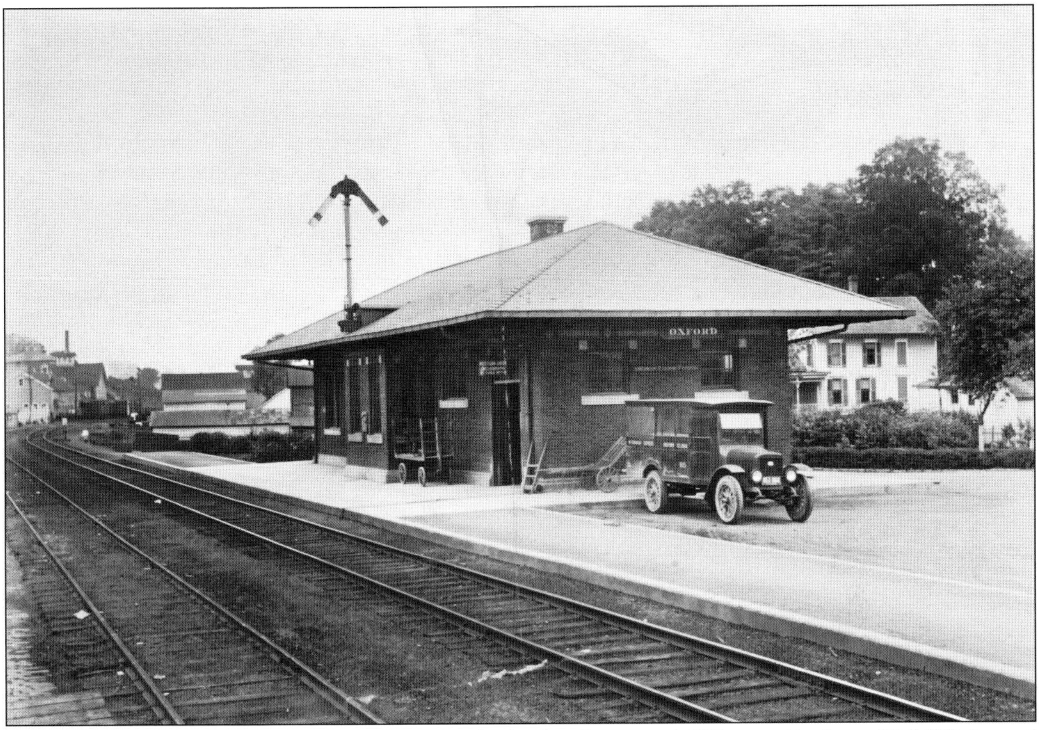

By 1870, there were two railroads serving Oxford. The Ontario & Western Railway (O&W) skirted the village a mile to the east, and the DL&W came directly through town on the east side. This photograph shows the second DL&W depot soon after it was built in 1914.

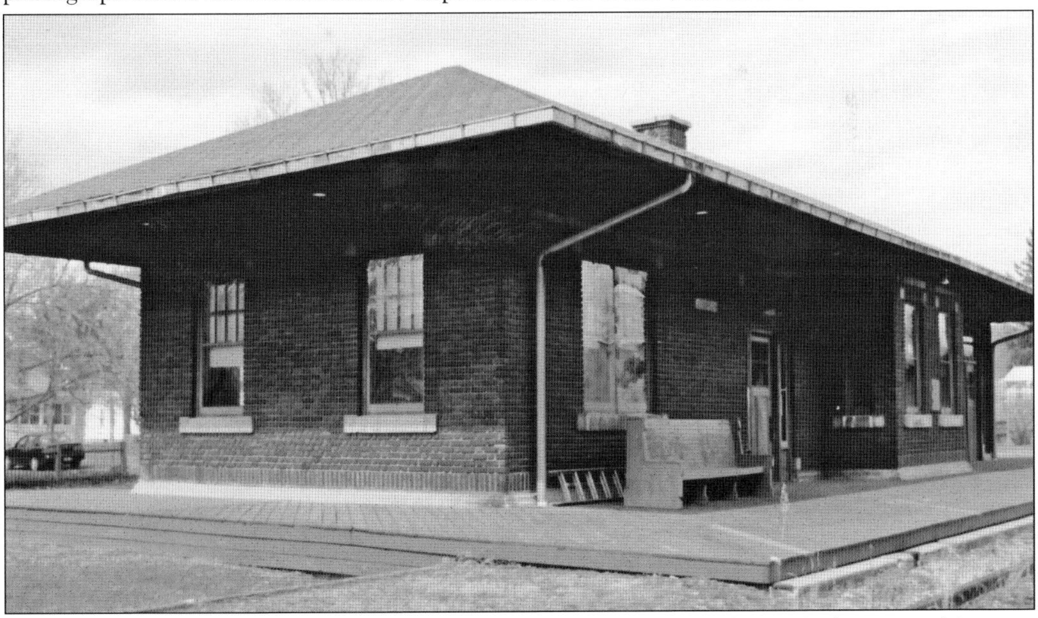

This is a recent photograph of the DL&W depot, which now houses the Oxford Historical Society. After passenger service was discontinued in 1957, the DL&W deeded the depot to the Village of Oxford in 1979. The Oxford Historical Society was then given a 99-year lease in return for providing maintenance.

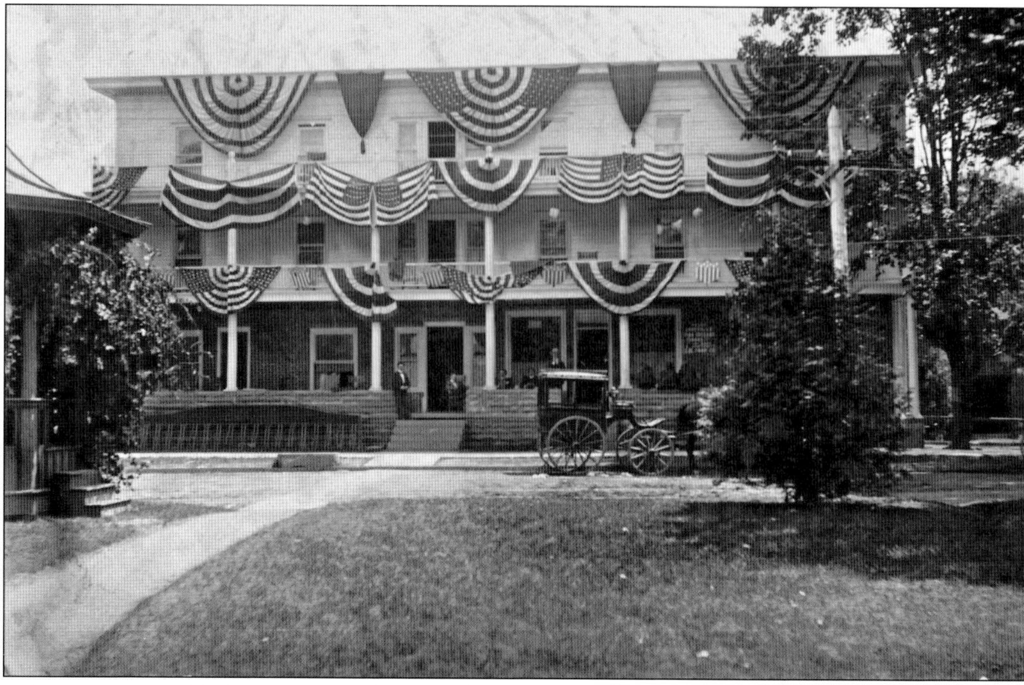

Taken around 1885, this photograph shows the Park Hotel on Washington Park. It was a beautiful building with a bluestone wall along the front that supported the columns. It had originally been the Perkins House. It was sold after a fire and later restored.

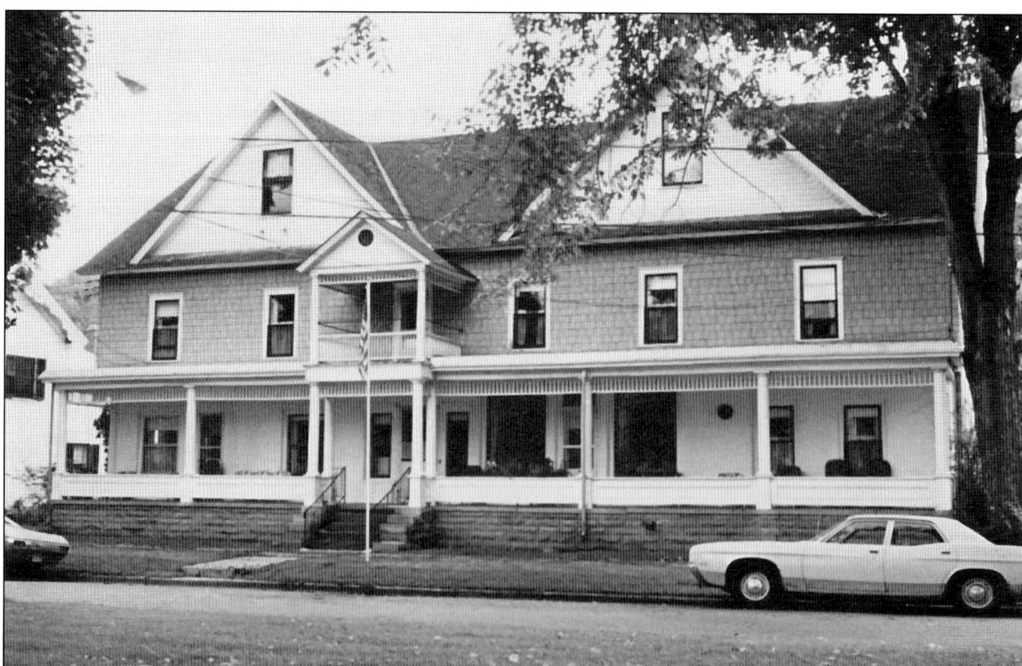

Here is a recent photograph of the same building that housed the Park Hotel. There have been major changes to the building, but the bluestone wall is still standing. It now houses the Bida nursing home.

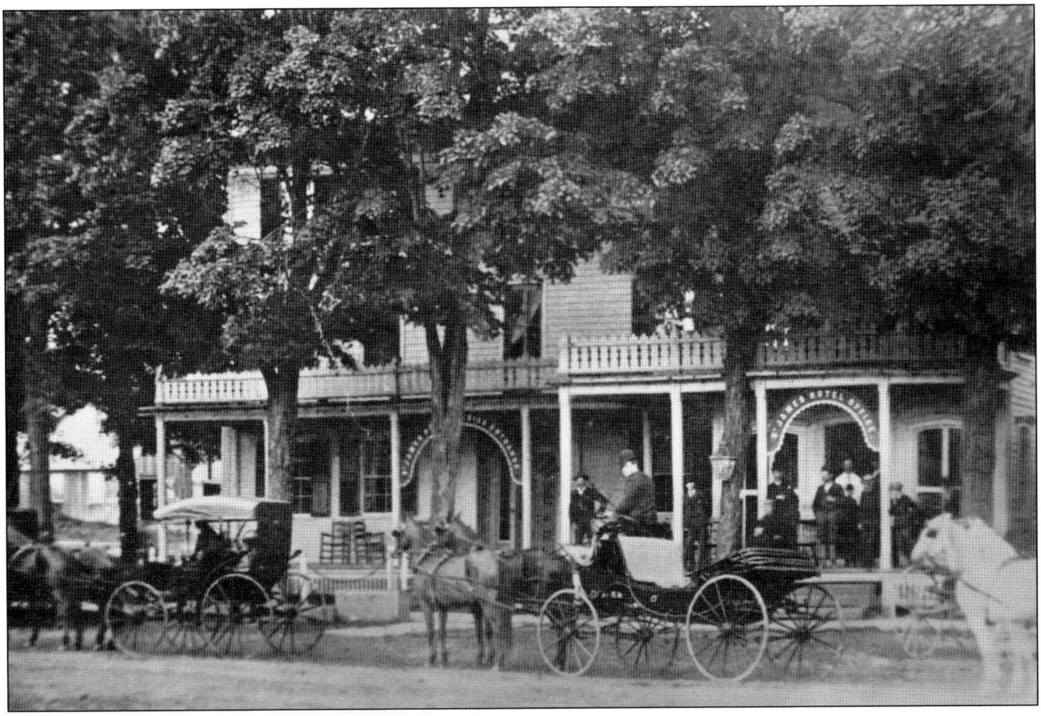

Pictured in the 1870s is the St. James Hotel. It was an elegant and popular hotel. The Oxford Historical Museum has an interesting guest log that survived the fire in 1914. The fire ruined the hotel, but it did not destroy the entire structure. It was rebuilt and now houses Chubb's Restaurant and Bartle's Pharmacy.

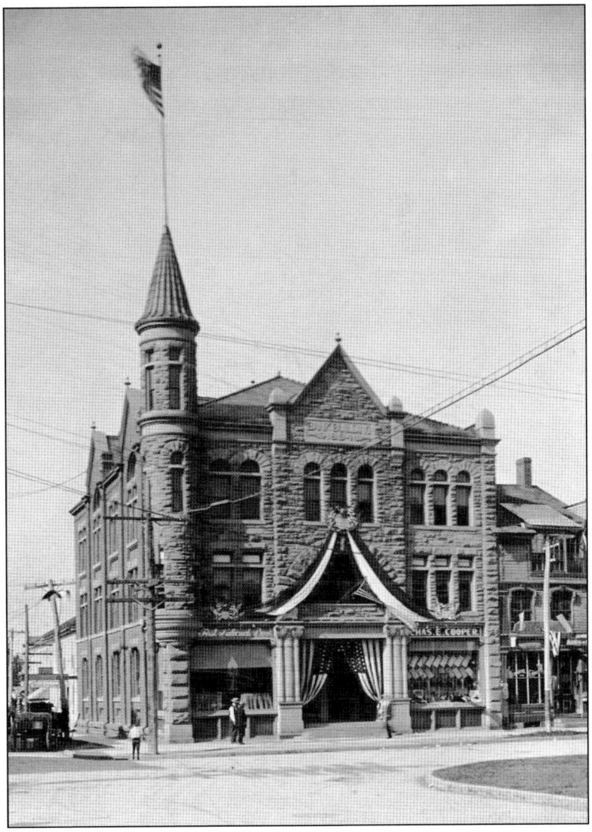

This photograph shows the First National Bank building soon after its completion in 1894. Architect Isaac Perry designed the bank as well as the New York State capitol. It was built out of Oxford bluestone and has not changed at all in appearance. The bank, however, left the building; the First National branch became part of Norwich Bank and Trust, which built a smaller office north of the Tuttle Block on New York State Route 12.

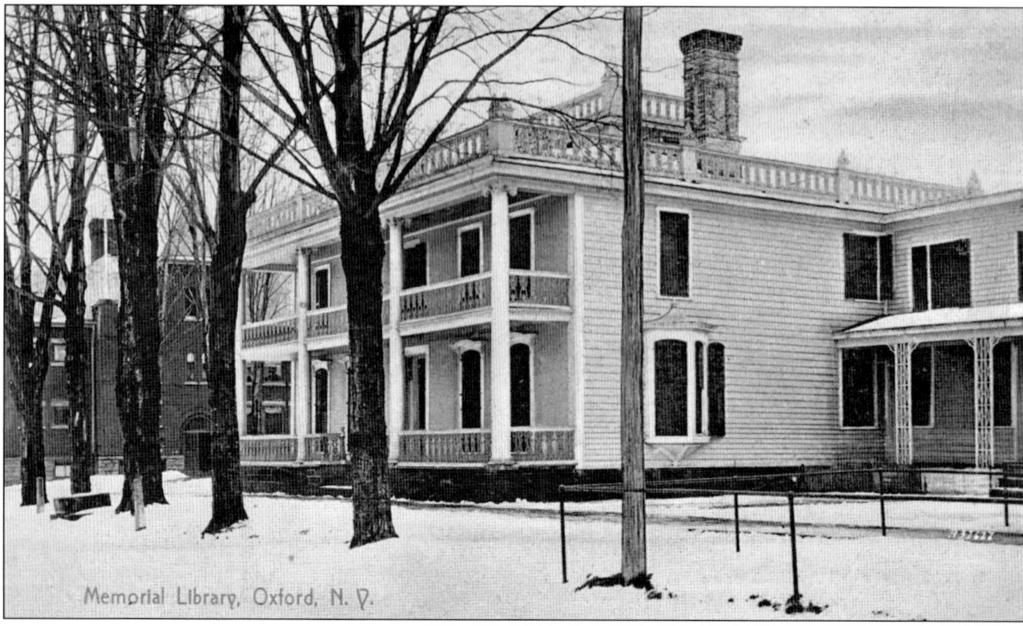

Here is the Oxford Memorial Library in the 1920s, which was the mansion Theodore Burr built in 1811. In 1900, the building was given to the Village of Oxford to be used as a library; it was a gift to honor the memory of Eli Lyon Corbin and Abigail Taintor, who was Corbin's wife. The library was recently restored with a $1 million construction contract, and it now includes a Community Room. Banks and community businesses, as well as citizens, were very generous in donations to renovate the library.

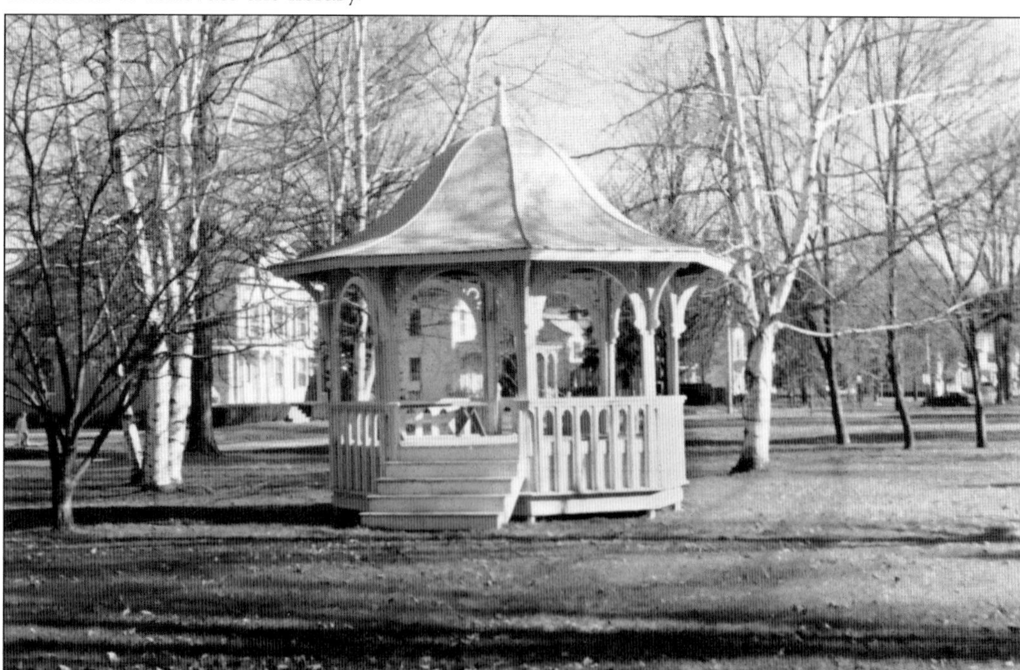

The iconic pagoda stands in Washington Park. Built in 1875, it has hosted many band concerts and wedding ceremonies under its roof.

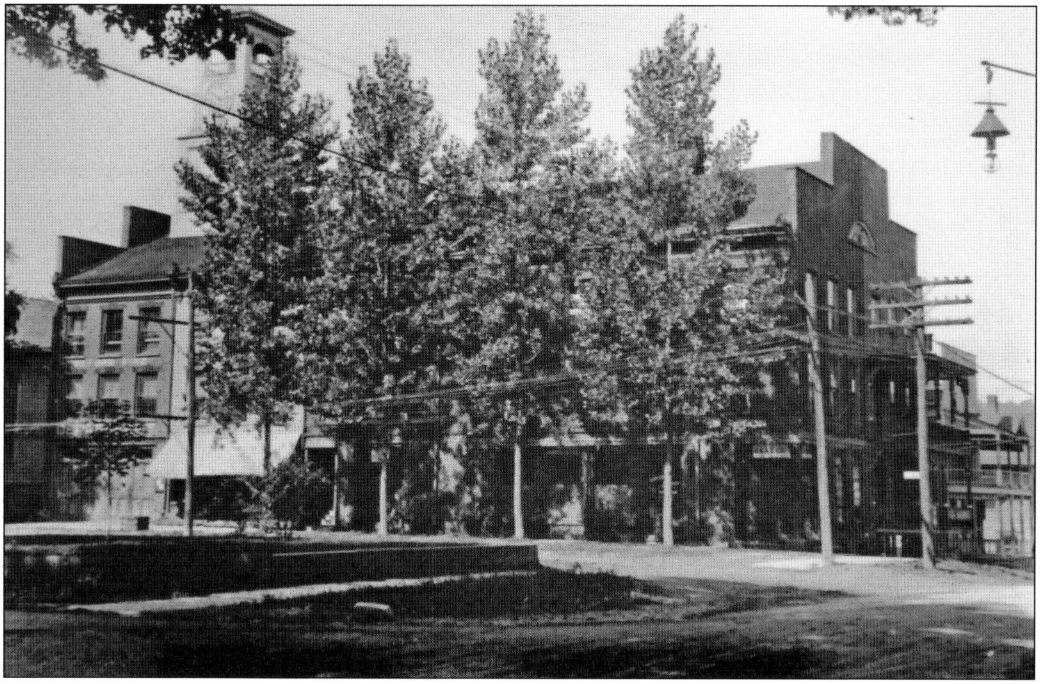

A c. 1900 photograph shows the Ira Willcox Building, which housed several stores. The fire companies kept their equipment at the left end of the building, which was under the clock tower. The electric light at upper right helps date the picture.

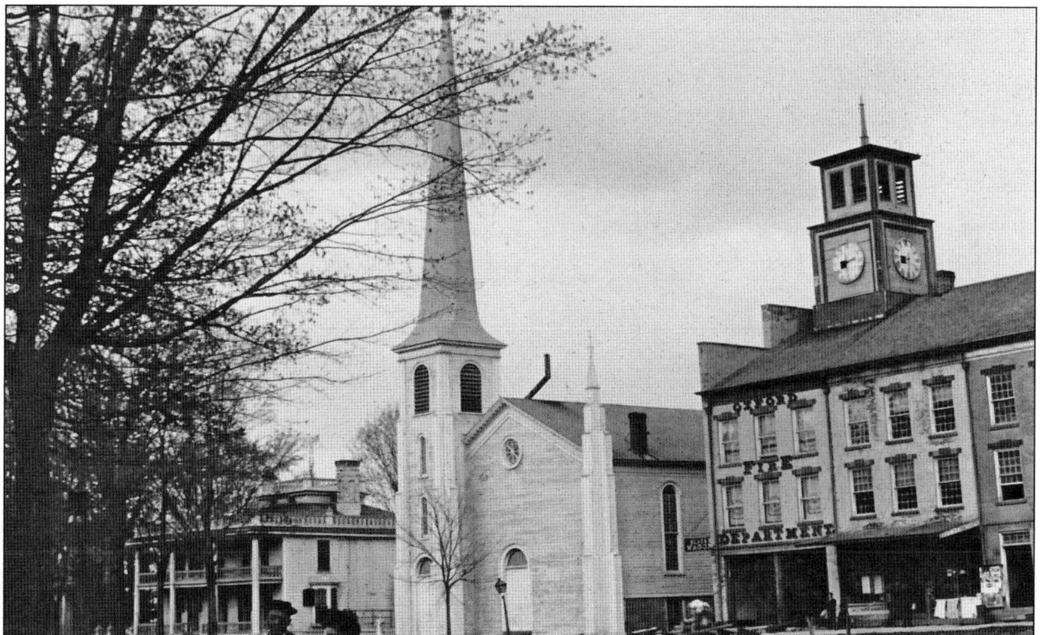

This c. 1915 photograph shows a closer view of the Ira Willcox Building. The clock tower would be replicated atop the new fire station 60 years after this shot. The Baptist Church, with its tall steeple, was still there and was later moved across the street in 1953. Oxford Memorial Library is on the left.

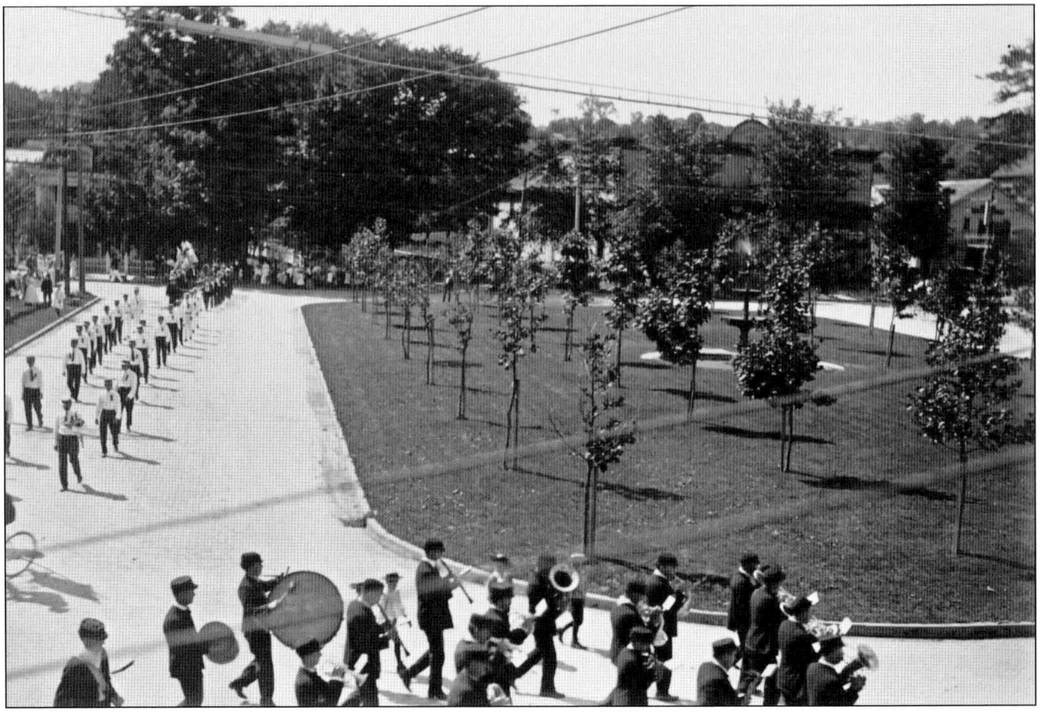

Turning north on Canal Street, the Oxford Community Band, with a couple of boys in the ranks, is leading a Firemen's Parade on Lafayette Park.

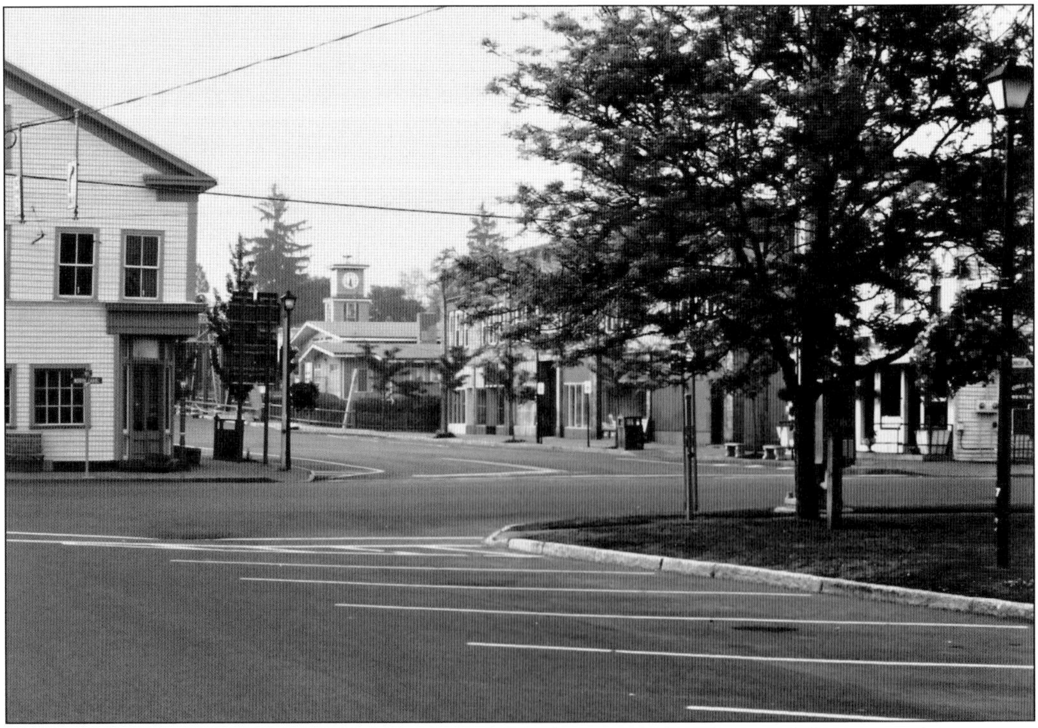

This recent photograph of the same location at Lafayette Park is from a different angle.

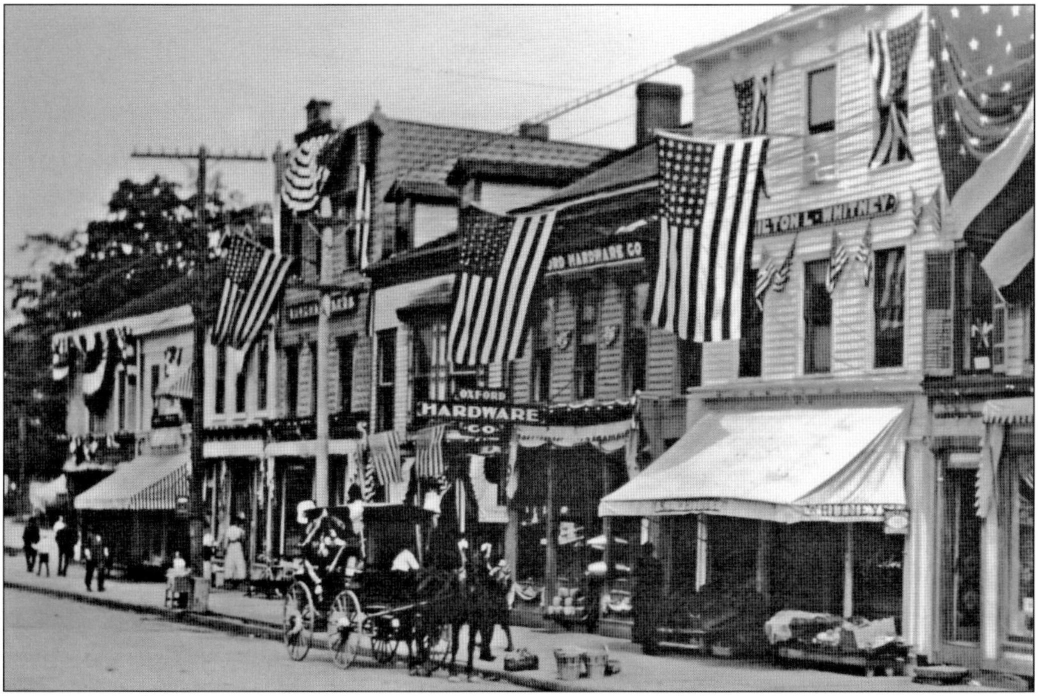

A 1908 photograph shows East Main Street during Old Home Week. Activities for the weeklong event included banquets, a parade, a band concert, a beautiful baby contest, and a maypole dance. It celebrated 100 years of the village charter; it was repeated a century later in 2008.

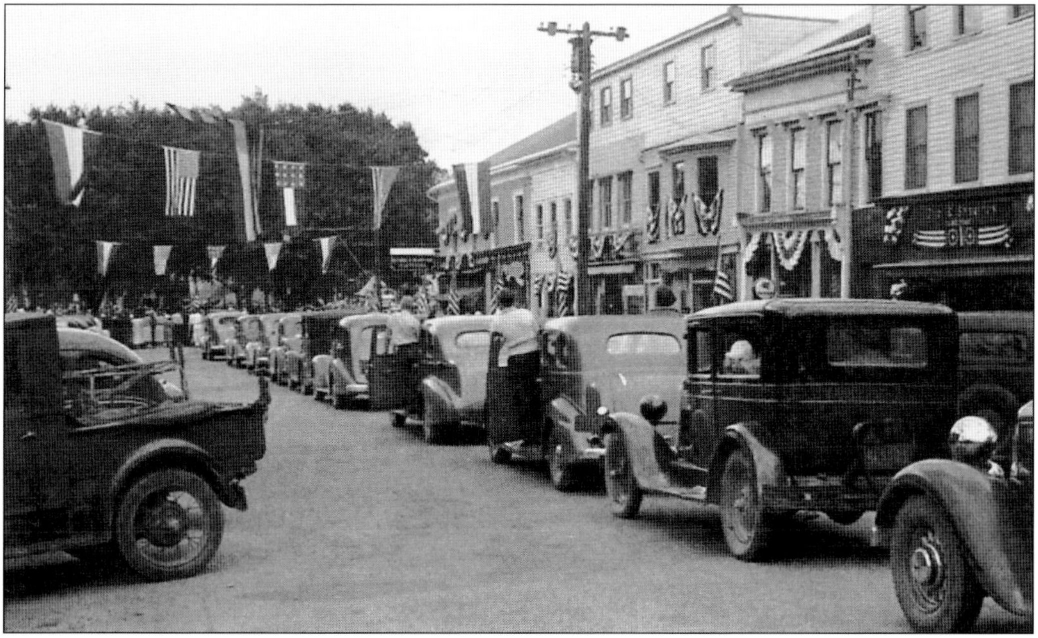

Taken in 1939 or 1940, this photograph shows the same location on East Main Street. Although the stores are the same, the traffic is new. Cars are backed up because people are waiting for the Independence Day Parade to pass by the park. Two impatient drivers have stepped onto their running boards for a better view.

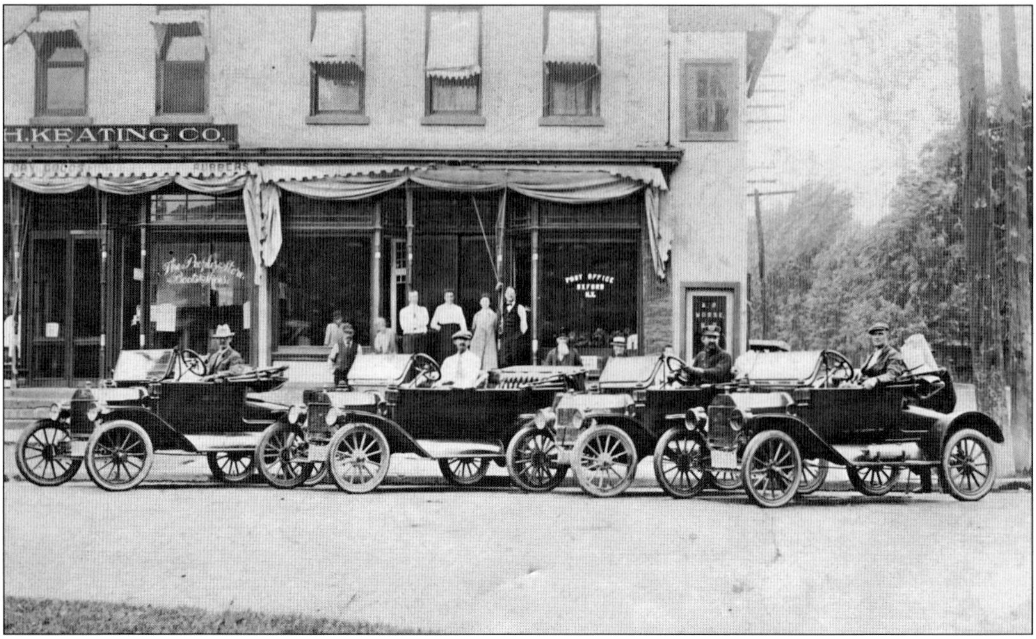

The drivers of these automobiles are mail deliverers, and they were about to set out on their routes. The post office and Hoppie's Lunchenette can be seen in the Clarke Building, which is located in background of this c. 1915 photograph.

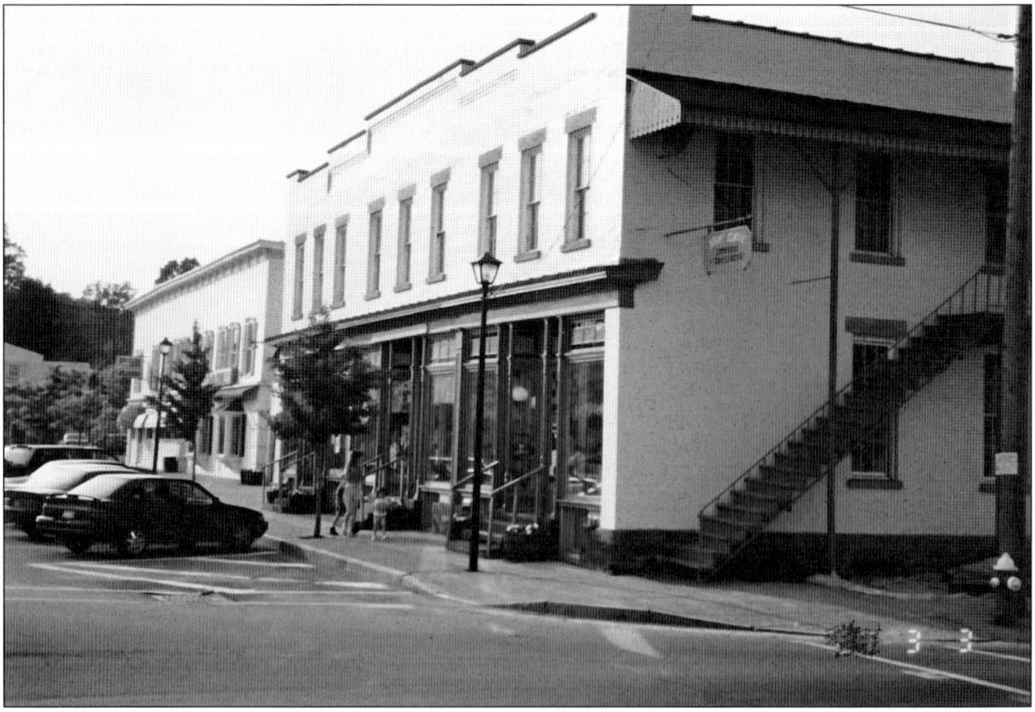

This is a recent photograph of the Clarke Building. Hoppie's Lunchenette is now located right on the corner, which is two doors from Six-On-The-Square and three doors from the Clachen Coffee House. Farther to the left are Bartle's Pharmacy and Chubb's Restaurant.

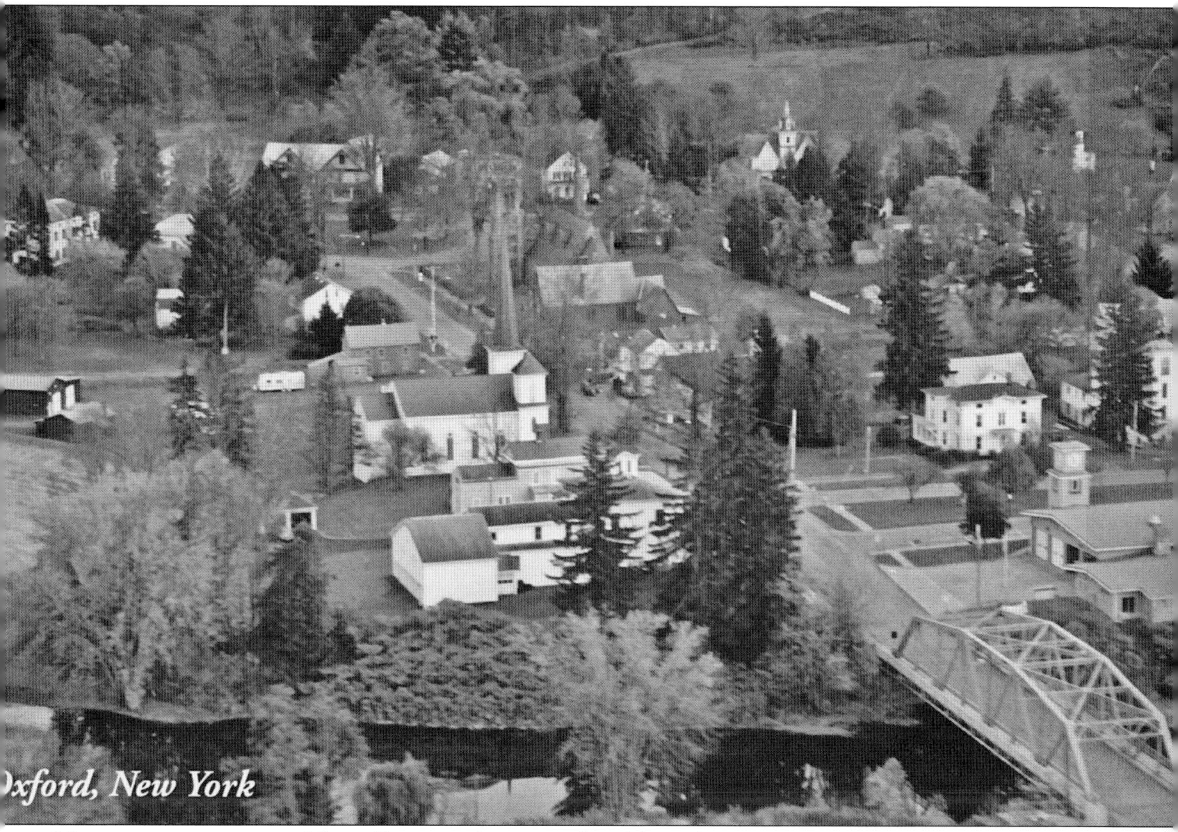

Here is a recent view of the village on the east side of the Chenango River and river bridge. The large building just across the river is the Behe Funeral Home. The Congregational Church is just beyond the funeral home, and St. Paul's Church is just above the center of the picture.

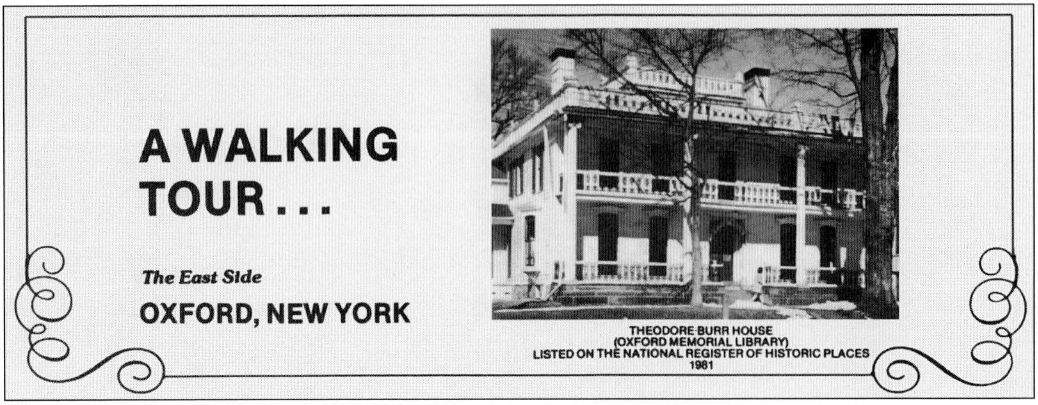

This is the walking-tour brochure for the east side of the village. Oxford historian Charlotte Stafford did a lot of research to verify the accuracy of the comments. It is filled with facts and a few anecdotes, which makes for an educational walk. Charlotte was the indefatigable lady who compiled data for the tours and often led them herself. She had an inimitable style and sense of humor, which made such a walk a memorable event.

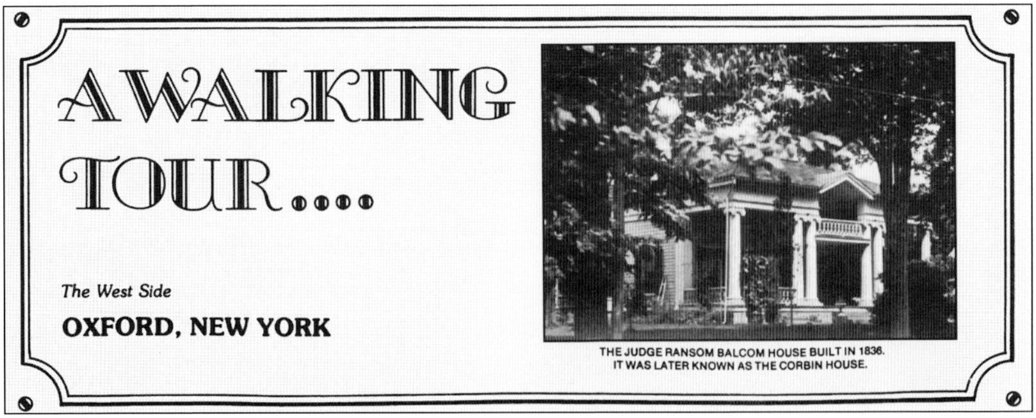

The west side walking-tour brochure contains dozens of historical facts that complement the architectural pointers. These brochures are available at the Oxford Historical Depot-Museum.

Nine

Clubs and Organizations

Oxford has many clubs and organizations. The list of associations in the community, in addition to church affiliations and school organizations, is long and impressive. Unfortunately, many groups that were once prominent and influential have dissolved and disappeared. In the 1880s, for example, there was the YMCA of Oxford and the large chapter of the Women's Christian Temperance Union. There were also two bicycle clubs and a long-standing chapter of the International Order of Odd Fellows among the many others that have faded over the years.

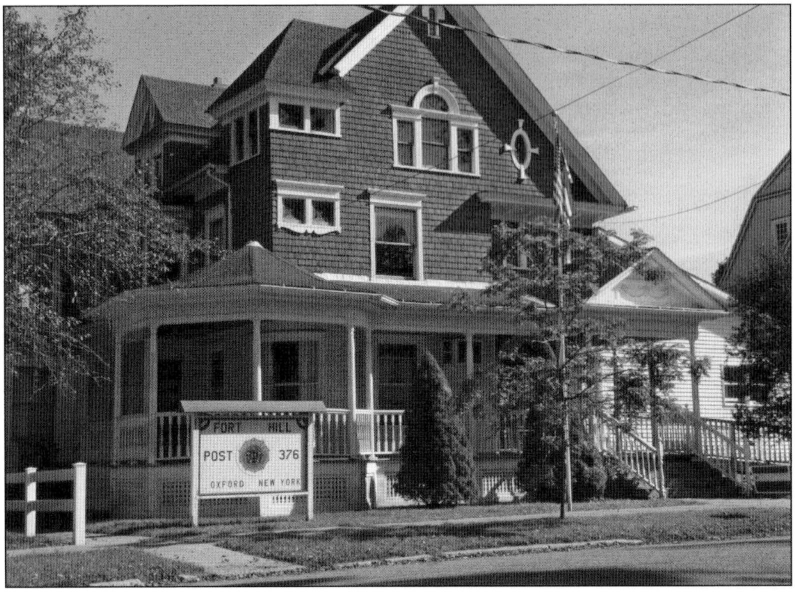

This is a recent photograph of Oxford's American Legion, which is an organization of veterans and an active social center. The legion's color guard participates in all local parades and leads the annual contingent to Riverview Cemetery on Memorial Day.

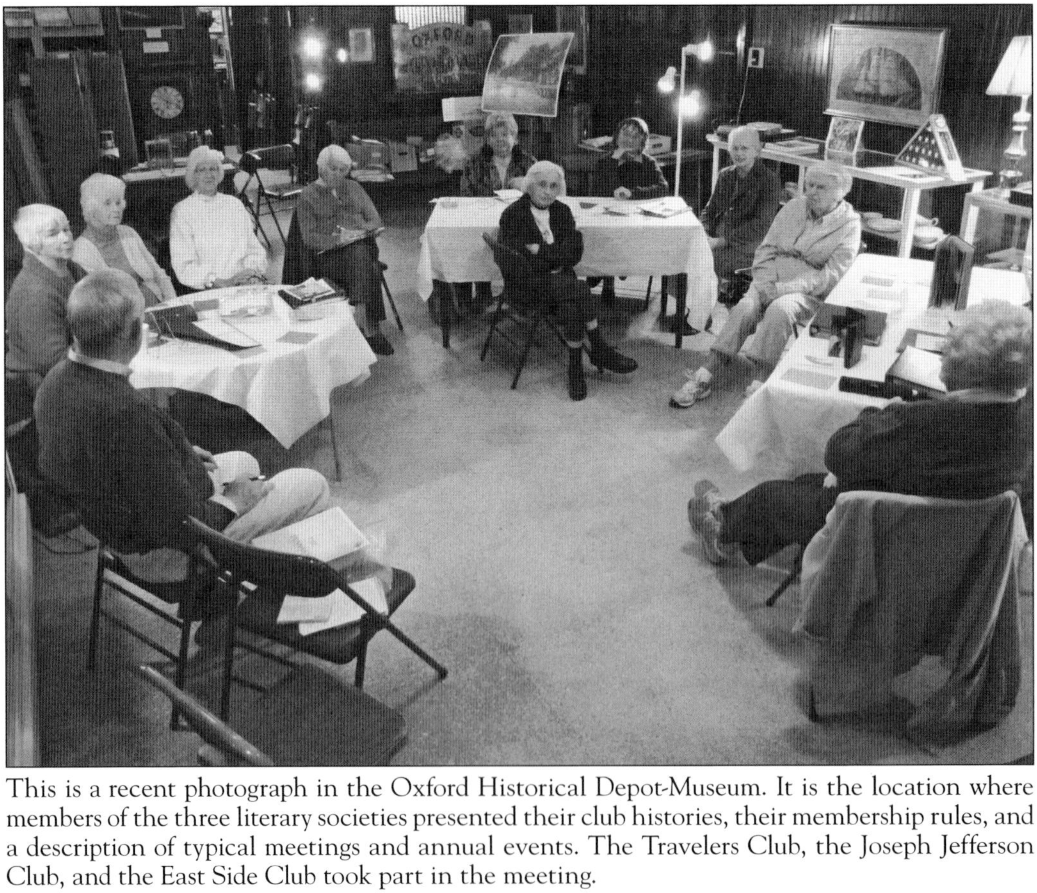

This is a recent photograph in the Oxford Historical Depot-Museum. It is the location where members of the three literary societies presented their club histories, their membership rules, and a description of typical meetings and annual events. The Travelers Club, the Joseph Jefferson Club, and the East Side Club took part in the meeting.

Ten

Faces and People of Oxford

To know Oxford means to know its people and their faces. Although historical figures are important, the local residents of Oxford also make the town what it is.

One famous resident was Oxford Academy student Horatio Seymour. He left Oxford for a few years and eventually became the governor of New York for two terms. Seymour was also the presidential candidate for the Democratic Party. Another famous resident, who mostly spent his life in Oxford, is Dr. Matthew Boname.

Many of Oxford Academy students also exemplified the word "pride," which is used in the first line of Oxford's alma mater. For example, classmates Colby Cooper, Tony Bancroft, and Conan Kennedy were recently appointed to the three major military academies: Cooper by West Point, Bancroft by the Naval Academy, and Kennedy by the Air Force Academy. Bancroft's older brother Jamie is already attending the Naval Academy. Another example of exceptional students is the Woodford twins, who are both in their high school's honor society and have won section four track championships.

In conclusion, Oxford has many memorable natives who continue to help create the town into what it is today. The following photographs are of a few residents who made their mark on their townspeople and town.

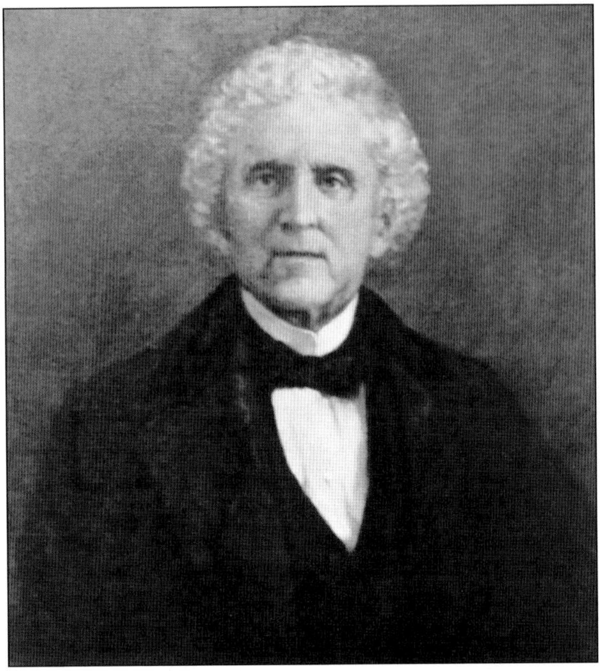

Henry R. Mygatt grew up in Oxford and worked in his father's tannery. He graduated from Oxford Academy and attended Union College. Mygatt returned to Oxford as a clerk in the office of James Clapp. Clapp was another Oxford resident who was a student of Aaron Burr during the time of the Hamilton and Burr duel. Mygatt was a clerk until he passed his bar exams. He was an excellent lawyer, and he even won a case in front of the US Supreme Court. He was the mentor for several aspiring law students and a great benefactor of the academy.

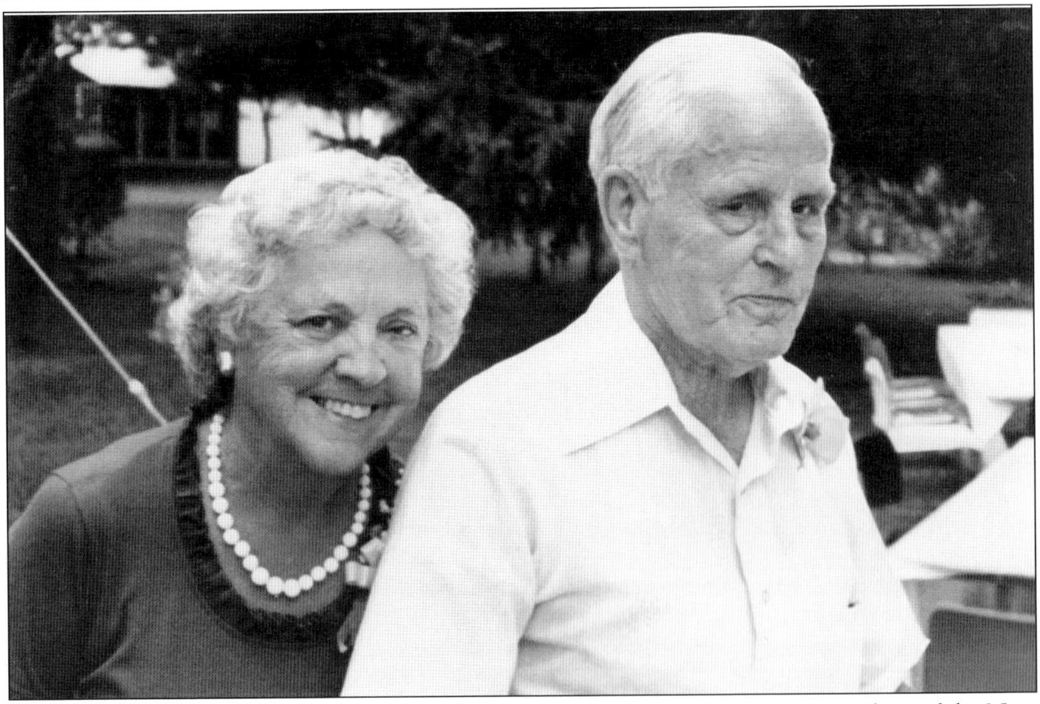

Here are Cylde and Pauline Cole posing after Cylde retired as Oxford superintendent of the New York State Public High School Athletic Association. He was also an outstanding coach during the late 1930s and 1940s; his teams won championships in every sport he coached. He established wrestling programs in Oxford and in Watertown, and he was known as the "Father of New York Wrestling." He is a member of the Ithaca College Hall of Fame as both an undergraduate athlete and a coach.

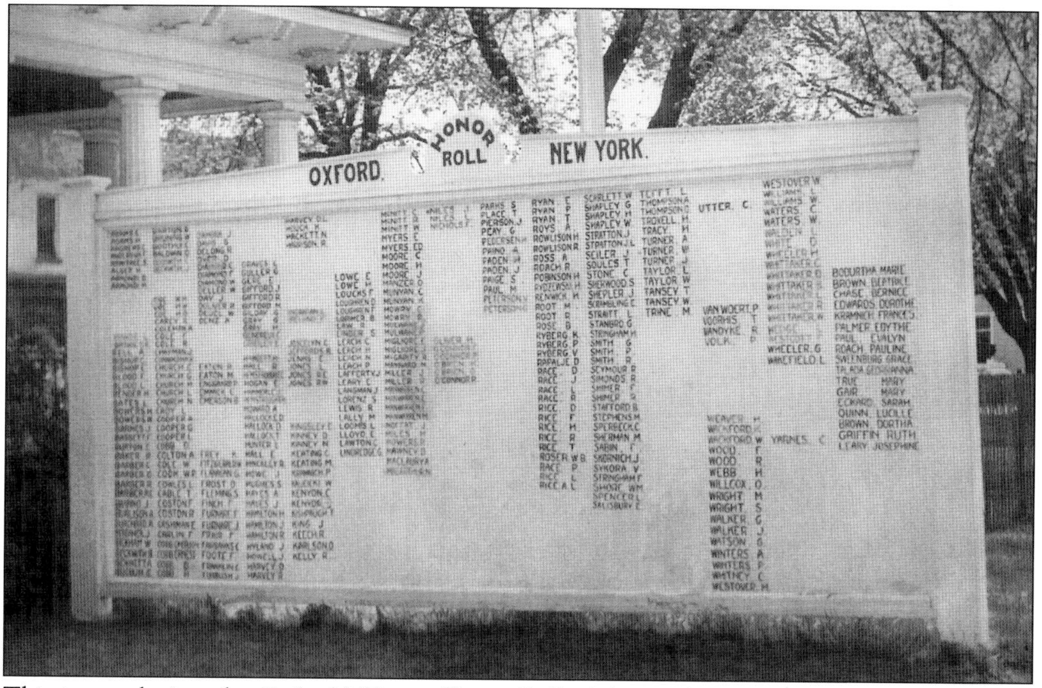

This image depicts the Oxford Military Honor Roll of those who served in the military during World War II. It was placed near the bandstand on Lafayette Park. It lists 362 names, including 17 women.

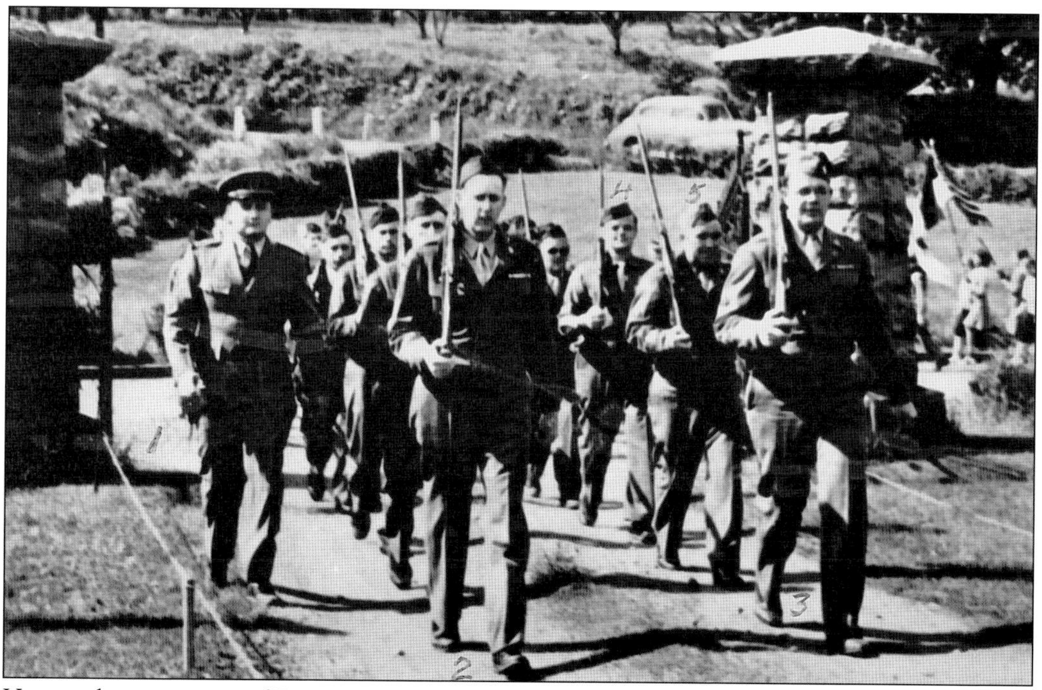

Here is the main gate of Riverview Cemetery and the military contingent that was part of the Memorial Day service in 1949. Veterans included in the photograph are Calvin Generoux, Leonard Tefft, Elmer Gere, and Lynn Loomis.

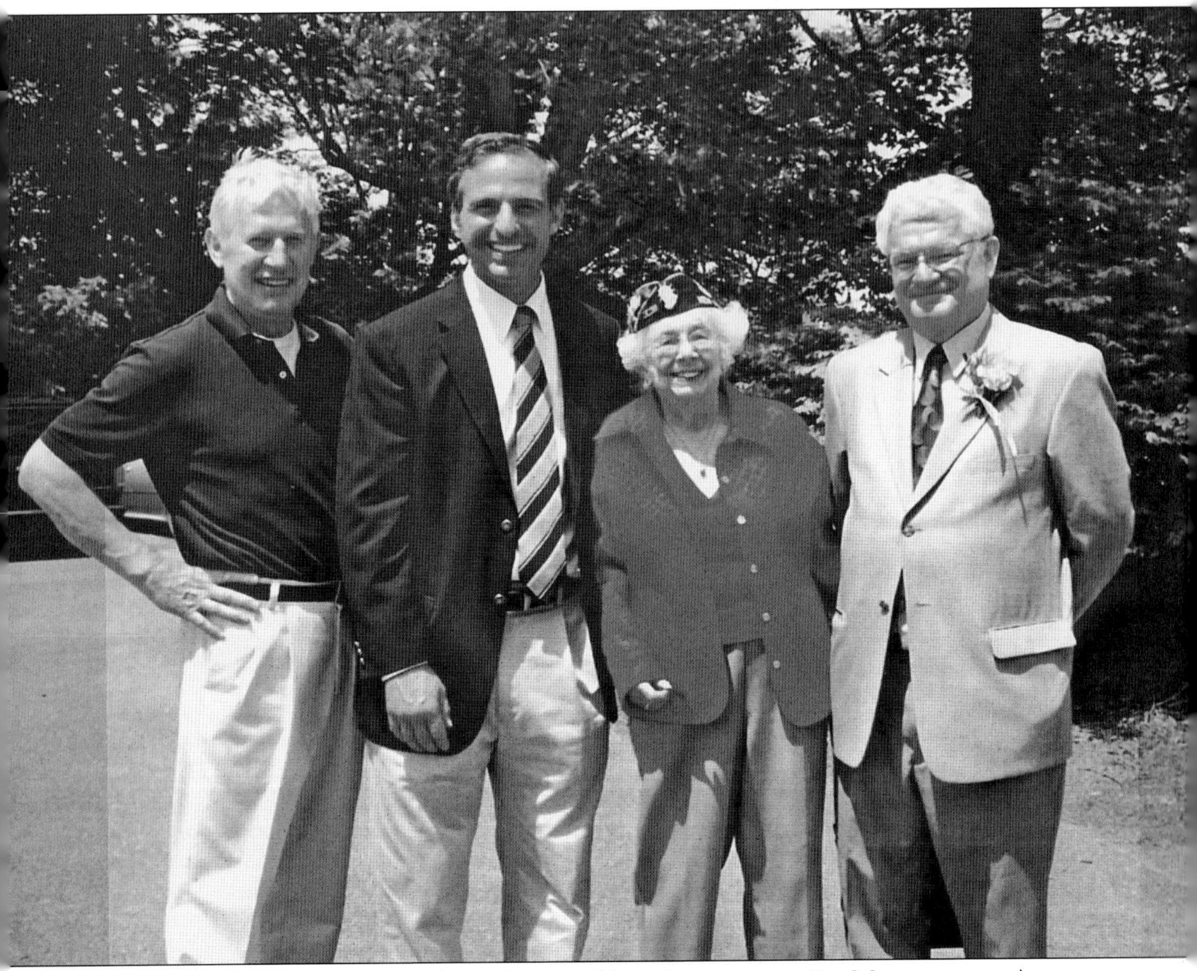

Posing for the camera are a military hero and her three escorts. Pat Marso was an Army nurse during World War II. She was involved for many years with the WRC Home, where her husband was superintendent. She has served many years as the commander of the Oxford Legion and is a long-standing champion of veterans' causes. The photograph was taken in 2008 during a dedication of a renovated section of the Oxford Library. Her escorts are, from the left to right, library board member Fred Lanfear, Congressman Mike Arcuri, and Mayor Terry Stark.

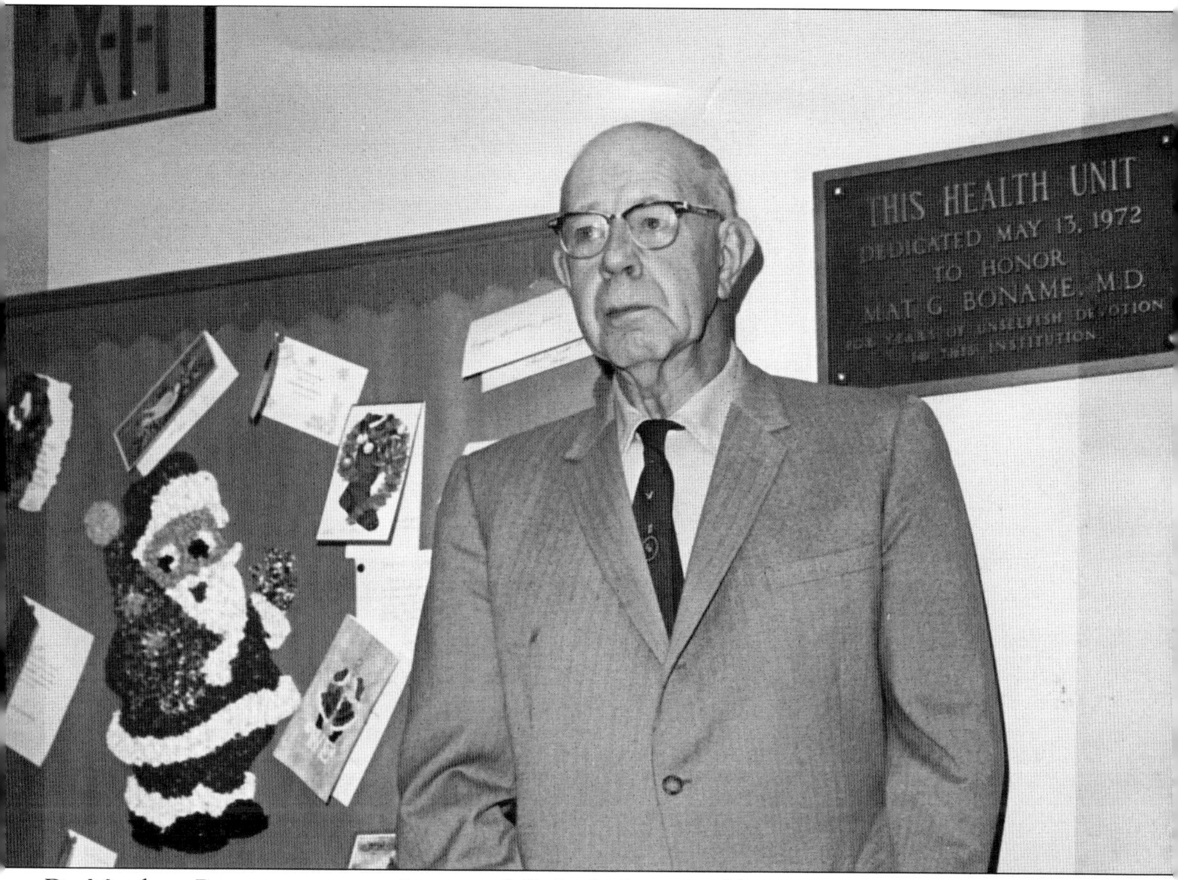

Dr. Matthew Boname was a native son of Oxford who served his community as a practicing physician for over 60 years. He graduated from Oxford Academy and Union School in 1920. He was also a graduate of Syracuse University and Syracuse Medical School. In 1928, he began his medical practice in Oxford and was still seeing patients in the early 1990s. He served over 30 years as the Chenango County Coroner. For over 35 years, he was also the health officer for the Oxford schools. He held regular office hours and conducted many home visits in any weather and any time of day. There were many stories about of his late-night responses. For many years, he suffered excruciating pain from trigeminal neuralgia until a new surgical procedure at Syracuse alleviated the problem. His story was featured in *Time* magazine on July 11, 1984.

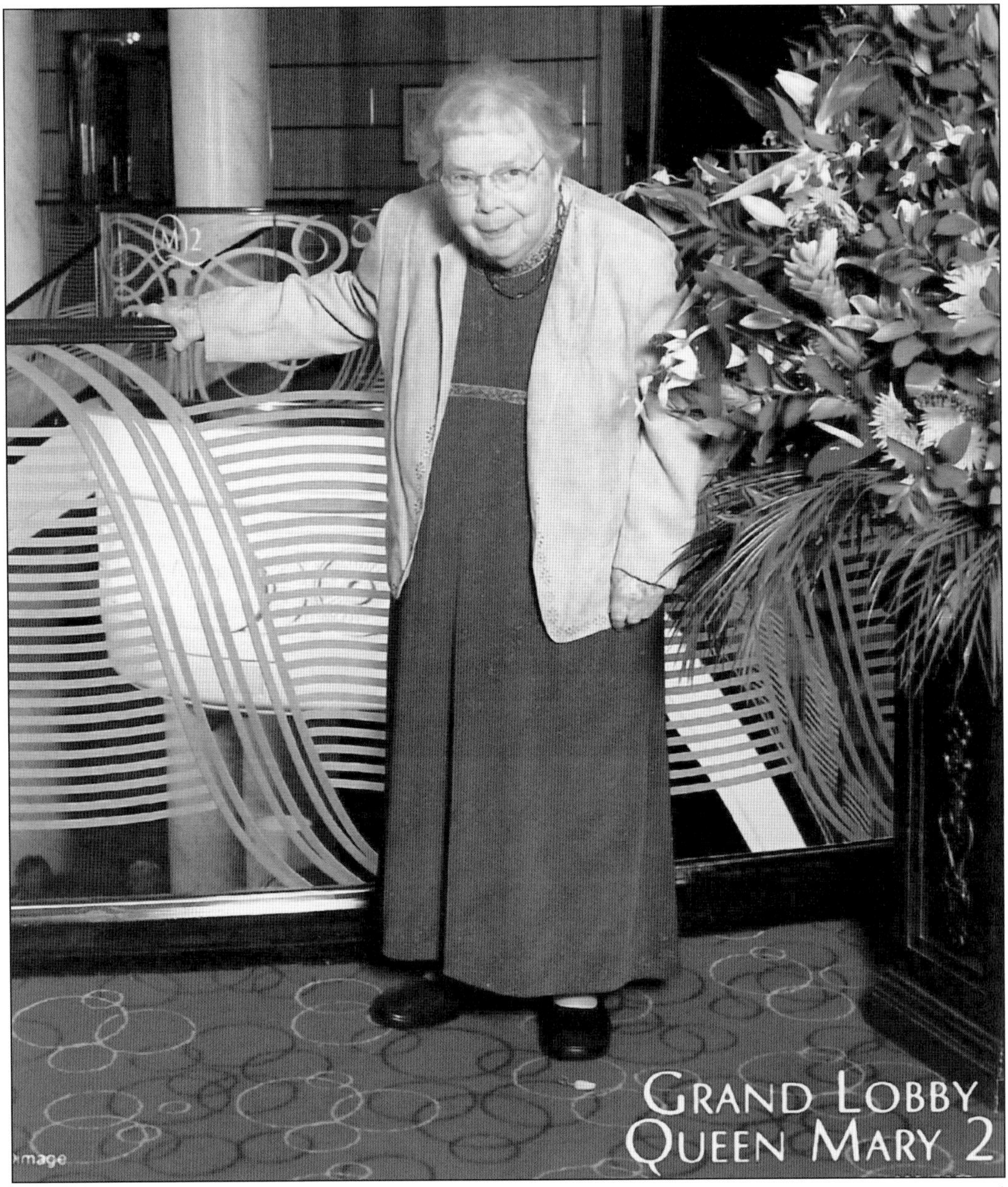

Charlotte Stafford descended from a line of Oxford achievers. Her great-uncle Sam was a Civil War hero and a lawyer who defended veterans' rights. Her grandfather was a craftsman who built the family's home, which was where she was born and raised. Her father owned and published the *Oxford Review-Times* for over 40 years. She was deeply attracted to Oxford history and lore. She majored in history and French at Elmira College and later earned a master's degree in library science at Albany University. After her career as school librarian in Binghamton and Norwich, she retired to her family's home. For 33 years, she became known as Oxford's town historian, and her work established a genealogical research center. She rejuvenated the Oxford Historical Society and established the Oxford Historical Museum. She wrote an index to the *Annals of Oxford* and *A Chronology of Oxford Happenings, 1788–1950.* The photograph shows Stafford posing for her 90th birthday as she celebrated her birthday on an Atlantic cruise on the *Queen Mary II.*

This photograph shows wrestler John "J.P." O'Connor, who was the great-grandson of Patrick O'Connor. Patrick, who was a stone worker, was an early advocate for workers' rights in the Oxford quarries. As a model for Oxford students, J.P. set records of scholarship and athletic accomplishments in high school and college. He is one of the only three wrestlers to win four wrestling championships in New York. He attended Harvard University as a pre-medical major and won 37 wrestling matches in his freshman year, which gave him recognition as an Academic All-American. He placed in three NCAA tournaments, and in 2010 he won the national championship in his weight class. He is one of only three national champions in Harvard's history. Currently, J.P. is entering medical school and is considering a career in sports medicine.

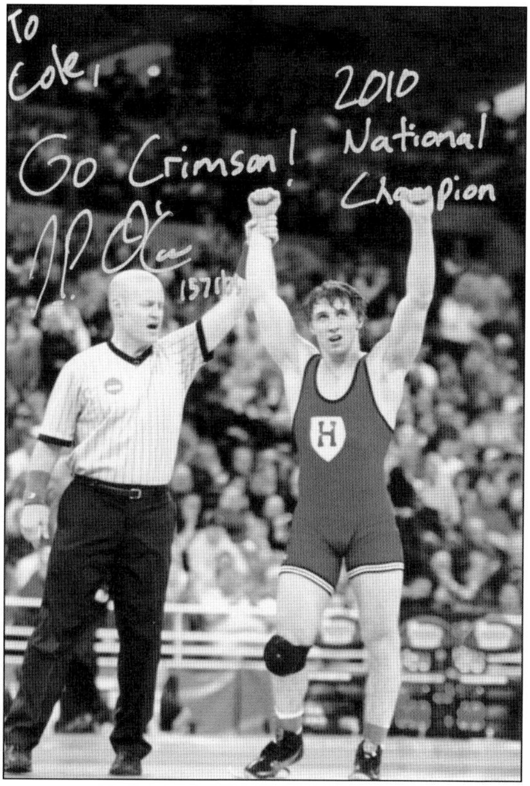

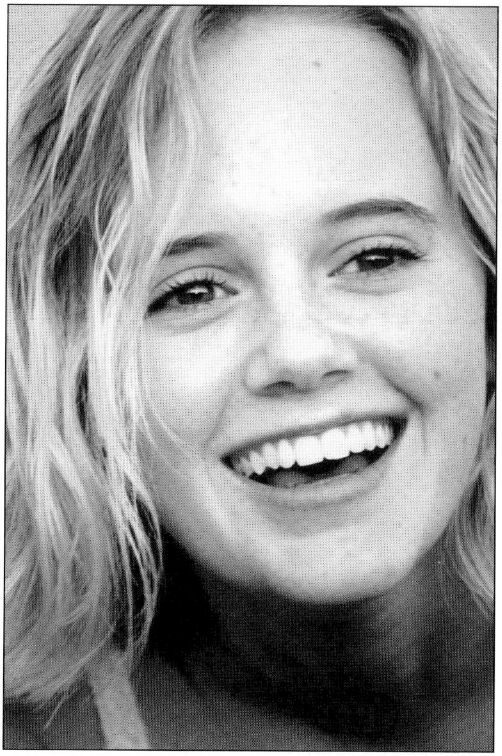

Brandi Estelow was known as a true daughter of Oxford. Both sides of her family go back generations in Oxford and have influenced the town greatly. She was an honor student in high school and an outstanding athlete on the field hockey team. She graduated high school in 2004. She enrolled at Hartwick College and planned to become an RN nurse. Unfortunately, Brandi never finished college because she was diagnosed with malignant mesothelioma, a rare form of cancer. She passed away on September 24, 2009. As a model to Oxford students, it was Brandi's courageous struggle that imprinted her in Oxford history.